Praise for Joby Warrick's

THE TRIPLE AGENT

"Warrick has reconstructed, in vivid and telling detail, the sequence of events that led Humam al-Balawi to kill seven CIA operatives in a suicide attack in Afghanistan in December 2009. . . . It is a chilling tale, told with skill and verve."   —*The Economist*

"*The Triple Agent* is a superlative piece of reporting and writing. . . . Unforgettable. *The Triple Agent* is one of the best true-life spy stories I have ever read."   —David Ignatius, columnist for *The Washington Post* and author of *Bloodmoney*

"A startling and memorable account of daring, treachery, and catastrophe in the CIA's war against al-Qaeda. . . . A powerful and fast-paced story of our time."   —David E. Hoffman, Pulitzer Prize–winning author of *The Dead Hand*

"An extraordinary story of intrigue and betrayal. . . . Warrick shows how the pressure for results led the CIA to take shortcuts when it came to handling an agent who some feared, correctly, was too good to be true."   —*Foreign Affairs*

"Potent, swift. . . . Warrick is very, very good. He burrows deep inside not only the CIA, which might be expected, but also the Mukhabarat and ISI, Pakistan's main spy agency."   —*The Washington Post*

"A fascinating . . . postmortem on the 2009 ambush on the American compound at Knost, Afghanistan. . . . Riveting. . . . Sketches careful, illuminating portraits of those who died." —*The Plain Dealer*

"Warrick demonstrates the initiative that has marked his newspaper career. . . . An alarming narrative, especially because of its understated, never-shrill tone." —*Kirkus Reviews*

"Riveting. . . . A must-read." —Associated Press

"Insightful and riveting. . . . Mr. Warrick adds a wealth of new detail to a narrative that reads like the best spy fiction." —*The Washington Times*

"[An] accessible and fast-paced debut. . . . [Warrick] gives this story a cinematic feel with suspenseful foreshadowing, rich character development . . . and a remarkable amount of heart." —*Publishers Weekly*

"A grim reminder that the U.S. war on terror as it has been conducted is deadly, expensive, and mostly futile." —*Houston Chronicle*

"*The Triple Agent* is by turns harrowing and heartbreaking, fascinating and frightening. . . . . A tale that reads like a thriller and stretches from the dusty back alleys of Waziristan to the plush executive floor at Langley." —James Bamford, author of the bestselling *The Puzzle Palace*, *Body of Secrets*, and *The Shadow Factory*

"Were Shakespeare alive, he would find ample material for a high tragedy among the players in . . . *The Triple Agent*. All the ingredients are there, including betrayal, shame, heroism, and more than one person with a recklessly determined hubris worthy of King Lear himself. Yet as those who have operated in the world of human intelligence will viscerally feel, this is not cathartic fiction, but a factual account of a modern-day human intelligence operation gone terribly wrong, involving real men and women, with all the failings thereof." —*Foreign Policy*

JOBY WARRICK

THE TRIPLE AGENT

Joby Warrick covers national security for *The Washington Post*, where he has been a reporter since 1996. He is a winner of the Pulitzer Prize. He lives in Washington, D.C.

The
TRIPLE
AGENT

The al-Qaeda Mole Who Infiltrated the CIA

JOBY WARRICK

ANCHOR BOOKS
A Division of Penguin Random House LLC
New York

FIRST ANCHOR BOOKS EDITION, MAY 2012

Copyright © 2011, 2012 by Joby Warrick

All rights reserved. Published in the United States by Anchor Books,
a division of Penguin Random House LLC, New York, and distributed in Canada by
Random House of Canada, a division of Penguin Random House Canada Limited, Toronto.
Originally published in hardcover in slightly different form in the United States by
Doubleday, a division of Penguin Random House LLC, New York, in 2011.

Anchor Books and colophon are registered trademarks of Penguin Random House LLC.

The Library of Congress has cataloged the Doubleday edition as follows:
Warrick, Joby.
The triple agent : the al-Qaeda mole who infiltrated the CIA / Joby Warrick. —1st ed.
p. cm.
Includes bibliographical references and index.
1. Balawi, Humam Khalil al- 2. Qaida (Organization)—Biography.
3. United States. Central Intelligence Agency—Biography.
4. Counterinsurgency—Middle East.
5. Suicide bombers—Afghanistan—Khowst—Biography.
6. Informers—Jordan—Biography. 7. Spies—Jordan—Biography.
8. Physicists—Jordan—Biography. I. Title.
HV6433.M52Q345 2011
363.325092—dc22
[B] 2011002639

Anchor Books Trade Paperback ISBN: 978-0-307-74231-5
eBook ISBN: 978-0-385-53419-2

Author photograph © The Washington Post
Book design by Michael Collica

www.anchorbooks.com

Printed in the United States of America

For the families of the fallen,
and for my family

All warfare is based on deception.

—Sun Tzu

CONTENTS

CONTENTS

AUTHOR'S NOTE

Quotations in this book that are designated by quotation marks are the recollections of individuals who heard the words as they were spoken. Italics are used in cases in which a source could not recall the precise language or when a source relayed conversation or thoughts that were shared with him by a participant in the events described.

LIST OF PRINCIPAL CHARACTERS

The White House

President Barack Obama
James L. Jones, national security adviser
John Brennan, chief counterterrorism adviser to the president
Rahm Emanuel, White House chief of staff

Central Intelligence Agency Headquarters, Langley, Virginia

Michael V. Hayden, CIA director, May 2006 to February 2009
Leon Panetta, CIA director, February 2009 to June 2011
Stephen Kappes, CIA deputy director
Dennis C. Blair, director of national intelligence

Amman, Jordan

Darren LaBonte, CIA case officer, Amman station
_____, CIA station chief, Amman station (identity classified; name withheld)
Ali bin Zeid, captain, Jordanian General Intelligence Department (GID), aka the Mukhabarat
Ali Burjak, aka Red Ali, Mukhabarat counterterrorism chief, bin Zeid's boss

Humam Khalil al-Balawi, physician and blogger
Khalil al-Balawi, Humam's father
Defne Bayrak, Humam's wife

In Afghanistan

Jennifer Matthews, CIA base chief, Forward Operating Base Chapman ("Khost")
Harold Brown Jr., CIA case officer, Khost
Scott Roberson, CIA security chief, Khost
Dane Paresi, security contractor, Xe Services LLC, aka Blackwater, Khost
Jeremy Wise, security contractor, Xe Services LLC, aka Blackwater, Khost
Arghawan _____, Afghan detail security chief, Khost (last name withheld)
_____, CIA deputy chief of station, Kabul station (identity classified; name withheld)
Elizabeth Hanson, targeter, Kabul station

Al-Qaeda and the Taliban in Pakistan

Osama bin Laden, al-Qaeda founder and leader
Ayman al-Zawahiri, al-Qaeda's No. 2 commander, deputy to Osama bin Laden
Osama al-Kini (given name Fahid Mohammed Ally Msalam), senior al-Qaeda commander for Pakistan
Abdullah Said al-Libi, an al-Qaeda operations chief, leader of al-Qaeda's "Shadow Army" in Pakistan
Sheikh Saeed al-Masri (given name Mustafa Ahmed Muhammad Uthman Abu al-Yazid), al-Qaeda's No. 3 commander
Baitullah Mehsud, leader of Pakistani Taliban alliance, Tehrik-i-Taliban Pakistan (TTP)
Hakimullah Mehsud, deputy TTP leader, cousin to Baitullah Mehsud

Atiyah Abd al-Rahman, al-Qaeda senior leader and Islamic scholar

Abu Musab al-Zarqawi (given name Ahmad Fadeel al-Nazal al-Khalayleh), Jordanian-born leader of al-Qaeda in Iraq, killed in U.S. missile strike in 2006

Abu Zubaida (given name Zayn al-Abidin Muhammed Hussein), first "high-value" terrorist operative captured by the CIA after the attacks of September 11, 2001, and the first to be subjected to waterboarding

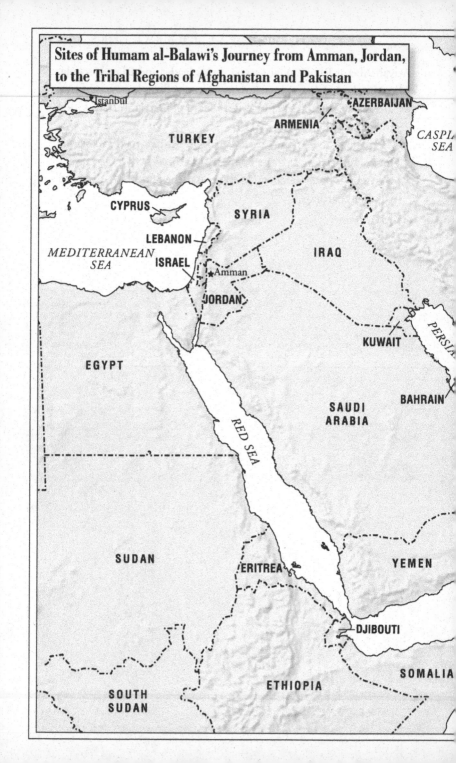

Sites of Humam al-Balawi's Journey from Amman, Jordan, to the Tribal Regions of Afghanistan and Pakistan

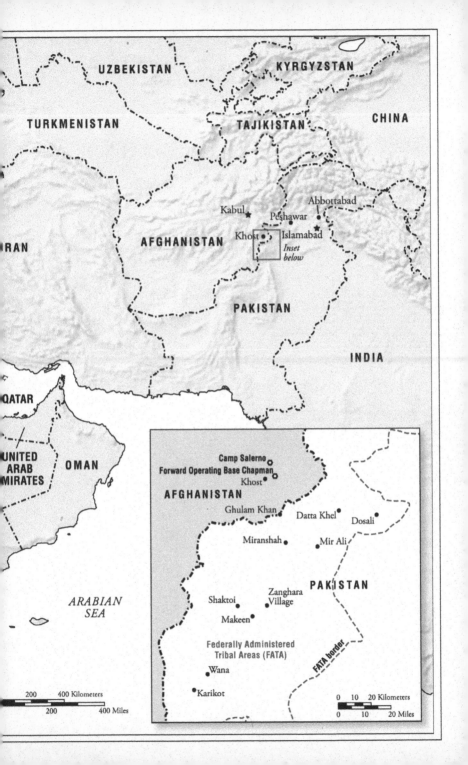

UZBEKISTAN   KYRGYZSTAN

TURKMENISTAN   TAJIKISTAN   CHINA

                                    Abbottabad
                    Kabul ★   Peshawar
                            Khost • ⬚ Islamabad
IRAN   AFGHANISTAN   Inset
                                       below

                    PAKISTAN

                                    INDIA

QATAR

UNITED   OMAN
ARAB
EMIRATES

ARABIAN
SEA

                        Camp Salerno ◌
            Forward Operating Base Chapman ◌
                        Khost •
            AFGHANISTAN
                    Ghulam Khan •   Datta Khel •
                                            Dosali •
                        Miranshah •   Mir Ali •

                                    PAKISTAN

                            Zanghara
                    Shaktoi • Village •
                        Makeen •

                    Federally Administered
                    Tribal Areas (FATA)   FATA border
                    • Wana
                    • Karikot

200   400 Kilometers   0   10   20 Kilometers
200   400 Miles   0   10   20 Miles

PROLOGUE

Khost, Afghanistan—December 30, 2009

For ten days the CIA team waited for the mysterious Jordanian to show up. From gloomy mid-December through the miserable holidays the officers shivered under blankets, retold stale jokes, drank gallons of bad coffee, and sipped booze from Styrofoam cups. They counted distant mortar strikes, studied bomb damage reports, and listened for the thrum of Black Hawk helicopters ferrying wounded. And they waited.

Christmas morning arrived on a raw wind, and still they sat. They picked at gingerbread crumbs in the packages sent from home and stared at the ceramic Nativity figurines one of the officers had set up in lieu of a tree. Then it was December 30, the last dregs of the old year and the tenth day of the vigil, and finally came word that the Jordanian agent was on the move. He was heading west by car through the mountains of Pakistan's jagged northwestern fringe, wearing tribal dress and dark sunglasses and skirting Taliban patrols along the treacherous highway leading to the Afghan frontier.

Until now no American officer had ever seen the man, this spectral informant called "Wolf," whose real name was said to be known to fewer than a dozen people; this wily double agent who had penetrated al-Qaeda, sending back coded messages that lit up CIA headquarters like ball lightning. But at about 3:00 P.M. Afghanistan time, Humam Khalil al-Balawi would step out of the murk and onto the fortified concrete of the secret CIA base known as Khost.

The news of his pending arrival sent analysts scurrying to finalize preparations. Newly arrived base chief Jennifer Matthews, barely three months into her first Afghan posting, had fretted over the details for days, and now she dispatched her aides to check video equipment, fire off cables, and rehearse details of a debriefing that would stretch into the night.

She watched them work, nervous but confident, her short brown hair pulled to the side in a businesslike part. At forty-five, Matthews was a veteran of the agency's counterterrorism wars, and she understood al-Qaeda and its cast of fanatical death worshippers better than perhaps anyone in the CIA—better, in fact, than she knew the PTA at her kids' school back home in Fredericksburg, Virginia. Hard-nosed and serious, Matthews was one of the agency's rising stars, beloved by upper management. She had leaped at the chance to go to Khost in spite of the quizzical looks from close friends who thought she was crazy to leave her family and comfortable suburban life for such a risky assignment. True, she would have much to learn; she had never served in a war zone, or run a surveillance operation, or managed a routine informant case, let alone one as complex as the Jordanian agent. But Matthews was smart and resourceful, and she would have plenty of help from top CIA managers, who were following developments closely from the agency's Langley, Virginia, headquarters. Their advice so far: Treat Balawi like a distinguished guest.

Matthews signed off on a security plan for the visit, though not without carping from some of the Special Forces veterans in her security detail. Her primary concern was not so much for the agent's physical safety—the men with the guns would see to that—but rather for preserving his secret identity. The CIA could not afford to allow him to be seen by any of the scores of Afghans working at the base, except for the trusted driver who was now on his way to pick him up. Even the guards at the front gate would be ordered to turn away to avoid the risk that one of them might glimpse Balawi's face.

Matthews picked a secure spot for the meeting, a gray concrete building in a part of the base that served as the CIA's inner sanctum, separated by high walls and guarded by private security contractors armed with assault rifles. The building was designed for informant meetings and was lined on one side by a large awning to further shield operatives from view as they came and left. Here, surrounded by CIA officers and free from any possibility of detection by al-Qaeda spies, the Jordanian would be searched for weapons and wires and studied for any hint of possible deception. Then he would fill in the details of his wildly improbable narrative, a story so fantastic that few would have believed it had the agent not backed it up with eye-popping proof: Humam al-Balawi had been in the presence of al-Qaeda's elusive No. 2 leader, the Egyptian physician Ayman al-Zawahiri, one of the twisted brains behind dozens of terrorist plots, including the attacks of September 11, 2001. And now Balawi was going to lead the CIA right to Zawahiri's door.

When the debriefing was over, a medical officer would check Balawi's vitals, and a technical team would outfit him for the dangerous mission to come. Then everyone could relax, have a bite to eat, perhaps even a drink.

And there would be a surprise, a birthday cake.

The Jordanian had just turned thirty-two on Christmas Day, a trivia plum that Matthews had been pleased to discover. In fact his special birth date had very nearly caused him to be named Isa—Jesus, in Arabic—before his parents changed their minds and decided instead on Humam, meaning "brave one." And now this same Humam was speeding toward Khost with what could well be the agency's greatest Christmas present in many a season, an intelligence windfall so spectacular that the president of the United States had been briefed in advance.

As she waited for the Jordanian, Matthews's head swirled with questions. Who was this man? How did anyone get close to Zawahiri, one of the most reclusive and carefully protected humans on the planet? So much about the Balawi case was confusing. But Matthews had her orders, and she would not fail or flinch.

Balawi would be given a fitting reception. There were no birthday candles at the CIA's forward base in violent eastern Afghanistan. But the Jordanian would have his cake.

That is, if he ever showed up.

By 3:30 P.M. the entire team was ready and waiting outside the interrogation building. Another thirty minutes dragged by without news from the Jordanian, and then an hour, and now the sun was slumping toward the tops of the mountain peaks west of Khost. The temperature dropped, and the nervous adrenaline congealed into plain nervousness.

Had something happened? Had Balawi changed his mind? There were no answers and nothing to do but wait.

The group of men and women beneath the metal awning had grown to fourteen, an oddly large gathering for an informant meeting. Normally, the imperative to shield a spy's identity dictates that no more than two or three officers are ever allowed to see him. But as was quickly becoming clear, there was nothing normal about the Balawi case. There was a sense of destiny, of history being made, one CIA participant in the events later recalled. "Everyone," the officer said, "wanted to be involved in this one."

Gradually the officers segregated themselves into small groups. The security detail, two CIA employees, and a pair of guards working for the private contractor Xe Services LLC, commonly known as Blackwater, stood near the gate, talking in low voices, M4s slung over their backs. Three of the men were military veterans, and all four had become chummy. Pipe-smoking Dane Paresi, a former Green Beret and one of the oldest in the group at forty-six, had joined Blackwater after a career that included stints in multiple hellholes, most recently Afghanistan, where his conduct under fire had earned him the Bronze Star. Iraq veteran Jeremy Wise, thirty-five, an ex-Navy SEAL with an infectious grin, had signed up with the security contractor to pay the bills after leaving active service and was struggling to figure out what to do with his life. Security team leader Harold E. Brown Jr., thirty-seven, was a former army intelligence officer and devoted family man who taught Roman Catholic catechism classes and led Cub Scouts back in Virginia. Scott Roberson, thirty-eight, had been a narcotics detective in Atlanta in a previous life, and he was looking forward to becoming a father in less than a month.

Nearer to the building, two men in civilian jeans and khakis chatted with the ease of longtime friends. Both were guests at Khost, having flown to Afghanistan from Jordan to be present at Balawi's debriefing. The big man with ink black hair was Jordanian intelligence captain Ali bin Zeid, a cousin of King Abdullah II of Jordan and the only one in the group who had ever met Balawi. Darren LaBonte, an athletic ex–Army Ranger who sported a goatee and a baseball hat, was a CIA officer assigned to the agency's Amman station. The two were close friends who often worked cases together and sometimes vacationed together along with their wives. Both had been anxious about the meeting with Balawi, and they had spent part of the previous day blowing off steam by snapping pictures and puttering around on a three-wheeler they had found.

A larger group clustered around Matthews. One of them, a striking blonde with cobalt blue eyes, had been summoned from the CIA's Kabul station for the meeting because of her exceptional skills. Elizabeth Hanson was one of the agency's most celebrated targeters, an expert at finding terrorist commanders in their hiding places and tracking them until one of the CIA's hit teams could move into place. She was thirty but looked even younger, bundled up inside a jacket and oversize flannel shirt against the December chill.

The wind was picking up, and the late-afternoon shadows stretched like vines across the asphalt. A frustrated boredom set in, and officers fidgeted with their cell phones.

Paresi set down his weapon and tapped out an e-mail to his

wife. Mindy Lou Paresi was airborne at that moment, flying back to Seattle from Ohio with the couple's youngest daughter after holiday visits with family. As he often did, Paresi would leave a message that his wife would see when she landed, just letting her know that he was OK.

"E-mail me when you get to the house," he wrote. "I love you both very much."

Jeremy Wise stepped away from the others to make his phone call. The Arkansas native was feeling strangely anxious, so much so that he wondered if he was coming down with something. He dialed his home number, and when the answering machine picked up, the disappointment clearly registered in his voice. "I'm not doing very well," he said, speaking slowly. He hesitated. "Tell Ethan I love him."

Bin Zeid was the only one with a direct line to Balawi, and his phone had been distressingly silent. The big man now sat quietly, clutching his mobile between thick fingers. It was bin Zeid who had gone over the arrangements with the agent—Balawi had been his recruit after all—and now the possibility of failure loomed over him like a leaden cloud. On top of it all, both he and his CIA partner, LaBonte, had personal reasons for wanting out of Afghanistan in a hurry. LaBonte's entire family, including his wife and their baby daughter, was waiting for him in an Italian villa they had rented for the holidays, and the delays had already eaten up most of his vacation. Bin Zeid, who was newly married, had made plans to spend New Year's Eve with his wife back in Amman.

When his phone finally chirped, it was a text message from dark-haired Fida, asking her husband if he was positive he would be home the following evening. Bin Zeid tapped out a terse reply. "Not yet," he wrote.

Just after 4:40 P.M. bin Zeid's phone finally rang. The number in the caller ID belonged to Arghawan, the Afghan driver who had been dispatched to the border crossing for the pickup. But the voice was Balawi's.

The agent apologized. He had injured his leg in an accident and had been delayed, he said. Balawi had been anxious about his first meeting with Americans, and he asked again about the procedures at the gate. *I don't want to be manhandled*, he kept repeating.

You'll treat me like a friend, right? he asked.

By now a column of dust from Afghawan's red Outback was already visible from the guard tower. The driver was moving fast to thwart any sniper who might happen to have a scope trained on the road in time to see an unescorted civilian vehicle heading for the American base. In keeping with the CIA's instructions and, coincidentally, with Balawi's wishes, there would be no fumbling or checking IDs at the gate. On cue, the Afghan army guards at the front gate rolled back the barriers just enough to let Arghawan roar past. The Afghan driver then veered sharply to the left and followed a ribbon of asphalt along the edge of the airfield to a small second gate, where he was again waved through.

Now Matthews could see the station wagon entering the compound where she and the others were waiting. Matthews had asked bin Zeid and LaBonte to greet Balawi while she and the other officers kept a respectful distance, spread out in a crude reception line beneath the awning. She began making her way to a spot at the front of the line, straightening her clothes as she walked.

Security chief Scott Roberson and the two Blackwater guards unslung their rifles and made their way across the gravel lot, but the arriving Outback cut them off. The car rolled to a halt with the driver's door positioned directly in front of the spot where Matthews was standing. Arghawan was alone in the front seat, his face nearly obscured by the thick film of dust that coated the windows. The figure sitting directly behind him in the backseat was hunched forward slightly, and Matthews strained to make out the face. The engine was cut, and in an instant Roberson was opening the rear door next to Balawi.

The man inside hesitated, as though studying the guards' weapons. Then, very slowly, he slid across the seat away from the Americans and climbed out on the opposite side of the car.

Now he was standing, a short, wiry man, perhaps thirty, with

7

dark eyes and a few matted curls visible under his turban. He was wearing a beige, loose-fitting kameez shirt of the type worn by Pashtun tribesmen and a woolen vest that made him look slightly stout around the middle. A long gray shawl draped his shoulders and covered the lower part of his face and beard. The man reached back into the car to grab a metal crutch, and as he did, the shawl fell away to reveal a wispy beard and an expression as blank as a marble slab.

As the others watched in confused silence, the man started to walk around the front of the car with an awkward, stooped gait, as though struggling under a heavy load. He was mumbling to himself.

Bin Zeid waved to Balawi but, getting no response, called out to him.

"*Salaam, akhoya.* Hello, my brother," bin Zeid said. "Everything's OK!"

But it wasn't. Blackwater guards Paresi and Wise had instinctively raised their guns when Balawi balked at exiting on their side of the car. Paresi, the ex–Green Beret, watched with growing alarm as Balawi hobbled around the vehicle, one hand grasping the crutch and the other hidden ominously under his shawl. Paresi tensed, finger on the trigger, eyes fixed on the shawl with instincts honed in dozens of firefights and close scrapes. One shot would drop the man. But if he was wrong—if there was no bomb—it would be the worst mistake of his life. He circled around the car keeping the ambling figure in his gun's sight. Steady. Wait. But where's that hand?

Now he and Wise were shouting almost in unison, guns at the ready.

"Hands up! Get your hand out of your clothing!"

Balawi's mumbling grew louder. He was chanting something in Arabic.

"*La ilaha illa Allah!*" he was saying.

There is no god but God.

Bin Zeid heard the words and knew, better than anyone, exactly what they meant.

1

OBSESSION

McLean, Virginia—One year earlier

For nearly three years the whereabouts of Osama bin Laden and his top generals had been Michael V. Hayden's daily obsession, a throbbing migraine that intruded on his consciousness at odd hours of the night. But as he turned the page on his final month as CIA director, it was a different Osama that was costing him sleep. Before New Year's Day was over, Hayden would have to decide whether the man would live or die.

The man was called Osama al-Kini, and he had been the subject of an increasingly frantic search. The boyish onetime soccer player from Kenya had moved up in al-Qaeda's ranks, starting as a truck driver and bomb maker and rising to become a top operations planner with a flair for the spectacular. He was preparing a list of targets for a wave of strikes across Western Europe when the CIA caught a lucky break. In late December, the agency had spotted one of al-Kini's top deputies in a town in northwestern Pakistan, and now it was following him, with eyes on the ground and robot planes circling silently above. Cameras whirring, it trailed him as he wandered through the bazaars, sat for tea, or climbed the hilly street to the abandoned girls' school where he sometimes stayed the night. Agents watched for hours, and then days, waiting to see who would come to meet him. As the graveyard shift at the CIA's Langley, Virginia, headquarters rang in the first minutes of 2009, the watchers sensed that they were finally getting close.

New Year's Day found Hayden attempting to enjoy a rare day off. He tried to relax with family and even took in a couple of football games, but the phone summoned him back to the hunt. From his basement office, with its twenty-four-hour security detail and secure line to headquarters, he mulled the latest updates from Pakistan. *Keep watching*, he ordered. Then, when late evening arrived without further news, Hayden decided to turn in for the night. He switched on his TV and sat on the bed. It was the Orange Bowl game from Miami, and Virginia Tech was pounding Cincinnati. He stretched out and tried to concentrate on the game.

At sixty-three, Hayden was no one's vision of a killer. The retired four-star general had been a career intelligence man in the air force who moved up to become head of the National Security Agency, overseeing the country's vast overseas eavesdropping network. In 2006 he was President George W. Bush's pick for the CIA's third director in two years, inheriting a demoralized spy agency in need of a wise uncle to pay bail and clean up the damage. Hayden's charge, simply put, was to restore stability and even a kind of bureaucratic blandness to the CIA after multiple scandals over the alleged kidnapping and torture of suspected terrorists. One of his stated ambitions going in: to get the CIA out of the headlines. "The agency needs to be out of the news, as source or subject," he told the *Washington Post* in an interview.

Hayden was born to Irish Catholic parents in Pittsburgh and maintained lifelong ties to that working-class city, returning home on fall weekends to root for the Steelers or for the football squad at his alma mater, Duquesne University. He liked talking in sports analogies, and, as CIA director he enjoyed mingling with young analysts in the agency cafeteria, his bald pate and easy smile making him a reassuring, rather than an intimidating, presence for junior staffers. The mechanics of finding and eliminating specific terrorist threats seemed to fall more naturally to Hayden's chief deputy,

Stephen R. Kappes, a legendary case officer who had made his mark matching wits against the Soviet KGB in Moscow.

But now, in his third year as director, Hayden was in charge of the most relentlessly lethal campaign in the spy agency's history. After the terrorist attacks of September 11, 2001, the CIA had devoted itself to hunting down bin Laden and his followers with the aim of capturing, imprisoning, and interrogating them. Now the agency had a different goal: killing the terrorists and their allies wherever they could be found. The agency had slowly built up a fleet of pilotless aircraft, called Predators, capable of firing missiles by remote control. In mid-2008, as the Bush administration entered its final months, the CIA unleashed the planes, commonly referred to as drones, in an all-out war against al-Qaeda. CIA missiles blasted terrorist safe houses and training camps week after week, and the finger on the trigger was Hayden's.

The transformation had been years in the making. In the middle years of the decade, as the Bush administration poured troops and resources into Iraq, al-Qaeda had staged a comeback in the mountains of northwestern Pakistan. The demoralized bands of Arab fighters who had streamed out of Afghanistan in late 2001 regrouped under their old generals, bin Laden and his operations chief, Ayman al-Zawahiri, and a new generation of aggressive commanders replaced those who had been killed or captured. From new sanctuaries in the rugged no-man's-land between the two countries, they quietly began reopening training camps, raising money, and plotting new attacks against the United States and Western Europe. The agency's wire intercepts crackled with vague but ominous talk about surveillance missions and dry runs targeting airliners, shopping centers, tourist resorts, and hotels—threats most Americans would never hear about.

By 2007 al-Qaeda's ability to wreak havoc nearly rivaled the group's pre-2002 peak. In some ways, the threat was even worse: Al-Qaeda had effectively merged with some of Pakistan's extremist groups, while spawning new chapters in North Africa, Iraq, and the Arabian Peninsula. Al-Qaeda's propagandists harnessed the Internet's formidable powers to spread al-Qaeda's hateful gospel to millions of Muslims through Web sites and chat rooms. New streams of cash and recruits spilled into northwestern Pakistan and to regional affiliates from Yemen to Southeast Asia. Many of the newcomers signing up for jihad carried Western passports and could slip undetected into American and European capitals. Some had blond hair and light skin.

What Hayden saw as he surveyed the world in early 2008 truly frightened him. So early that year, during his weekly intelligence briefings at the White House, he began to make the case to President George W. Bush.

"This is now a bona fide threat to the homeland," Hayden told the president during one Oval Office visit. Another September 11–style terrorist strike was inevitable, he said, and it would come from the tribal region of Pakistan.

To prevent such an attack, the United States must take the fight to the enemy, Hayden argued. That meant attacking al-Qaeda on its home turf inside Pakistan, disrupting its communications, killing its generals and field commanders, and depriving it of sanctuary. Only the CIA had the legal authority to reach targets deep inside Pakistan, and the agency already possessed the perfect weapon, the Predator. It was time to take the fetters off the CIA's fleet of unmanned hunter-killer planes, he said.

Bush and his advisers listened sympathetically. The problem, everyone knew, was Pakistan. Islamabad was a crucial ally, and it officially opposed foreign missile strikes on its soil, no matter the target. Pakistani officials argued that American air strikes only worsened the terror problem by radicalizing ordinary Pakistanis and driving more of them to join with the extremists—a concern shared by some U.S. terrorism experts as well. In private discussions, Pakistani intelligence officials chided the Americans for what they perceived as two dangerous obsessions: an overdependence on expensive technology, and an absurd fixation on the person of Osama bin Laden.

"Al-Qaeda is not very strong, but you've made it into a ten-foot-tall giant," one senior Pakistani government official recalled telling a visiting Bush administration delegation. "How can a handful of core al-Qaeda leaders seriously threaten the greatest empire in the world?"

Eventually, Pakistani leaders agreed to allow a limited number of Predator strikes, and for months Washington and Islamabad engaged in an awkward dance over when an attack was permissible. If the CIA discovered a potential target, the agency could pull the trigger only after both governments agreed. In practice, it rarely happened. "If you had to ask for permission, you got one of three answers: either 'No,' or 'We're thinking about it,' or 'Oops, where did the target go?' " said a former U.S. national security official who was involved at the time. A whole year passed without a single significant success against al-Qaeda on its home turf. "We're at zero for '07," Hayden complained to the White House.

After months of debate Bush decided in July 2008 to give the CIA what it wanted. News reports later characterized the policy change as an informal agreement by Pakistan to allow more U.S. air strikes in remote tribal regions that were largely outside of Islamabad's control. In reality, the shift was much simpler: The CIA stopped asking for permission. The new policy, communicated to Pakistani officials in a meeting that month, required only "simultaneous notification" when the strikes occurred.

Over the next six months Predators hit targets in Pakistan thirty times, more than triple the combined number of strikes in the previous four years.

U.S. elections in November 2008 signaled the coming end of Republican control of the White House and likely Hayden's tenure at CIA. But in the final weeks, as the clock ran down on the Bush presidency, the number of Predator strikes soared, prompting speculation within the agency that Hayden was hoping to flush Osama bin Laden himself out of hiding as the Bush administration's final payback for September 11. It was amid the scramble for big targets in the final days of 2008 that a familiar name popped up in one of the agency's phone intercepts.

The name belonged to an East African man named Sheikh Ahmed Salim Swedan, a midlevel al-Qaeda operative linked to several terrorist bombings. But Swedan was most interesting because of whom he worked for, the former soccer player known as Osama al-Kini, now the senior al-Qaeda commander in Pakistan. The two men had been on a bloody two-year rampage, killing hundreds of people in a series of increasingly spectacular attacks in Pakistani cities. On January 1, 2009, they were preparing to take their brand of mass murder on the road.

All by himself, Swedan would have made a worthy target. At the time he stumbled into the CIA's surveillance net, he was on the most wanted lists for both the CIA and FBI and had been indicted in New York for assisting the 1998 bombings of U.S. embassies in Kenya and Tanzania. His apparent hideout in late 2008—an abandoned girls' school on the outskirts of a village called Karikot—had also drawn keen interest. The CIA's informants identified the building as a training academy for al-Qaeda's bomb makers.

Hayden mulled his options and decided to wait. As important as he was, Swedan was only a deputy, and he wasn't going anywhere. On the morning of January 1 he was under constant surveillance, not only by CIA operatives on the ground but also by a pair of Predators flying above the village. Sooner or later Swedan would have to communicate with his boss, and then Hayden would have a much bigger prize.

The CIA had been waiting for such an opportunity for more than a decade. Like his deputy, Osama al-Kini was also linked to the 1998 African bombings and had a five-million-dollar bounty on his head. Slim and athletic with tightly curled locks, al-Kini had been part of Osama bin Laden's entourage since the early days and had been promoted to operations planner. By 2007 he was al-Qaeda's top regional commander for all of Pakistan, and he was good at his job. His cell assisted the Pakistani Taliban in the assassination of former prime minister Benazir Bhutto and carried out bombings and suicide attacks against police stations, army camps, a civilian court, and a naval academy. Then, in September 2008, he achieved something far more ambitious, a massive truck bombing at Islamabad's luxurious Marriott Hotel. The blast killed more than fifty workers and guests, wounded two hundred others, and made headlines around the world.

Al-Kini was now muscling his way into al-Qaeda's senior ranks while putting his personal stamp on the organization. Aggressive and charismatic, he was popular with the group's younger fighters, and he was beginning to pose a challenge to al-Qaeda's more experienced leaders, particularly a commander named Sheikh Saeed al-Masri, a cruel-tempered Egyptian who controlled the group's purse strings and claimed the top leadership spot after Zawahiri. Most ominously, al-Kini was preparing to go international, dispatching some of his top trainees to Western Europe. CIA officials concluded that the Kenyan was attempting to lay the groundwork for a network of terrorist cells across Europe that could begin casing major hotels and other landmarks for future attacks.

It was this threat that weighed most heavily on Mike Hayden on January 1 as he waited for news from northwestern Pakistan. The CIA director had not yet fallen asleep when the phone rang at 10:30 P.M. with fresh word from the hunt. Hayden rolled out of bed and trudged to his basement office to get on a secure phone line.

It was already daylight in Pakistan, and one of the CIA's Predators had been hovering nearby as Swedan left the girls' school for an early appointment. As the CIA watched, Swedan met with a man he appeared to know, and the two traveled back to the girls' school together. The second man's face was obscured, but everything about him matched the description of the terrorist commander the CIA had been looking for. The duty officer at the Counterterrorism Center had made a judgment call and phoned Hayden for his consent. *Permission to strike?*

Hayden had a standard set of questions for situations such as this, and he proceeded to go through them.

How long have you watched this location?

What is the history of this location, and how many times have you looked at it?

Have you seen women and children in this compound, ever?

From its vantage point a half mile above the village, the lead Predator, which had followed the two men, had already locked its video tracking system on the girls' school while awaiting further instructions. The odd-looking aircraft with its narrow fuselage and bowling alley–length wingspan cut lazy circles in the sky above the town, moving at speeds barely above those of freeway traffic. With a full tank and the usual complement of missiles, it could have continued to hover for fourteen hours without a pause. Instead, with a subtle shift in the engine's pitch, the aircraft widened its arc to line up its body with the building below. In Langley, the live video feed flickered on a pair of flat-screen TVs in the operations center, while the aircraft's two-man crew, in a separate building, made small adjustments to the aircraft's movements with joysticks and the click of a computer mouse.

Hayden thought for a moment. Swedan was inside the building; that was certain. The man with Swedan was doubtlessly an accomplice and very possibly al-Kini himself. The building was a known training facility for al-Qaeda that probably contained explosives and was far enough from the village to ensure that no one else would be harmed. Three for the price of one, Hayden thought.

One or two of the Predator's Hellfire missiles would probably do the job, but Hayden wanted to be doubly sure.

Use the GBU, he ordered. At the command, the Predator's flight crew bypassed the aircraft's fourteen-pound Hellfire missiles and switched on a far larger weapon hidden inside the bomb cavity, a five-hundred-pound laser-guided GBU-12 Paveway. The weapons officer checked the guidance system, made one last tweak, and pressed a button. He counted backward as the missile hurtled toward the village at a speed slightly faster than sound. Three, two, one, the operator called. And then: "Impact."

The building in the black-and-white screen erupted in a massive fireball.

The drone lingered for hours, to record the recovery of two mangled corpses. A local Taliban official confirmed the deaths of the two men he called foreign fighters and "close friends."

By then, the drone operators had ended their shift and climbed into their cars for the journey home, a commute made refreshingly easy by Washington standards because of the holiday.

Hayden sat on his bed to watch the last few minutes of the football game and then fell into a deep sleep. The next morning an intercepted phone call in Pakistan confirmed the death of Osama al-Kini, the last high-ranking al-Qaeda leader to be killed by orders of the Bush administration.

The whereabouts of the other Osama remained unknown.

Weeks later, Mike Hayden was officially out of a job. Newly elected President Barack Obama had opted for a fresh start by naming an old Washington hand, Leon Panetta, to run the CIA. Panetta had no significant intelligence experience but was a proven manager, having been chief of staff in the Clinton White House. One of his first decisions was to retain Hayden's popular deputy, Steve Kappes, as the agency's deputy director and to keep the agency's entire counterterrorism team intact.

Hayden's initial meeting with his successor was cordial, if occasionally awkward. Panetta had gotten off to a poor start inside the CIA by publicly criticizing the agency's harsh treatment of al-Qaeda captives, some of whom had been locked in secret prisons and subjected to waterboarding, an interrogation tactic that mimics the sensation of drowning. Panetta testified in his confirmation hearing that he believed such techniques constituted torture, a criminal offense.

Hayden made a curt reference to the controversy. "You should never use 'torture' and 'CIA' in the same paragraph," he advised dryly. But the retired general was mostly interested in talking about something else. Using notes he had written on an index card, he cautioned Panetta against being lulled into underestimating al-Qaeda.

Although the terrorist group was being hammered in northwestern Pakistan by Predator strikes—a practice Obama had already heartily embraced—it remained capable of hitting Americans in ways that were both unexpected and potentially devastating. Just three months earlier, a Taliban-allied terrorist group from Pakistan had launched commando-style attacks on Mumbai, raking hotels, rail stations, and other buildings with automatic weapons and grenades, and killing more than 170 people.

Hayden now looked directly at Panetta. This was the important part.

"I don't know if you understand this yet, but you are America's combatant commander in the war against terrorism," he said. More than the Pentagon, the FBI, or anyone else, Hayden continued, the CIA was responsible for hunting down terrorists in foreign countries and stopping them before they could strike. Other CIA directors had carried out similar missions in bygone years, but now the job was different: For the first time in the agency's history, "stopping" the bad guys meant killing them.

"You will be making decisions," Hayden said, "that will absolutely surprise you."

Panetta listened politely, but Hayden's final point struck him as a bit dramatic. At military posts, a change of command was often greeted with ceremonial flourish: boot clicks and salutes and theatrical rhetoric. It would be weeks before Panetta fully understood what Hayden meant.

On his way out, Hayden stopped by the White House for a final meeting with the newly elected president. In an Oval Office briefing with Barack Obama, the general mentioned a pair of targets the agency had been monitoring in northwestern Pakistan. Hayden had authorized a strike, and the agency's team was waiting for the right moment, he told the president.

Later that morning, after the meeting had moved into the White House's Situation Room, Hayden was asked about the Pakistani operation. What about those two targets?

Hayden made a quick call on his secure phone.

"Check," he said, "and check."

Hayden left the meeting a few minutes later amid appreciative smiles and handshakes.

They certainly seem supportive, he thought, appraising the young president and his security team with guarded approval.

He had officially passed the baton. Now it was their turn.

2

HAUNTED

London—January 19, 2009

A winter squall was whipping through central London's Grosvenor Square, scattering newspapers and tourists and pelting Franklin Roosevelt's caped statue with sheets of rain. Jennifer Lynne Matthews peered from her office window into the thick weather, barely able to see.

It was another soggy Monday in London and the start of the final stretch of a nearly four-year stint as the CIA's chief liaison on counterterrorism to Britain. Soon she would be on her way either back to Virginia or to an entirely different location—perhaps even Afghanistan—and the uncertainty was making her anxious. The morning's cable traffic had brought unsettling news. The FBI was chasing a possible threat by Somali terrorists to blow up the inaugural parade for the newly elected president, Barack Obama, due to begin in less than twenty-four hours. In Afghanistan, insurgents had attempted an unusually sophisticated double suicide bombing just outside the CIA's secret base near the city of Khost. First, a minivan was blown up at the front gate, killing and wounding mothers and young children who had been waiting in line to see the base doctor. As guards and troops rushed to help the wounded, a truck, sagging under the weight of a massive bomb, came barreling down the main highway. A few well-aimed gunshots by an

Afghan soldier had killed the truck's driver and averted a bigger disaster.

She studied the item, habitually fingering the thick shock of brown hair that spilled across her forehead. Was this the kind of place she wanted to be? Matthews was forty-four now but looked younger, her body lean from years of running and her angular features showing no trace of wrinkles. She was nowhere near retirement, but after two decades of CIA work, her career choices were becoming increasingly momentous. If nothing else, another overseas posting would mean a better pension when the time finally came.

Still. *Afghanistan.*

Matthews sat back in her chair and stared into the gloom outside her window. Office workers were slogging through the square with their umbrellas, and some of them would be heading to pubs later that day for celebrations marking the end of George W. Bush's presidency. Glad though she was to see certain members of Bush's security team leave town, Matthews would not be celebrating. She reserved great disdain for Bush's former defense secretary, Donald Rumsfeld, one of a half dozen men she blamed for letting Osama bin Laden slip away when the CIA had had the terrorist in its crosshairs. But the prospect of an Obama presidency had been more unsettling to some of her former comrades in the agency's Counterterrorism Center. Candidate Obama had condemned the agency's past use of waterboarding and had even called it torture, suggesting that investigations, public hearings, and even criminal charges were on the agenda.

Matthews knew about waterboarding. She had spent weeks by the side of Abu Zubaida, the man who became renowned as the first high-value al-Qaeda prisoner to be subjected to the procedure, in a controversial, secret prison overseas. As one of the CIA's leading al-Qaeda experts she had fed questions to the interrogators as they did their work. She had been pregnant at the time and became so sick afterward that her doctors worried about the health of her unborn baby.

But underlying her anxiety about the torture case was an even deeper secret, one that had gnawed at her for four years and followed her to London when she accepted the CIA's liaison post in 2005. Thousands of miles from CIA headquarters, in the heart of one of the world's great cities, she had plunged into her new role with an intensity that left her physically and emotionally spent, yet it was clear when a lawyer friend from the CIA General Counsel's Office stopped by for a visit that the old pain still raged.

"I can't get this thing out of my head," she told him, fighting back tears. Matthews had gone over the details many times, with this friend and others. The lawyer offered reassurance but quickly concluded that it was hopeless. "She was haunted," he later said.

The reasons for Matthews's anguish were well known within the CIA, where roughly two dozen other officers carried the same burden. After the September 11, 2001, terrorist attacks the CIA's internal watchdog, the Office of the Inspector General, had launched a wide-ranging investigation into how the intelligence agency had failed to uncover the al-Qaeda plot to hijack four airliners and crash them into buildings. Other U.S. departments shared in what was arguably a government-wide failure, but the agency's probe homed in on CIA missteps that had allowed two of the nineteen hijackers to enter the United States undetected.

Leading the probe was career CIA analyst John L. Helgerson, a quietly amiable former college professor who surprised his peers by becoming one of the most aggressive and fiercely independent inspectors general in the agency's history. Helgerson concluded that the CIA's Counterterrorism Center had failed to respond to a series of cabled warnings in 2000 about two al-Qaeda operatives who later became part of the September 11 plot. The first warning came in January of that year, when the two operatives, Nawaf al-Hazmi and Khalid al-Mihdhar, were observed attending a meeting of suspected terrorists in Malaysia. Soon afterward the CIA learned that one of the men had obtained a U.S. visa, and the other had apparently already entered the United States. The cables were seen by as many as sixty CIA employees, yet the two operatives' names were never passed along to the FBI, which might have assigned agents to track them down, or shared with the State Department, which could have flagged their names on its watch list. In theory, the arrest of either man could have led investigators to the other hijackers and the eventual unraveling of the 9/11 plot.

Helgerson's report named individual managers who it said bore the greatest responsibility for failing to ensure that vital information was passed to the FBI. The report, never released in full, also recommended that some of the managers be reviewed for possible disciplinary action.

Jennifer Matthews was on that list.

The report ignited a furor at CIA headquarters as top agency officials pushed back sharply against Helgerson's call for individual accountability. It was unfair, Helgerson's critics argued, to tarnish a few managers for what had been a collective failure. The agency's director at the time, Porter Goss, decided the matter by formally rejecting disciplinary reviews. He then ordered that Helgerson's list of names remain classified.

From the reprieved officers came a collective sigh of relief. But Matthews would not be consoled. It galled her that she, one of a handful of dedicated al-Qaeda experts in the CIA before 2001, had been accused of failing to take al-Qaeda seriously. Matthews believed the opposite was true: She had been among the few who had recognized the threat posed by Osama bin Laden in the 1990s. Like others in the agency's al-Qaeda unit, she faulted the country's political leaders for missing numerous chances to kill or capture the Saudi terrorist.

It was abhorrent to Matthews that her name would be forever linked to one of the worst intelligence failures in U.S. history. The jagged sliver continued to bore into her psyche years later in London, long after public interest in the agency's pre–September 11 failures had dried up.

As Matthews sat in her sparsely furnished office overlooking Grosvenor Square, she could see how it would all unfold. A leak that revealed her name as one of the culpable. A media flurry. A ruined career. And, most painful to contemplate, public disgrace.

"The worst part was that her children would know," said the CIA lawyer who visited with her. "She would be indelibly tarnished, forever linked to the failures of September 11."

London had served as a welcome respite for Matthews and her family, at a time when she really needed it. She had relished her long weekends and holidays traveling with the family around Europe. She savored repeat performances of her favorite musical, *Les Misérables*, on the London stage, and she bought cases of French wine to add to a growing collection back home. At work, Matthews was caught up in the investigations of several international terrorism plots, including the 2006 al-Qaeda plan to blow up commercial airliners using liquid explosives. British colleagues came to respect her knowledge of the subject matter and quickly adjusted to her take-no-prisoners style. "I could always tell which of my office mates had met with Jennifer on any day," one British intelligence officer would later recall. "It was always the busiest person in the room."

But now it was over, and Matthews was torn over what to do next. Most of the typical slots for someone with her background involved a desk somewhere back in Langley, an unappealing prospect for multiple reasons. Career-wise she was near the top of the government's civilian pay scale, yet she lacked the experience in key areas necessary to make the jump into upper management, the so-called senior executive service, where minimum salaries start at $111,000 a year.

During trips to Washington she rode the elevator to the CIA's seventh-floor administrative wing to seek advice. The guidance was consistent: There were gaps in Matthews's résumé that had to be filled before she could advance. Matthews was already an experienced manager who had led ably in London and Langley. But in two decades of counterterrorism work, she had never served in Kabul or Baghdad, front-line posts that were central to the CIA's core mission. If Matthews really wanted to move up, she had to go to war.

But not all war zone jobs were the same, she discovered. A stint in Baghdad's Green Zone would mean three years of hard work away from family. But within the constellation of CIA facilities were a few dismal outposts where conditions were so harsh or so dangerous that a one-year assignment was considered equivalent to three years anywhere else.

A base chief's slot was due to open up in the early fall in just such a place, Matthews was told. It was in the wilds of eastern Afghanistan not far from Tora Bora, in what historically had been considered one of the roughest locales in that most violent of countries. It also was next door to a pair of Pakistani provinces that were the heartland of the Taliban and the location of the last confirmed sighting of Osama bin Laden.

Matthews knew the place. It was called Khost.

Other officers already were vying for the position, but Matthews quickly claimed the inside track. Several of the CIA's most senior officers supported her for the job, telling Matthews that her one-year stint would be as beneficial to the agency as it would be to her own career.

Some of her closest friends and mentors were divided on whether she was suited for such a position. Some worried that it was too much, too soon. Matthews had no experience in dealing with the security demands of living and traveling in a war zone. She also had little background in the science of running covert agents, a separate tradition within the spy agency with its own highly specialized training and skills. Much of the Pakistani work at Khost involved working with networks of undercover operatives.

Then there was the personality factor. CIA peers who worked with Matthews regularly knew her to be passionate and direct, but also impatient and stubborn.

"She didn't take questions well, and she had no patience for people who didn't know as much about a subject as she did," recalled a former covert officer who met with her regularly at Langley. "She had this way of sighing audibly, as if to say, 'I know this; why don't you?' "

Yet it was hard to argue that she lacked experience. Matthews had helped run operations against al-Qaeda from Washington and London for nearly fifteen years, and her role in the CIA's takedown of Abu Zubaida had been roundly praised. Matthews's team had led the agency's two-year search for al-Qaeda's former logistics man, tracking him at last to a safe house in the Pakistani city of Faisalabad, where he was surrounded and captured by dozens of Pakistani commandos and CIA paramilitary officers.

Moreover, Matthews's superiors saw in her exactly the qualities the agency needed in its escalating war against al-Qaeda: leadership skills, mental toughness, enthusiasm, ambition, and an unquestioned mastery of the subject matter. One of her bosses had a pet name for her: STRAC. It was an old Navy acronym that stood for "Standing Tall, Ready Around the Clock." The CIA had big plans for Matthews, it was clear, and the point of sending her to Afghanistan was to help her gain the experience she needed. With the agency stretched thin by years of deployments to Iraq and Afghanistan, it was getting harder to find willing volunteers whose job skills lined up perfectly with the opening. But in Matthews's case, the candidate in question seemed to have the important ones, said a retired senior officer who weighed in on her professional appraisal.

"She was so smart and so careful," the officer said. "The best people are simply the best people. An excellent case officer can also be an excellent analyst, and vice versa."

Matthews, by all accounts, spent even less time worrying about her fitness for the job. Khost offered everything she was looking for: both a way to move up and a path to personal redemption. The mere fact that some were questioning her ability made her even more determined, friends said.

Matthews did finally seek the advice of one dissenter, a retired CIA officer whom she respected, someone who knew the bureaucracy well and was unfailingly blunt in his opinions. The two spent an afternoon together on his porch overlooking the Virginia foothills. Then they got on his computer to look at satellite images on Google Earth. In the photographs, the CIA base at Khost is clearly identifiable because it sits on an airfield with a packed-dirt runway, expanded by the Soviets in the 1980s to support bombing sorties against Afghan rebels dug in to the mountains. Just east of the base was the border crossing at Ghulam Khan, gateway to Pakistani strongholds controlled by notorious warlords and militants such as Jalaluddin Haqqani, Baitullah Mehsud, and perhaps bin Laden himself.

The retired officer attempted to distill his advice in a way that he hoped would penetrate Matthews's reflexive defenses. For the CIA's sake and for yours, he told her, Khost is the last place you should want to go.

"I understand the drive you're feeling to go there," the officer told her, according to his account of the conversation. "But you're not thinking clearly. This is a paramilitary environment, and you have no experience with that."

He ticked off a list of other concerns. Khost ran covert agents, something that Matthews knew little about. The drone strikes she helped orchestrate could kill innocent civilians and possibly expose her to legal jeopardy. Even her gender would work against her, he said, as Afghan tribesmen would be loath to negotiate as equals with a woman, particularly one wearing fatigue pants and a T-shirt.

Matthews's eyes flashed at the suggestion that she as a woman would be at a disadvantage. The conversation became heated, and the more the two argued, the more adamant Matthews became.

"She already knew she was going to Afghanistan," Matthews's adviser later said. "I tried to talk her out of it, but she was hearing something else. She thought I was saying she couldn't handle it."

Unable to dissuade Matthews, the retired officer instead wished her good luck. It was the last time they would meet.

3

THE DOCTOR

Amman, Jordan—January 19, 2009

The raiding party gathered in the street just before 11:00 P.M. and waited, as always, for the bedroom lights and TV sets to flicker out. Darkness would mean fewer witnesses, and a sleeping household would allow the agents of Jordan's feared Mukhabarat intelligence service to work quickly, with a minimum of noise and fuss. There would be no knock at the door and no spoken commands. Just a crash of metal against wood and a single coordinated movement that would sweep the hapless suspect from his bedclothes to the back of a waiting car.

The target on this raw January night was a four-story house on Urwa Bin Al-Ward Street, a narrow alley in a Palestinian immigrant neighborhood of neatly scrubbed stone houses the color of beach sand. Just before midnight, two black sedans moved from their parking spot on cue and pulled into the alley with headlights off, while a third parked diagonally across the street to block traffic. Police and Mukhabarat agents in dark clothing dispersed to take positions around the front and rear of the house, and a small breach team gathered by the front door to await the signal. One of them, a stout intelligence captain wearing a black commando sweater, clutched a warrant with orders for the arrest of a young physician named Humam Khalil Abu Mulal al-Balawi. The man they were seeking was thirty-one years old and had never been accused of anything more serious than a traffic violation. Yet in forty-eight hours Balawi had emerged as one of the most dangerous men in all Jordan.

Just as the raid was set to begin, a scuffle broke out between some of the Mukhabarat's officers and a group of young men walking home from a party. The men gathered around the strange car straddling the alley and began hectoring the driver for blocking the street. Another plainclothes officer arrived, and soon there were shouts and shoving.

I'm calling the police, one of the men was yelling.

Inside the house, the commotion roused the suspect's father, Khalil al-Balawi. The sixty-six-year-old retired schoolteacher had dozed off while reading on the living room sofa and awoke to angry voices just outside his front window. The bearded pensioner peered through the curtain and, seeing nothing, tied his robe and hobbled to the front door. He had opened it only a crack when the door burst inward, flinging him back. Three figures in leather coats brushed past him without a word, while a fourth moved toward the old man as though to block him.

Balawi, still foggy, guessed that the intruders were trying to escape the fight under way in the street. But now three of the men were bounding up the stairs, toward the apartments where Balawi's adult children lived with their families. He started to protest but felt a viselike grip on his shoulder. It was a large man in a black sweater.

"Mukhabarat," the man said quietly, using the Arabic term for the spy service known officially as the General Intelligence Department, or GID. He handed Balawi a creased document. "We're here for Humam."

Balawi felt his knees buckle. Was he dreaming? From upstairs came desperate sounds: A child's piercing scream. Bangs and thumps. His daughter-in-law's voice shouting, then pleading, then wailing. Finally a single thought crystallized in his brain: This is a mistake. It was the wrong house, the wrong Humam. His son was a healer, not a criminal.

"Whatever you're looking for—it doesn't exist!" he stammered to the captain. "We don't have weapons or drugs. We don't keep anything against the law!"

The officer's hazel eyes met the old man's with a look that seemed to convey sympathy, but he said nothing. Khalil al-Balawi's mind raced. Was it possible that Humam had a secret life? Was he stealing from the clinic? No, not possible, he thought. *Humam is a homebody. He has no use for money. He doesn't go to the nightclubs in the Western hotels downtown. He barely leaves the house.*

More shouts and thumps. Then two of the officers thundered down the steps with what Khalil al-Balawi recognized as his son's belongings. One carried a desktop computer, and the other was struggling with a box crammed with books, papers, and a rack of computer disks. The first man set down the computer and presented the elderly Balawi with a handwritten list under a heading that read, "Prohibited items." It was an inventory of the electronics and paper records seized as evidence.

"Sign here to say we didn't break anything," the man ordered.

Khalil al-Balawi was wide awake now, and his skin flushed beneath his red beard. "Where are you taking him? What's this about?" he demanded.

"You can ask about him tomorrow," the officer replied, "at the Mukhabarat."

The old man stared at the pen that had been thrust into his hand, then looked up to see his son being led down the stairs by one of the officers. Humam Khalil al-Balawi was wearing a knee-length kurta shirt, pajama pants, and he was walking slowly, eyes fixed on the steps. At five feet seven he was slightly taller than his father, but narrow at the waist and shoulders, and he had the delicate skin of a man who keeps company with books and computers. His brown curls and wispy beard were matted from sleep, so that he looked more like a scrawny teenager than an accomplished physician with a practice and two kids of his own.

At the bottom of the staircase the procession stopped. To his father, the younger Balawi seemed oddly, inexplicably detached, as though he were sleepwalking. Then he caught his son's eyes. They were inordinately large and as soft and brown as a doe's. They were also incapable of hiding emotion, quick to betray fear or anger or whatever passion Humam happened to be feeling. But on this day they were ablaze with something the older man could not immediately grasp. It wasn't fear, or nervousness, or even anger, exactly, but something more akin to contempt, like a champion boxer who had just taken a sucker punch.

"It was defiance I saw," the elder Balawi said afterward. "I knew the look. It was very *Humam.*"

Neither man spoke. There was a brief jostling at the door, and then the old man watched the officers shove his son into the back of one of the cars. In an instant, Dr. Humam al-Balawi, the gifted scholar and pediatrician who had dreamed of practicing in the United States, disappeared behind tinted glass, along with his reputation and all traces of his former life. From now on, no matter what else happened, he would live his life as a man who had been marked by the Mukhabarat.

The only unknown was where precisely his path would end. Humam could choose defiance and see his career destroyed, the family name tarnished, and his children reduced to poverty. Or he could cooperate and endure the ignominy of becoming an informant for the government. Some Jordanians who chose the latter course had gone slowly insane, isolated from friends and mistrusted by coworkers. Others had fled the country, and still others had simply disappeared behind the walls of the Mukhabarat's fortresslike headquarters, never to be heard from again.

Khalil al-Balawi shivered as he stood in the doorway in his thin robe, watching the slow-motion demolition of his son's life and his own hopes for a quietly comfortable old age. He strained his eyes, hoping for a last glimpse, but the windows of the dark sedan revealed nothing. The lead car with Humam inside made a tight U-turn in the alley, rounded the corner, and was gone.

"Your handcuffs will be as silver bracelets. The hangman's noose will be a medal of honor."

The Arabic characters skittered across the computer screen as Humam al-Balawi typed, pressing the keys softly to avoid waking his wife and two girls asleep in the room next door. It was June 2007, nineteen months before his arrest, and he was doing the thing he loved most. In a few hours it would be daylight and he would be on his way to the children's clinic to prescribe antibiotics and treat tummy aches and fevers. But at this moment, in the quiet of the family kitchen, he was Abu Dujana al-Khorasani, cyberwarrior for Islam and scourge of the Americans and their Arab lackeys around the world.

"Brothers, download these videos until your Internet cable gets overheated because of how hot the clips are," Balawi wrote, pausing to insert coding that would allow readers to view a collage of Iraqi insurgent attacks on U.S. troops whose Humvees erupted in clouds of flame, smoke, and shrapnel. *"Watch how the Americans get killed as if they were in PlayStation video games."*

Balawi read the sentences back to himself and, satisfied, clicked a button to transmit. In seconds, his column would appear as the billboard item on the Web site al-Hesbah, one of the leading outlets for radical Islamic views and teachings in the Arabic-speaking world.

"Abu Dujana" was a mere invention, a fake identity created by Balawi initially so he could express himself in chat rooms without fear of getting arrested. But over time the character had evolved a personality of its own. Where the young physician was respectful and reserved, Abu Dujana was aggressive, blunt, and bitingly sarcastic, an evil twin with a devilish sense of humor. He was also an instant hit. New postings by Abu Dujana al-Khorasani were among the most widely read items on al-Hesbah and received the most comments. Soon he was asked to serve as moderator of the Web site's discussion groups, a position that put him in charge of the daily online conversation and gave him a showcase for his own columns.

Abu Dujana had been thrust into a small elite of jihadist writers and pundits with large online audiences and global reach. Yet no one knew who he really was. The speculation among his most ardent online followers was that he was a Saudi and very likely a senior official within al-Qaeda. But in fact even the al-Hesbah managers who gave Abu Dujana the moderator's job did not know his true name or nationality. Nor did the Mukhabarat or the CIA, which employs teams of specialists to monitor jihadist Web sites full-time and write reports deciphering and analyzing their content. Balawi's father and brothers joked about his love affair with his computer, but even they knew nothing about the secret life he created on the flickering blue screen.

The transformation would occur at home, usually at night or on weekends, when he was free from his duties at the clinic. Balawi would hunch over his small desktop computer for hour after hour until his eyes reddened and his wife, Defne, began to worry. Already Balawi had a reputation for being a recluse, rarely going out or socializing with friends or even attending Friday prayers at the local mosque. Balawi would deflect Defne's questions by insisting that he had to study, but when she came into the room, the books would be tossed to the side and her husband would be where he always was, perched on his favorite chair with eyes locked on the computer screen. The more Abu Dujana grew, the smaller Balawi and his old life became.

"He was preoccupied," Defne said later. "He was living in fantasy in another world."

Balawi had written online columns under several other fake names before Abu Dujana al-Khorasani made his first appearance in 2007, just as Balawi was hitting his stride as an essayist. The pseudonym itself was a mash-up of historical names instantly recognizable to devout Muslims; *Al-Khorasani* means "from Khorasan," the ancient name for the vast swath of Muslim lands stretching from the old Persian empire to the Hindu Kush mountains, encompassing much of modern-day Afghanistan. Abu Dujana was a seventh-century Arab warrior who was a favorite of the Prophet Muhammad's. A skilled swordsman who relished the mayhem of hand-to-hand combat, he was also arrogant and showy. Before battle he would don a red headband and taunt his enemies by strutting mockingly in front of their lines.

Abu Dujana the pundit was a showman as well, prone to verbal bluster and fireworks. His first articles quickly cemented his reputation as one of the most engaging and colorful writers in the online community of radical Islam. He raged against all the usual targets—Israel, the West, and U.S.-friendly Arab governments— but his writings also reflected an understanding of Western culture and a knack for appealing to younger Muslims who grew up with instant messaging and social networks. In one passage he would excoriate ordinary Muslims as being unthinking clones, "like Dolly, the cloned sheep," and in another he would write wistfully about a future in which even the Barbie doll "will wear the veil and recite the Koran when you touch it."

He would also entice his audience with images of battlefield carnage, fresh from amateur jihadi photographers in Tikrit or Ramadi, served up with a gleefully ghoulish commentary that became Abu Dujana's trademark.

"Welcome to the al-Hesbah café," he wrote to open one Internet session. "Go to the menu and pick today's dish:

"Roasted Humvee with sauce of human remains.

"Exploded tank by an IED [improvised explosive device] with no survivors.

"Or a pastry made of Americans' brains taken out with snipers' bullets."

Thousands of Muslims sampled Abu Dujana's offerings and paused to read his words. And each week the appetite for his articles grew larger still. Abu Dujana—whoever he was, wherever he was—was becoming a true celebrity.

He had to be stopped.

Inside the headquarters of the secretive National Security Agency in suburban Washington is a computer search engine unlike any other in the world. Code-named Turbulence, it is a five-hundred-million-dollar-a-year network that continuously vacuums up terabytes of data from across the Internet and scours them for possible security threats. When specific targets are identified—a new Web site or an unknown militant group, for instance—it can burrow into a single computer on the other side of the world to steal files or drop off eavesdropping software. Agents on the ground can then follow up with portable surveillance gear so sensitive it can detect individual strokes on a computer keyboard from hundreds of feet away.

The precise methods used for tracking a specific target overseas are a closely guarded secret. But what is known is that sometime in late 2008, such tools were used to hunt down a popular jihadist blogger who called himself Abu Dujana al-Khorasani. Working backward through a maze of servers and trunk lines spanning continents, U.S. officials narrowed the search to Jordan, then to Amman, and finally to a single house in a working-class neighborhood called Jabal Nuzha.

The man's true identity came as a shock, most especially to Jordan's Mukhabarat intelligence service: One of radical Islam's rising stars was an obscure pediatrician living right under its noses.

What happened next was up to the Mukhabarat. While the CIA and its foreign counterparts closely monitor jihadist Web sites and occasionally shut them down, more often they prefer to quietly study them for insights into how terrorist movements are evolving. The Mukhabarat would have to decide if the man who called Muslims to holy war as the fictitious Abu Dujana posed a flesh-and-blood threat to Jordan and beyond. Someone would have to go to school on Humam Khalil al-Balawi, and that person ultimately turned out to be a midlevel officer who understood the phenomenon of Internet jihad as well as anyone in the agency's counterterrorism division. His name was Ali bin Zeid, but he was known among his peers as Sharif Ali, an honorific that denoted noble birth. Bin Zeid was a direct descendant of Jordan's first monarch, Abdullah I, and a cousin to the king.

Just thirty-four, bin Zeid was already a ten-year veteran of the intelligence service, with a number of medals and commendations to his credit, including one from the CIA. Sensitive to perceptions that his royal blood accorded him privileges, he worked long hours and never mentioned his ties to the crown unless there was something to be gained for his entire unit. Once, during a training exercise in the desert, he pulled rank to arrange for a special lunch delivery to his campsite: Big Macs and fries for everyone in his company. But he was also serious and intense. His weapon of choice was a fat .44 Magnum pistol known as a Desert Eagle, which he hoped would even the odds in case he encountered a would-be assassin looking to make his mark by killing a son of the monarchy.

The stocky, thick-chested bin Zeid was also more Western than most of his colleagues, having attended college in Boston and worked as an intern for Massachusetts' junior U.S. senator, Democrat John Kerry. He spoke immaculate East Coast–accented English, and he was tight with his American counterparts in the CIA's station in Amman, particularly a former Army Ranger named Darren LaBonte. The two men were frequently partners when the two agencies worked together on terrorism cases, and they had traveled the world together, from Eastern Europe to the Far East. Both newlyweds with young wives, they sometimes spent lazy weekends in a foursome on the Red Sea near Aqaba in bin Zeid's boat.

Bin Zeid and LaBonte would brainstorm about difficult cases, and few were more perplexing than that of the mysterious doctor the Jordanian was assigned to watch. The Mukhabarat had gathered reams of material on Balawi and had trailed him for weeks on his excruciatingly dull ten-mile trek from central Amman to the United Nations' Center for Motherhood and Children, where he worked in the Marka refugee camp. Bin Zeid read the files and daily reports and pondered them, set them aside, then read them again.

Who was this guy? bin Zeid wondered aloud to his colleagues.

Nothing about Balawi fitted the usual pattern for terrorist or supporter of outlaw groups. There had been no brushes with the law, no record of violence, no known association with radical groups or even with Jordan's Muslim Brotherhood, the creaky eighty-year-old social movement that by now was noted mostly for its fund-raising dinners for Iraqi orphans and widows.

Instead the files depicted a young man of extraordinary ability and achievement. Balawi came from a stable college-educated family with no hint of scandal. He was faithful to his wife and doted on his two young girls. He had a do-gooder streak a mile wide, yet he showed no outward signs of religious fanaticism.

His school records were singularly impressive. A graduate of Amman High School with top honors and a 97 percent grade point average. Winner of a college scholarship from the Jordanian government. Fluent in English.

After high school, he had been a shoo-in for the University of Jordan's biosciences program, but he chose instead to go abroad to study medicine. He won admission to the University of Istanbul and, though he initially spoke not a word of Turkish, earned both a bachelor's degree and doctorate of medicine in six years. Balawi had returned to Jordan with a Turkish wife, a college-educated journalist, and settled in an apartment in his father's house. A wide array of career choices beckoned him, but he eventually decided to turn down a hospital assignment for one of the least glamorous medical positions in the city: tending to mothers and young children at the sprawling Marka camp, home to tens of thousands of ethnic Palestinians who had moved there as refugees after the Arab-Israeli War in 1967. The camp's denizens quickly took a liking to the soft-eyed doctor, who was gentle with children yet also oddly serious for such a young man.

"He wasn't flirty like some of the others," said one single mother from the camp who saw Balawi frequently. "He seemed very shy, and he didn't joke a lot."

The portrait that emerged of Balawi was that of a social introvert who lived modestly and rarely went anywhere other than work. He drove a banged-up Ford Escort that doubled on most days as a free taxi service for any neighbors or patients who happened to need a lift. The Mukhabarat's spies found nothing that suggested he was quietly meeting with Hamas or other radical groups or even knew who they were.

Still, there was the matter of Abu Dujana al-Khorasani. Balawi's secret online hobby had become a big deal, even bigger, no doubt, than Balawi had ever dreamed. More disturbingly, his writings seemed to suggest a hidden connection with al-Qaeda. Abu Dujana had always lionized the terrorist group and its founder, Osama bin Laden, but lately he seemed to be speaking *for* them. Anytime al-Qaeda's No. 2 leader, Ayman al-Zawahiri, came out with a new statement or video message, Abu Dujana was there with fresh analysis, annotating and interpreting Zawahiri's stilted Arabic. His essays defending al-Qaeda's tactics so closely reflected Zawahiri's own views that they might have been written by Zawahiri himself. Whether al-Qaeda intended it or not, Abu Dujana had become a mouthpiece and booster for the terrorist group. And Muslims around the world were paying attention.

Worse, Abu Dujana's views were skewing increasingly radical. He had launched a personal crusade to rehabilitate Jordanian terrorist Abu Musab al-Zarqawi, the thuggish leader of al-Qaeda in Iraq who made videos of himself cutting off the heads of American hostages. Jordanians had poured into the streets to denounce Zarqawi in 2005 after he launched a series of coordinated attacks on hotels in Amman, killing sixty people, many of them women and children who had been attending a wedding reception. But Abu Dujana called him a "tiger" who embodied a robust, energetic faith that true Muslims should aspire to. Most recently, amid torrents of bile over Israel's military assault on Gaza on December 27, 2008, he began hinting about moving into an operational phase. "When will my words taste my blood?" he wrote.

Humam al-Balawi, the doctor, ambled along as before. But Abu Dujana was hurtling down a dangerous path, inciting others to violence and threatening to join them. By mid-January 2009, Ali bin Zeid and his bosses had made up their minds: Abu Dujana had to go. Whether Balawi survived or perished along with his jihadist avatar was up to him.

In the dark, the headquarters of the Mukhabarat looms over western Amman like a medieval fortress, with high walls of limestone blocks that have leached over the years to produce an oozy reddish stain. The oldest part of the complex was once one of the most feared prisons in the Middle East, a labyrinth of stone-walled cells reserved for suspected terrorists and other enemies of the state. The few who ventured inside told stories of dark passageways, of whips made of knotted electric cords, of shrieks and screams coming from the interrogation room late at night. Among some in Jordan, the building had earned a grim nickname, the Fingernail Factory.

Times were different now, at least on the surface. Jordan's media-savvy, pro-Western monarch, King Abdullah II, disliked seeing reports from human rights groups of torture by the country's intelligence service. He dismantled the old prison and, in 2005, fired the Mukhabarat's ruthlessly efficient director, Saad Kheir, a man with genteel English manners and the icy regard of a rattlesnake.

But despite the happy talk about detainee rights and due process, the spy agency could ill afford to be seen as soft. Jordan, with a population of just over six million, was a moderate Arab state allied with the United States and officially at peace with Israel, policies that automatically made it a target for most of the region's Islamic terrorist groups as well as Iran, which funded many of them. The country has long been a way station for Iraqi criminal gangs, Iranian provocateurs, Hamas, and Hezbollah. It has endured savage attacks from al-Qaeda, including Zarqawi's 2005 killing spree in which suicide bombers blew themselves up in three Amman hotels. Zarqawi, who had spent five years as the Mukhabarat's prisoner in the 1990s, had tried repeatedly to exact revenge by destroying the agency itself. In 2004 the Mukhabarat narrowly averted an attack on its headquarters after Zarqawi loaded a couple of trucks with enough explosives and poison gas to wipe out tens of thousands of people. In the end, it was a Mukhabarat informant—a Zarqawi foot soldier in Jordanian custody—who gave up the location of Zarqawi's safe house near Baqubah, Iraq. On June 7, 2006, a pair of U.S. fighter jets dropped two five-hundred-pound bombs on the building, killing Zarqawi along with his wife and child and four others.

What Humam al-Balawi knew of the Mukhabarat and its reputation is unclear. But somewhere between his house and the intelligence headquarters, Abu Dujana and all his bluster had faded from sight. Balawi was handcuffed and sandwiched between Mukhabarat agents, who had squeezed into seats on either side of him. One of them reached over and shoved a cloth hood over his face, pulling the drawstring tight.

The foul-smelling covering not only blinded him but also made it hard to breathe. Metal cuffs bit into his wrists and forced him to lean forward in his seat.

Your handcuffs will be as silver bracelets.

The convoy wound through nearly deserted streets, past the mosque Balawi had attended since boyhood, past the empty bazaar, and past the elementary school with its concrete playground. It eased onto the modern highway that leads to central Amman, whizzing by shopping malls and gleaming hotels with bars lit in neon at this hour and past the expensive fitness clubs where men and women were said to work out together, paying money to sweat in air-conditioned rooms in their booty shorts, sports bras, and muscle shirts.

The procession turned north to enter a new section of town known as Wadi as-Seer, a district of broad avenues and heavy limestone buildings with military guards but no signs to identify the occupants. Balawi felt the car stop, twice, at security checkpoints, and then the vehicle was inside a gate. It rolled through a series of connected courtyards until it halted outside a large stone building that serves as headquarters for the Mukhabarat's "Knights of Truth," the elite counterterrorism division. Unseen by the hooded Balawi were the imposing portraits of the last two Jordanian kings and the black flag of the intelligence service, bearing its motto in Arabic script: "Justice has come."

4

HUMILIATION

Amman, Jordan—January 20, 2009

Who is Abu Dujana al-Khorasani?

Balawi was groggily aware of the question and was forming his words when he felt the sharp sting of a slap across his cheek. He was fully awake now, and the hood was finally gone. He was in a small cell with solid white walls, sitting on a wooden stool, the room's only furnishing other than a battered desk, a fluorescent light, and a metal pin to which his legs were shackled. Two men were standing on either side of him, and one of them drew an arm back as though to hit him again.

Who is Abu Dujana?

You already know that it's me, Balawi said, wearily.

It was barely midmorning, and already Balawi had endured four rounds of interrogation. The aim was to quickly exhaust him, and it was working. An hour in the interrogation room, then two hours in his cell, then back under the lights with fresh interrogators. Between sessions he would try to sleep, but the moment his eyes closed the guards were at him again, shouting curses and banging doors. Then he was back in the interrogation room again, questions flying at him like swarms of blackflies.

Who controls the al-Hesbah Web site? Who are the other writers? Where do they live? Who is your contact?

When this inquiry yielded nothing, the Mukhabarat's men probed Balawi's personal life, his family history, his brothers, his Turkish in-laws, his school years abroad. Questions were reasked, twisted slightly, and asked again. Sometimes they carried implicit warnings, reminders of the Mukhabarat's ability to touch Balawi where he lived.

Where did you get your medical license? Are you sure it's valid?

Your father is not Jordanian, is he? Are his papers up-to-date?

What about your Turkish wife? Your children are Turks, too, aren't they?

The threats were real, as Balawi well knew. His father was one of more than a million Palestinians to whom Jordan has played reluctant host since the first Arab-Israeli War in 1948 sent them in search of refuge. For a noncitizen, crossing any of dozens of invisible lines could mean forfeiting the right to a Jordanian passport or residency papers. Work permits, including professional licenses, can be voided over mere suspicions. The message was clear: Cooperate or lose everything.

By now Balawi could distinguish among his interrogators. The division chief, dubbed the Red Devil by other detainees, was Ali Burjak, the part-Turkish senior officer who was one of the most feared men in Jordan. Heavy and short, with reddish, close-cropped hair, he had famously broken some of the country's most hardened criminals and terrorists, and he also had tangled with journalists, opposition figures, and others who had fallen afoul of the state. He took special delight, it was widely said, in humiliating his captives, sometimes by forcing them to confess gratuitously to incest or other sexual crimes.

Working with Burjak was a small team of counterterrorism specialists from the Knights of Truth. They were considered the elite of the Mukhabarat, in part because they worked most closely with foreign intelligence agencies and also because they did everything: conducting surveillance; intercepting phone signals; making arrests; interrogating captives. The group took orders from Burjak and his deputy, a man called Habis. The other officer who stood out was the stout, hazel-eyed captain who had been present during the arrest. Though quieter and less abrasive than some of the others, he was treated by his peers with a deference that seemed disproportionate to his captain's bars. The men called him Sharif Ali.

When the Mukhabarat's men ran out of questions, Balawi was led back to his cell, which was newly built and clean but tiny, measuring nine by six feet, and furnished with a cot and blanket, a two-way mirror, and a metal commode and sink. The hood was again pulled over his face, and the cell's thick metal door was slammed shut, leaving Balawi alone in complete darkness. He felt his way to the cot, sat, and waited.

Minutes passed, then an hour. Or was it two? From his darkened cocoon, there was no way to tell.

The hooding was standard treatment, a way of softening up Balawi for an extended cycle of interrogation and isolation that was just getting under way. Nearly all detainees are blindfolded, sometimes for days at a time. Unable to see, and hearing only muffled sounds through the cell's steel door, they quickly become disoriented and lose all sense of time. In medical studies, volunteers subjected to similar forms of sensory deprivation begin hallucinating in as little as fifteen minutes. Longer periods induce extreme anxiety, helplessness, and depression. In one study, British scientists discovered that people held under such conditions for forty-eight hours could be made to experience any symptom by mere suggestion. A comfortably dry room could suddenly become freezing cold, or filled with water, or alive with snakes.

Balawi tried reciting prayers to keep his mind focused. But as he later admitted, he was pricked with fear about what was coming and when it would arrive. He would be beaten, no doubt, and probably worse. Was he tough enough to take it? Would he crack and give up the names of contacts? What if they threatened to hurt his wife or the girls? What if they went after his father? Balawi waited, straining for any meaningful sound—footsteps, jangling keys, the tap of a truncheon against cinder block as the guards paced the long corridor.

At some point Balawi remembered his dream. A few weeks earlier he had had a vision of seeing Zarqawi. Balawi had idealized his fellow Jordanian and had wept like a child when the terrorist was killed in the U.S. missile strike in 2006. But in the dream Zarqawi was alive again and, to Balawi's surprise, visiting his father's house.

"Aren't you dead?" Balawi asked him. Zarqawi's face fairly glowed in the moonlight, and he was busy preparing for something. Balawi guessed it was a bombing.

"I was killed, but I am as you see me, alive," Zarqawi said.

Unsure of what to say to the man whose videotapes he had endlessly watched on the Internet, Balawi fumbled for the right words. *Would Zarqawi accept his help? What if Balawi gave him his car? What if they could become martyrs together?*

Zarqawi said nothing, and the dream abruptly ended. Balawi awoke unsettled and days later was so haunted by the strange encounter that he told several friends about it. What could it mean?

Everyone agreed that the dream was an omen. One friend told Balawi that the vision was a warning, a signal that he was about to be arrested. But another said Zarqawi was conveying a blessing. Balawi, he said, had been called by God for special service, an act of jihad for which he had been specially chosen.

"You will mobilize in Allah's path," the friend said.

Twenty-four hours after his arrest, Balawi was showing the strain of a second day without sleep. His voice rasped with exasperation, but there was no fight in his eyes. Across the table from him, the Mukhabarat's men were just getting started.

Who is Abu Shadiyah? Who is Yaman Mukhaddab?

The questioners this time were Ali bin Zeid and a younger officer, and the subject had turned to the identities of other bloggers and commentators who shared the same Web space as Abu Dujana. Balawi could plausibly claim ignorance. Like him, the writers used fake names, and almost no one knew who they really were or where they lived. As far as Balawi knew, the other bloggers might be U.S. intelligence agents. Some of them almost certainly were.

Then a new question: *Tell us about your plans for a martyrdom operation.*

The younger of the interrogators pulled a page from Balawi's file and began to read aloud. Balawi recognized his own words, from an essay he had written after watching a news broadcast about the recent Israeli air strikes in Gaza. News footage showed Israeli women and girls on a rooftop watching as U.S.-made F-16 attack planes pounded targets in Gaza City. The women were taking turns with a pair of binoculars, chatting and laughing as though they were witnessing a polo match. Laughing! As he watched, Balawi felt revulsion sweep over him until it slowly turned inward, filling him with a mixture of rage and loathing, much of it aimed at his cowardly self.

That had been two weeks before. Now Balawi was silent. Spent.

"When will my words drink from my blood?" continued the interrogator, reading from the printed sheet. "I feel my words have expired, and to those who preach jihad, I advise you not to fall into my dilemma and the nightmare I have that I may die one day in my bed."

Ali bin Zeid regarded the detainee for a long moment. *Tough talk. But this man is no Zarqawi.*

Bin Zeid had worked with real terrorists, hard-core jihadis so fanatical that they welcomed death and refused to break no matter what the Mukhabarat threw at them. Balawi had run out of steam on the first day. His words were full of bluster, but the man with the drooping eyelids in front of him was soft and weak.

He was also jarringly familiar, like someone bin Zeid might have known in school. They were roughly the same age. Both were college educated and had lived abroad. They both descended from tribes with ancestral roots in the Arabian Peninsula and claims of ties to the Prophet Muhammad. Their families were well traveled and understood the world outside Jordan. Balawi was married with young girls; bin Zeid was a newlywed hoping to have children soon.

Bin Zeid could even appreciate, in an abstract way, the deep resentments that animated Balawi's online persona. Despite his government's official policy of peaceful coexistence with Israel, bin Zeid had often experienced a twinge of bitterness on mornings when he sat on his back porch, high on a ridge overlooking the Dead Sea, and gazed at the fertile plains to the north and west, lands that had once belonged to Arabs. Nearly all Jordanians had been angered when Israeli tanks rolled into Gaza in late December, killing more than five hundred Hamas militants and civilians in what Arabs viewed as a wildly disproportionate response to Palestinian rocket attacks.

But somewhere Balawi had fallen off a cliff, bin Zeid and his colleagues reasoned. Against all logic and his own self-interest, he had embraced a virulent philosophy that threatened to destroy everything that Jordan had achieved in a half century of faltering progress toward modernity. He had risked his reputation and his own family in the service of fanatics living in caves two thousand miles away.

How such a thing could happen to such a clever, world-wise young man as Balawi was unfathomable. But this much was clear: Abu Dujana would cease to exist, and Balawi's life would radically change. From now on the doctor and the Mukhabarat would be permanently tethered. Balawi's ability to work, travel, own a house, or clothe his children would depend on the spy agency's generosity and Balawi's good behavior. And if the Mukhabarat needed something—no matter how big or small—Balawi would have no choice but to comply.

The man in the prisoner's chair had not yet fully grasped this new reality, but he would. From the looks of him, it would not take much longer.

On the third day of Humam al-Balawi's incarceration, his father and oldest brother, Muhammad, hired a taxi and made the trip across town to Wadi as-Seer and the Mukhabarat headquarters. A

Jordanian soldier armed with an M4 assault rifle motioned the car to stop a few dozen yards from the main security gate, forcing the old man to walk the rest of the way while his eldest son waited behind. The weather had been cold and gray all week, and a northeast wind tugged at Khalil al-Balawi's white kaffiyeh as he crossed the parking lot and headed toward the small building where visitors were screened for weapons and bombs.

At the guard station, Khalil al-Balawi gave his name and asked to speak to a Mukhabarat officer, a Colonel Fawas, who was expecting him.

"I am here to pick up my son," he said.

He was handed a number on a scrap of paper and shown to a waiting area, a small room with white marble floors and a few leather chairs. A large portrait of King Abdullah II, in military parade dress and festooned with sashes and medals, looked down disapprovingly.

All my life I have managed to avoid this place, he thought, *until today*.

By now the family had deduced the reason for Humam's arrest. The government's agents had seized computer equipment, and Defne had told them about her husband's fascination with Internet chat rooms. Khalil al-Balawi, a teacher of Arabic literature and religion before his retirement, knew little of such things. But he had learned from a Mukhabarat official that his son was cooperating and would be ready for release on Thursday, ahead of the Muslim weekend.

The old man had been so anxious he had hardly slept. As he waited, his mind raced, and he thought of Humam as a young boy: whip smart, stubborn, insatiably curious, and—out of all of his ten children—the one most like himself.

Papa, why did God create people?

Why, Humam, the purpose of man is to worship his Creator.

{Silence.}

Papa, why did God create ants?

An hour ticked past, and then two. Other numbers were called, and now the waiting room was nearly empty. Worried that something bad had happened, Khalil al-Balawi shuffled back to the guard station and—an old man in failing health to a goodhearted servant of His Majesty—pleaded politely for information. A phone call was made, and the explanation obtained.

"I'm sorry, *Ya ammo* Balawi, but your son is no longer here," the head officer said.

"Where is he?"

"He is at home, of course," came the reply. "He was dropped off an hour ago."

Khalil al-Balawi was soon tearing across Amman as fast as the afternoon traffic would permit, while he and Muhammad ran through a list of possible explanations for the abrupt change. Was Humam injured? Perhaps scarred? Since when did the Mukhabarat offer detainees a courtesy ride home?

As central Amman gave way to the city's poorer neighborhoods, the old man gave in to brooding. The Balawis were cursed. It was happening again.

Life had begun badly for Khalil al-Balawi, who was born into turbulence in 1943 in a village near Beersheba, in what is now southern Israel. By his fifth birthday his family had witnessed massacres, reprisal killings, and finally the all-out warfare that split Palestine into two states and sent tens of thousands of Arabs, the Balawis included, into exile. The small lot where he played as a boy was now a cotton field owned by a Jewish consortium, off-limits to the Balawis forever.

His laborer father had eventually settled in Jordan, and the family, particularly Khalil, a gifted student whose high academic marks and college degree were the pride of the Balawi clan, had prospered. But with few jobs available in Jordan, Khalil had moved with his new bride to Kuwait, where he had accepted a teacher's post. He was promoted to department head and was content to live out his days in safe, sensible Kuwait, with its moderate policies and flush, oil-fed economy. Then Iraqi leader Saddam Hussein's Republican Guard rolled into Kuwait City in August 1990 to kick off six months of military occupation, looting, and war. After the defeat of Iraq by a U.S.-led coalition in 1991, the Kuwaitis immediately expelled more than three hundred thousand Jordanians living in the country, because of their government's support for Iraq during the conflict. Khalil al-Balawi managed to save a few family treasures, but between the occupation and expulsion he lost everything else he owned.

In Jordan once again, he had scraped to put his children through college and was looking forward to a quieter time, surrounded by contented, prosperous children and grandkids. Now a half century of upheaval and misfortune could not match the pain he felt deep in his chest.

The car pulled up to the curb on Urwa bin al-Ward Street, and Khalil al-Balawi climbed out quickly and entered the house ahead of his eldest son. There in the living room, on the black sofa framed by the old man's books, was Humam.

"*Salaam alekum, Humam,*" the father said. "Peace be with you."

Humam said nothing. He could not bring himself to look into his father's eyes.

The two sat in silence. Finally Humam spoke, his head still bowed.

"I have cleared the family's name, Father," he said.

"Humam, you did not have to do anything," the old man said. "Our family name is clean."

Days passed before Humam uttered another word to his family. His father believed his son would eventually open up about what had happened, so he did not pry. Five days went by, then a week. Finally, on a day when the two were again alone in the living room, Khalil al-Balawi could no longer contain himself.

"Did they beat you?" he asked softly.

Humam lifted his head, finally, to meet his father's gaze. His cheeks were flushed, and when he finally spoke, his words, in Arabic, were a barely audible hiss.

"No," he said. "They humiliated me."

5

THE INFORMANT

Ali bin Zeid squeezed his big frame into his office chair and scowled at the computer screen. The half-written file, already coded "secret" but awaiting a conclusion that he would provide, if only he could decide what it should be, was still there. The report bore an Arabic caption that read "Assessment" and "Humam Khalil al-Balawi," and it was entirely routine. Except for this last part, the ending.

What potential is seen for this subject? That was the stumper.

Bin Zeid was tired, feeling the strain of the Mukhabarat's peculiarly erratic hours and the stress of so many difficult cases, including this one. It annoyed him that he rarely had time for a decent meal with his wife, let alone the honeymoon that he had been promising her for more than a year. The late-winter sun was just low enough in the sky to bathe his fourth-floor office in a golden glare that washed out electronic type and made the room stuffy. Bin Zeid turned away from the screen and again picked up Balawi's paper file. He began to read.

Humam al-Balawi had talked, eventually.

On his third day in the Mukhabarat's vise, and in a handful of secret meetings afterward, the physician gave up names of figures inside al-Hesbah and other jihadist Web sites. He told what he knew about networks of jihadist bloggers and their funding. He spoke so openly that the chains and cuffs came off, and the sessions became freewheeling conversations. Afterward he would sit quietly, face flushed, head cradled in his hands, awash in unspoken emotion.

Balawi swore to his interrogators that in his heart of hearts, he opposed terrorism in all its forms. It was a claim that seemed wildly at odds with his posts lauding such notorious butchers as Abu Musab al-Zarqawi.

"It is true that I like to express my feelings in my writing," he said at one point. "But I'm against violence, including military action. Our religion forbids terrorism." Balawi surveyed the skeptical faces around him. *It's not who I am*, he protested. The blogs, the fake persona, the cries for blood—none of it was real.

It's just a hobby, he said.

After his release the Mukhabarat's men fanned out to try to corroborate his information. They also deepened their scrutiny of Balawi himself, tapping his phones, trailing his movements, and reaching outside Jordan for evidence of ties to terrorist groups. The agency placed Captain Ali bin Zeid in charge of Balawi's file and passed the essentials to the CIA, which shared space with the Jordanians in a joint counterterrorism center in a building on the outskirts of Amman. The American intelligence agency would want to check the names Balawi provided against its own database.

The more they probed, the murkier and more dangerous Balawi's secret life appeared. Despite his claims about opposing violence, he had sought at least twice to join the Zarqawi-led Sunni insurgency in Iraq, the officers discovered. Why he had ultimately failed to do so was unclear. Perhaps his courage had flagged, or he had felt guilty about orphaning his children; possibly he had been forced to admit to himself that he was a poor candidate for guerrilla warfare, lacking in both physical strength and military training. As a backup plan, he canvassed friends and relatives to collect money for the insurgency and raised just over fourteen hundred dollars before abandoning the effort. After Israel's invasion of Gaza in 2008, he had tried to volunteer as a Hamas medic to treat Palestinian wounded.

Balawi had also had a flirtation, and possibly more, with a

known terrorist organization in Turkey, it was learned. While living in Istanbul as a student, he had attended meetings of the Islami Büyükdoğu Akıncılar-Cephesi, or Great Eastern Islamic Raiders' Front, a group that claims kinship with al-Qaeda and advocates the overthrow of secular governments in the Middle East, from Ankara to Amman to Cairo. Turkish police have credited the IBDA-C with several spectacular terrorist attacks, including bombings of two synagogues in Istanbul in 2003 that killed twenty-four people.

Balawi's interest in the group was something he apparently shared with the woman he eventually married, Turkish sources revealed. Humam and Defne Bayrak were first introduced in 2001 in an Internet chat room for young Muslims. After the two began dating, they connected with other couples at social events that were essentially recruitment sessions for the Raiders' Front: small-group lectures, fund-raisers to support Palestinian militants.

Defne, tall and lithe with a doll's porcelain complexion, had admired Humam's intelligence but really fell for his conservative politics, according to her own account. She had been living at her parents' house in Istanbul, working as a journalist and brushing up on her Arabic-language studies, when the Jordanian medical student burst into her life. Three months later, they were making wedding plans.

"I liked his personality, his piousness, his strict following of the religion," she said.

During their courtship the couple began to change. Neither had ever been considered devout in a traditional sense. Defne wore a head scarf in public, but so do a majority of Turkey's adult women. Humam had memorized large portions of the Koran as a child but regularly skipped Friday prayers at the mosque and referred derisively to his native Jordan as "that Islamic country." But as a couple he and Defne embraced a creed that was gaining popularity among Turkey's college-educated elite and whose chief tenet was rage against the non-Muslim West. Rooted in the same decades-old resentments expressed by millions of other Muslims, but peculiar to privileged young adults who came into maturity in the age of al-Qaeda, this brand of faith perceived CIA and Israeli intelligence plots behind the terrorist attacks of September 11, 2001. Its adherents saw the invasions and occupations of Iraq, Gaza, and Afghanistan as part of a Western crusade to destroy and corrupt Islam, loot natural resources, and slaughter thousands of innocents.

Humam and Defne's new passion was partly driven by personal and family history: Humam was a son of Palestinian refugees and treated refugee children; Defne had worked for conservative Turkish newspapers, translating Arabic news accounts about fighting in Iraq and Afghanistan. Defne, who friends say was the more strident of the two, had also translated laudatory books about al-Qaeda leader Osama bin Laden and former Iraqi leader Saddam Hussein. The former had been titled *Osama bin Laden, the Che Guevara of the East.*

But in each other Humam and Defne had found a partner whose political views reinforced and amplified their own. Later, when they had children, even choosing their names became a means of asserting their beliefs.

The couple named their older girl after Leila Khaled, a Palestinian woman who hijacked a TWA jetliner in 1969 and served time in a British jail. The younger was named after a Swedish-born Palestinian filmmaker named Lina Makboul. Her best-known work is a documentary titled *Leila Khaled: Hijacker.*

Now bin Zeid did what he often did when he needed to think. From the high perch of his pilot's seat in the cockpit of a Boeing 737, he checked his flaps and eased the throttle forward. The stripes of the runway began falling toward him in a quickening stream. He tugged on the yoke, and with a roar, the jet's nose tilted skyward, clearing the trees and hills and soaring into an endless expanse of blue.

Bin Zeid took off his headset and leaned back in his chair, staring at the computer screen. Physically he was still in Jordan, in the house he had built overlooking the Dead Sea. Bin Zeid had set up the flight simulator on his computer so that it was just like a real cockpit, with controls and pedals and even realistic engine sounds that he downloaded to match the specific plane he was flying. He would set a course for a distant city and then, once the wheels were up, sit in silence for an hour or more as the plane moved over empty seas. His hobby mystified some of his family members, but bin Zeid claimed it was therapeutic.

It helps me think, he would say.

That's your problem, was the usual retort. *Too much thinking.*

But bin Zeid craved space when working through a complicated puzzle. If he had a day to himself, he would slip into the desert in his Land Rover with his two dogs or head south to the Red Sea with his wife, Fida, to anchor his boat in a desolate cove with no other humans in sight. In photos he always seemed to be in the same place: alone on a beach chair in his shorts and floppy camouflage hat, eyes fixed on some indiscernible point on the horizon.

Bin Zeid had fallen in love with America as a land of endless horizons. During holiday weekends at Emerson College he would hit the road in his car, sometimes alone, sometimes with his brother, Hassan, who was attending school across town at Boston University. When time was short, he would drive to Cape Cod to wander the beaches or sit in the cheap seats at Fenway Park to ponder the mysteries of American baseball and the allure of the frankfurter. During longer breaks he would drive alone to snow-covered Montreal or discover a secluded lake hidden among the hills of Virginia's Blue Ridge Mountains.

His need to roam was one of many traits that set him apart and made him something of an oddity at the Jordanian intelligence service. CIA acquaintances joked that the hardworking, plain-living bin Zeid was the "most unroyal of the royals." But some Jordanian colleagues had trouble seeing past his ties to the monarchy and decidedly Western lifestyle. His superiors worried that family connections would eventually catapult bin Zeid to the top, pushing veterans aside and giving the royal family an even tighter grip on the spy agency. Fellow officers admired his energy but also were acutely aware of the gulf between their lives and his. It wasn't just money and privilege, though everyone knew about bin Zeid's Boston education and the small Bertram fishing yacht he and his brothers kept anchored in Aqaba Harbor. It was also bin Zeid's apparent detachment from the conventions that governed the life choices of most Jordanian men his age. Though a Muslim, he had married a woman from Jordan's tiny Christian minority, a dark-haired beauty named Fida Dawani. In a culture that considers dogs unclean, bin Zeid was openly affectionate toward Jackie, a German shepherd he had acquired as a puppy, and her shaggy offspring, Huskie. The two rode around Amman in bin Zeid's truck as though they were a couple of cattle dogs on a Wyoming ranch.

Bin Zeid could shrug off the comments about his pets, but he detested it when people treated him differently because of his royal blood. Although colleagues persisted in calling him Sharif Ali, he introduced himself as Captain at work and as just Ali to neighborhood shopkeepers. The local repairman who serviced bin Zeid's desktop computer took a liking to the affable young man who would linger in his shop to dissect the day's news, sometimes bringing in a pizza to share with the technicians. Years passed before he learned that low-key, jeans-wearing Ali was both a Mukhabarat officer and a cousin to the king.

At work, however, bin Zeid was all business. As a boy he had written in an essay that he planned to devote his life to serving his country, offering that it was "very important for an individual to be willing to die for his country." He went to work at the Mukhabarat soon after graduating from college and poured himself into the job. He was pulled into some of the agency's biggest terrorism cases, including the investigations into the Zarqawi-led suicide bombings in Amman in 2005. And increasingly, he became an indispensable conduit between the intelligence service and the CIA. The two agencies had worked closely since the 1960s, and by 2001 much of the Mukhabarat's budget was underwritten by its cash-flush American partner. From Langley's perspective, it was a smart investment: The Jordanian agency was a reliable partner, and its operatives were deemed among the best in the world.

Bin Zeid occupied a unique place within this special relationship.

He understood Americans and their language better than anyone in the Mukhabarat, and the U.S. agency routinely asked for him whenever the two countries worked together on joint investigations. When the two agencies clashed over tactics, it fell to bin Zeid to serve as mediator and bridge.

The Balawi case was a perfect example. Two weeks after his arrest, Humam al-Balawi remained a cipher to the Mukhabarat. Yes, he had given up names of jihadist writers, but his confessions were looking less impressive on closer examination. The writers were either minor players or prominent figures whose identities were already known. Balawi had kept clean since his release and halted his Web columns—he never had a choice about that—but bin Zeid saw no hard evidence that he had changed his views or could be trusted.

Yet the CIA and senior Mukhabarat officials were increasingly interested in the doctor. Abu Dujana al-Khorasani was an emerging opinion leader in the world of radical Islam, and now the man behind the persona was the property of the Mukhabarat. What could he accomplish if he were working for their side?

Jordan already employed hundreds of informants, who came in two varieties: low-level snitches of dubious reliability and elite double agents who were highly trained and spent years developing their cover. Balawi was neither of those, but surely there was a role for him. It fell to bin Zeid to assess what that role might be. To do so, he would have to become Balawi's new best friend.

Complicating matters was the pressure on him from above. Cultivating an informant takes time, yet time was suddenly in short supply. In Washington, the newly inaugurated Obama administration swept into office with a promise to redraw the country's counterterrorism priorities, starting with a renewed commitment to capture Osama bin Laden and his deputy, Ayman al-Zawahiri. The CIA was in a rush to find and deploy scores of new informants and operatives throughout the Middle East and around the world. In Jordan, Mukhabarat officers were being asked to write assessments describing promising new contacts and what they could potentially deliver.

As bin Zeid set out to write such an assessment for Balawi, he worried aloud to colleagues that inflating expectations could lead to disappointments and mistakes.

One evening after work bin Zeid put the case aside to watch a movie at a friend's house. The film was *Body of Lies*, a Hollywood spy thriller starring Russell Crowe and Leonardo DiCaprio. Set mostly in Jordan after the September 11, 2001, terrorist attacks, the movie depicts an amoral CIA official, played by Crowe, whose miscalculations repeatedly risk the lives of subordinates as well as Arabs who happen to get caught in the crossfire. As he watched the video, bin Zeid seemed mesmerized by the film's portrayal of American and Jordanian agents at war with Middle Eastern terrorists and sometimes one another.

When the DVD ended, the friend asked bin Zeid for his impressions. The two laughed about the convoluted plot twists; then bin Zeid turned serious.

"Here's what's true about it," he said. "It's the way it shows the Americans in too much of a hurry. Always, they want everything to happen right now."

Late February brought some of the coldest, iciest weather Amman had seen in years. Temperatures hovered near freezing for days, and a rare heavy snowfall closed schools and left an army of snowmen plodding the usually dusty sidewalks. Humam al-Balawi had spent much of his time out of the house during the cold snap, but one afternoon he returned from his appointments with a surprise announcement: He had sold his car.

His parents and brothers stared at him stunned. Humam's sturdy little Ford was one of his most cherished possessions. It was also his only means of getting to work at the distant Marka clinic.

"Why did you do that?" his father finally asked.

Humam shrugged. "It needs a lot of maintenance," he said. "I'm tired of keeping it up."

To judge from his appearance, Humam was more than just

tired. He said little these days, spending his time at home on his computer—the Mukhabarat had kindly returned it—or lost in his thoughts. He would disappear for hours at a time, saying vaguely that he was visiting the mosque or meeting with friends.

At the clinic, his patients had noticed his newly baggy clothes and sallow skin and worried about him. One who confronted him was Hannan Omar, forty-two, a mother with four children who sold snacks from a cart in the clinic lobby. When Omar's blood pressure had suddenly dropped a few months earlier, Balawi had hounded her for weeks to make sure she was taking her medicine.

"You've lost weight!" she said scoldingly to Balawi after he arrived for work one morning. "Are you sick?"

The doctor smiled weakly and said diabetes was making him thin. It was the last time she would see him; later she learned that Balawi had handed the clinic manager his letter of resignation.

Balawi was gradually checking out of his old life. In some ways, the old Balawi was already gone.

Defne Bayrak tried to understand what was happening to her husband but was getting only small glimpses. After his three days in the Mukhabarat's prison he was almost unrecognizable: jittery, sullen, distracted. Never one to pray openly, he now prayed all the time, asking for God's guidance with the smallest decisions. He sat in the apartment with an open Koran for hours at a time, and when the girls' noisy playing got to him, he would run—sometimes literally—down the block to the neighborhood mosque and the serenity of its prayer room.

Occasionally he would allow her to pull back the curtain slightly. Defne was able to extract a few details about her husband's detention, as Balawi described the sleep deprivation and how he was pressured to reveal the true identities of prominent writers. *I gave up no names*, he lied. He repeated to her what he told his father: that the Mukhabarat had not used torture but had sought to shame him. He would not say how.

He also talked about his new minder, an intelligence officer whose name was Ali and who was blood kin to the king. Since his release he had begun meeting with this officer for friendly chats, he told Defne, first over chai and then for longer sessions. For Balawi, there was no real choice but to agree to bin Zeid's coffee klatches. Gradually he became intrigued by what bin Zeid was saying.

They would meet in a prearranged pickup spot, with bin Zeid usually showing up in his blue-gray Land Rover. If it was dinnertime, bin Zeid would choose the restaurant and pick up the tab, which sometimes ran to seventy-five dollars or more—outlandishly expensive compared with the shawarma and kebab joints in Balawi's neighborhood. Once bin Zeid asked the physician to accompany him on an errand, and the two spent a half hour cruising Amman's massive Western-style Safeway supermarket, with its dizzying array of fresh and imported foods and the small room where customers could discreetly purchase wine and whiskey. After the checkout line, bin Zeid tucked a case of dog food under his arm and handed several bags of groceries to Balawi—a gift, he said, for the doctor and his family.

Bin Zeid's pitch was subtle, especially at first, but the message was always the same: *We need you to help us. For your sake. For your country's sake.* He dissected some of the more strident essays Balawi had written as Abu Dujana al-Khorasani, trying gently to upend the jihadists' use of the Koran to justify suicide bombings and terrorist attacks.

Osama bin Laden's vision of Islam is distorted, he would say. *The Koran forbids the taking of innocent lives.*

Bin Zeid even suggested that Jordan's King Abdullah II was a purer manifestation of Islamic principles than bin Laden. After all, the king, a man with Western affinities and a glamorous wife who traveled the world promoting education for women, was a Hashemite, a descendant of a clan that traced its lineage directly to the Prophet Muhammad.

Balawi nodded in tacit agreement. Maybe there was a way he could help the monarchy.

The precise role that Balawi might play was not immediately clear, but bin Zeid was clear about one thing: If the doctor could use his connections to help track down wanted terrorists, the potential reward could be immense. Enough to change his life and that of his entire family.

How much money? It depended on the target, but the CIA, the agency that wrote the checks, had put bounties on the heads of bin Laden and his wily No. 2, the Egyptian physician Ayman al-Zawahiri, promising sums that were difficult even to imagine.

How much, exactly? Defne would ask later, when her husband was at home. Humam had been contemptuous of the Mukhabarat agent when he related details of their meetings to his wife in the privacy of their apartment. But now he was distracted again, lost in his thoughts.

Millions, he finally said.

On the morning of March 18, Humam al-Balawi packed two small bags and prepared for what he said would be a brief trip. He announced that he had decided to apply to study medicine in the United States, but he first had to pass a qualifying exam. The exam was being offered in Istanbul.

The story was mostly plausible. Long before his arrest Balawi had talked about studying in America, and he had fretted about whether he could decipher the highly technical English on the exam that would determine his eligibility. But when the subject came up previously, the test was always to be in Amman. Still, Balawi was well connected in Turkey from his school days, and no one questioned his reasons for going there. He hugged his girls and wife and left the house with his younger brother, Assad, who agreed to drive him to the airport. Humam said nothing to his father about the trip, and he would not bring himself to say good-bye to him.

At Amman's Queen Alia International Airport, Humam motioned for his brother to bypass the check-in gate for Istanbul. Instead they queued up at an Emirates airline counter for a flight to Dubai, the transit hub of the United Arab Emirates. Humam dropped off his bags and asked that they be checked all the way through to his final destination: Peshawar, Pakistan.

Afterward Humam shook hands with his younger brother, who eyed him with a mixture of puzzlement and concern.

I think we should talk to our father about this, Assad al-Balawi finally said.

No, he is not to know, came the reply. *Will you promise?*

Assad consented.

Peace be with you, he said.

And with you.

Humam al-Balawi shoved his ticket and passport in his pocket, turned, and walked up the steps to the gate.

6

TARGETS

Langley, Virginia—May–June 2009

Throughout the spring America's invisible army of spy satellites and eavesdroppers spread its nets across northwestern Pakistan, arraying the world's most sensitive eavesdropping gear against one of the most backward regions on earth. Cameras scrutinized every mud house, barn, and goat stall across an area the size of Puerto Rico. Banks of computers trolled phone lines, Internet transmissions, and wireless signals, in an automated search for a single word or phrase that might signal trouble or lead to the capture of a long-sought foe.

In May one such phrase, plucked from routine phone intercepts, sent a translator bolting from his chair at the National Security Agency's listening station at Fort Meade, Maryland. The words were highlighted in a report that was rushed to a supervisor's office, then to the executive floor of CIA headquarters, and finally to the desk of Leon Panetta, now in his third month as CIA director.

Nuclear devices.

Panetta read the report and read it again. In a wiretap in the tribal province known as South Waziristan, two Taliban commanders had been overheard talking about Baitullah Mehsud, the short, thuggish Pashtun who had recently assumed command of Pakistan's largest alliance of Taliban groups. It was an animated discussion about an acquisition of great importance, one that would ensure Mehsud's defeat of Pakistan's central government and elevate his standing among the world's jihadists. One of the men used the Pashto term *itami*, meaning "atomic" or "nuclear." Mehsud had *itami* devices, he said.

After the shock subsided at Langley, skepticism crept in. Was it a translation error? A tall tale? A ruse? Some of the agency's most experienced hands were openly scornful. Baitullah Mehsud was a semiliterate gangster with a big mouth. His experience with bombs was limited to strapping a few pounds of homemade explosives on a hapless teenager and blowing up a bazaar. Mehsud lacked the resources to acquire a nuclear weapon, and no one would be stupid enough to give him one.

Still, the CIA would quietly dial up the volume on its surveillance of the hilly border region that was home to the Mehsud clan. The heightened listening continued fruitlessly for days, until one evening the agency's trawlers snagged something big: a secret meeting among members of Baitullah Mehsud's Taliban shura, or council. The advisers were overheard discussing an interesting ethical dilemma that had been recently thrust upon the group.

Was it permissible under the laws of Islam, the advisers were asking, *to use Baitullah Mehsud's new "devices"?*

Now the attention of the Obama administration's entire security infrastructure was fixed on a small patch of real estate in northwestern Pakistan. The Taliban had remorselessly slaughtered thousands of people, including many women and children, yet these devices had given them pause. The terrorist movement appeared to be taking the unusual step of acquiring religious cover for whatever it was about to do.

In Washington not a word about the new threat would be uttered publicly. But across the Obama administration, government agencies girded themselves to deal with a new crisis. The Energy Department, with its radiation-sniffing planes; the Pentagon; the Homeland Security chiefs responsible for ports and border security—all were put on heightened alert. At Langley, Panetta harangued his counterterrorism teams daily for specifics, his dark eyes flashing from behind his wire-rims. "What the hell are we talking about here?" he demanded. "Did they take something from one of those damned nuclear depots?"

Of all the devastating scenarios Panetta had ever allowed himself to imagine, the worst by far was a nuclear explosion in a U.S. city. There were only a handful of places in the world where agency officials feared that a terrorist might buy or steal a bomb or its key components, and nuclear-armed Pakistan topped the list. Yet it was all but inconceivable that a small-time rogue like Baitullah Mehsud could have gotten his hands on a functioning atomic bomb.

Panetta and his top aides eventually settled on a more plausible explanation: The Pakistani terrorist had acquired a *dirty bomb*. Sometimes called the poor man's nuclear weapon, a dirty bomb fuses conventional explosives with lethal quantities of radioactive waste, such as the radioactive cobalt used to remove cancerous tumors or irradiate food. Dirty bombs are far less deadly than an actual atom bomb, but they are cheap and easy to make, and they can spread radioactive contamination over wide areas. One well-made bomb detonated in lower Manhattan could kill scores of people, wreak economic havoc, and render parts of the city uninhabitable for months or even years. Was this the *itami* device the Taliban was planning to set loose?

Faced with a potentially grave threat, the five-month-old Obama administration prepared to take action, starting with the dispatching of a high-level delegation to Pakistan to secure that country's help in locating Baitullah Mehsud and his mysterious devices. "The entire U.S. policy-making community was very alarmed," said an administration official who participated in meetings convened to discuss the White House's response. "It was an all-hands-on-deck mentality."

It had already been a rough spring for Panetta, who, at seventy, sometimes found himself looking back wistfully at the comfortable semiretirement he had been enjoying before being summoned by Obama to head the CIA. The former California congressman had been suggested for the intelligence job by his longtime friend Rahm

Emanuel, Obama's newly appointed chief of staff, but his nomination quickly stirred up controversy. Panetta's prior brushes with the spy world had been limited mainly to the White House briefings he attended as staff director for the Clinton administration, and even Democrat stalwarts in the Senate publicly questioned if he had the necessary experience to lead the world's most powerful intelligence agency. Obama, seeing the pounding his candidate was taking on Capitol Hill, wondered aloud to Emanuel whether the nomination was worth the political price he was paying.

"Are you sure this was the right choice?" he asked.

Emanuel was convinced. Panetta was a shrewd manager who knew Washington and possessed formidable political skills. Though tough and profane, Panetta had an easy laugh and the natural charm of a small-town mayor—a combination that made him nearly impossible not to like. Panetta would protect the administration's interests while also finding ways to fight and win the agency's battles with other intelligence agencies, White House bean counters, the Pentagon, and Congress. "This will turn out," Emanuel assured the president.

Yet Panetta's troubles persisted. He angered Republicans and many CIA managers with his comments condemning waterboarding. Then, just two months after his arrival at Langley, he infuriated Democrats when he opposed the administration's decision to release Bush-era legal memos that justified the use of waterboarding. Panetta's stance on the so-called torture memos won him new friends inside the CIA, but it also put him at odds with powerful members of the administration he was now serving.

A bright spot for Panetta was the CIA's continuing successes against al-Qaeda, as the new administration embraced and even expanded the agency's campaign of missile strikes against terrorist bases in Pakistan near the Afghanistan border. In his daily intelligence briefings, Panetta could see the impact the strikes were having. For the first time in years, al-Qaeda's leaders faced a mortal threat within their own sanctuary, the prospect of instant annihilation from robot planes that hovered continuously overhead, their mechanical humming filling the evening silence and making men fearful in their own beds.

But for Panetta even these successes came at a price. The son of Italian immigrants, Panetta was a lifelong Catholic who regularly attended mass, and the responsibility for deciding life and death for other individuals—even suspected terrorists living thousands of miles away—weighed heavily on him. His predecessor, Mike Hayden, had warned that the job would require "decisions that will absolutely surprise you." It was true: Once a week, on average, Panetta was approving what amounted to a death sentence for a group of strangers on the other side of the globe. The CIA's new weapons systems were impressively precise, with capabilities that exceeded the accounts most people would read in newspapers. The agency's Predators could put a missile through the window of a moving car or nail a target the size of a dinner plate in a narrow alley at night without harming buildings on either side. The aircraft's operators could—and, on at least one occasion, did—change a missile's trajectory in midflight to avoid an unintended target that suddenly wandered into its path. According to the agency's closely held body count, its missile strikes had inadvertently killed nine people by the time Panetta took office, or an average of one unintended death for every forty al-Qaeda or Taliban fighters targeted.

Still, friends kidded Panetta about becoming a CIA hit man so late in his life. "Does your bishop know what you're doing?" one close friend quipped when Panetta talked about his work. But the CIA director wasn't amused.

"I don't take it lightly," Panetta protested.

Yet week after week, when Panetta was confronted with the choice, his personal qualms would fall away against what he perceived as the far greater evil. Al-Qaeda and its Taliban allies were contemplating acts of mass murder, unburdened by remorse. In all the world, only the CIA had both the means and the will to reach into the terrorists' mountain sanctuary to stop them.

Now, in his third month as CIA director, Panetta was facing the same life-or-death calculation for a Pakistani man who the CIA believed was preparing to detonate a dirty bomb. Until that spring the United States had never regarded Baitullah Mehsud as a significant threat to Americans, and the CIA was just beginning to redirect its vast surveillance network toward the task of searching for him. Inevitably, the agency would find Mehsud. When it happened, Panetta would know what to do.

One of the most talented of Langley's new crop of terrorist hunters arrived at work, as always, in flip-flops. Elizabeth Hanson liked wearing beach shoes, even in the dead of winter. The snap of her sandals as she padded around the CIA's corridors was as familiar to her colleagues as her blond mane, with the couple of rebellious curls that resisted her efforts to flat iron them into submission. She kept a pair of dressier shoes under her desk for the days when she was unexpectedly summoned to the executive floor to talk about al-Qaeda, and she could quickly turn on the glamour when the situation demanded it. But on normal working days Hanson believed in making herself comfortable: jeans, flip-flops, and sometimes even pigtails. After all, she routinely worked long hours, and when things were busy at the office, she often stayed up through the night, watching the live video feed from the CIA's Predator aircraft as they stalked one of her targets. And June was already shaping up to be a remarkably busy month.

She plopped down at her small cubicle desk, pushing aside papers to make room for her caramel macchiato, then switched on her computer monitor and began sifting through the morning's secret cables from Pakistan and Afghanistan. The agency's senior targeters were caught up in an urgent search for one Baitullah Mehsud, and that group included Hanson, who was developing a reputation for her ability to track down the country's most dangerous foes. Terrorist figures of greater importance than Mehsud had been on Hanson's list in the past, and some of them were no longer among the living.

Coworkers sang out greetings as they wandered by, and Hanson acknowledged them with a smile. It was early, but the CIA's Counterterrorism Center was humming with a kind of low-grade tumult that never completely subsided. The place was divorced from normal time distinctions of day and night, early and late, weekday and holiday. The cavernous main room was perpetually awash in a fluorescent brightness that compensated for the lack of windows. (Any portal to the outside world is viewed as a security risk, new hires are told.) The center's warrens of cubicles and flat-panel TV monitors took up much of the ground floor of the agency's sleek new headquarters building, a facility that was built, for security's sake, into a hillside. Workers in the Counterterrorism Center arrived on the fourth floor through a gleaming glass atrium festooned with scale-model spy planes and statues, then descended four levels below to the bunker where the agency's most sensitive operations are managed.

Hanson stood out in this subterranean world, and not just because of her footwear. Barely thirty, she had a kind of understated midwestern girl-next-door beauty that men adored and women admired. Coworkers loved her for her outsize sense of humor, which ranged from slyly sarcastic to scatological to downright silly. She could quote endlessly from comedies like *The Hangover* or put her coworkers in stitches with a dead-on impression of Beavis from the cartoon series *Beavis and Butt-Head*. The most mundane CIA-speak would be transformed into off-color puns ("OK, who had weekend doody?" and "Have you been debriefed?"), and when she needed a favor from a boss or colleague, she would preface the request by demanding, "I want a pony." A small circle of close friends knew her by a family nickname, Monkie, an artifact from her girlhood fascination with the famous sock puppet monkeys originally manufactured in her hometown of Rockford, Illinois.

Hanson's playful demeanor belied the utter seriousness with which she approached the core business of the Counterterrorism Center. For more than two years, she had worked as a targeter, a job that entailed tracking terrorists on the CIA's wanted list, by whatever means available, from a tiny cubicle a few miles outside

Washington. She had her own list of targets and access to raw data from every surveillance tool in the agency's sizable kit. Like an artist assembling a giant mosaic, she could summon bits of information from wiretaps, cell phone intercepts, surveillance videos, informant reports, and even news accounts, blending them with a mix of imagination and conjecture to develop a profile that the agency's spies, drone operators, and undercover case officers could use to physically spot the target. More recently Hanson had become a group leader for other targeters, overseeing multiple efforts to track down terrorist leaders. Often she spent hours monitoring the hour-by-hour surveillance of a terrorist target, and she personally made the call to the CIA director to request the go-ahead to launch one of the agency's Hellfire missiles. Hanson had helped track down some of al-Qaeda's most senior leaders, including Osama al-Kini, the man killed by a CIA missile on New Year's Day. And her intricate knowledge of Pakistani terrorist networks made her an indispensable source of expertise when agency officers were on the trail of lesser terrorists, some of them al-Qaeda's closest allies. These included the cagey Pashtun warlord Jalaluddin Haqqani, the longtime ally of Osama bin Laden's whose fighters were attacking U.S. troops around the eastern Afghan city of Khost; and, more recently, leaders of the Tehrik-i-Taliban Pakistan alliance headed by Baitullah Mehsud.

"Her career trajectory was straight up, like a rocket," said a CIA colleague who worked closely with her in the Counterterrorism Center. "She was helping put bad people out of business, permanently. It was getting to the point that it was getting harder to hide in the tribal areas."

Some coworkers compared Hanson with Jennifer Matthews, another female officer and onetime targeter who had shot up through the ranks. The two had worked together briefly and were friendly, but their paths had been markedly different. Matthews had joined a vastly different CIA in the late 1980s, a place where women still were relatively rare, the Cold War still raged, and most of the glamour jobs were held by male case officers who had secret meetings with informants in seedy bars in Vienna or Budapest. By contrast, Hanson was part of a class of new officers hired after September 11. Some referred to themselves as the Windows generation: young, highly educated, and confident in the power of their technology. Case officers and informants would always be needed, but in the post–September 11 era, they were no longer kings.

"It's now about connecting dots," said another of Hanson's coworkers. "It's about multitasking, going through reams of data from different sources. It's putting two and two together to stop a plot or to find a leader who is trying not to be found."

It was also about personal toughness. Friends recalled being startled one day when Hanson, then twenty-nine, got into a heated argument with an army colonel over a potential target. When the military officer tried to dismiss the young targeter, Hanson moved within inches of his face. "The target is correct, sir," she said. "Either you take it out, or we will."

As spring turned to summer, Elizabeth Hanson was preparing for a transfer to Kabul, Afghanistan, her first overseas posting with the CIA. But before her departure she would set her sights on the elusive and newly dangerous Baitullah Mehsud.

On the morning of June 22 the Obama administration's national security adviser, James L. Jones, traveled to Pakistan's capital, Islamabad, for urgent meetings with the country's civilian and military leaders. In press releases the meetings were described as routine consultations on Washington's Afghanistan strategy. In reality the top items on the agenda were Mehsud and his "devices."

Pakistani officials adamantly insisted that the country's nuclear stockpile was secure, but they could not rule out the possibility of a Taliban dirty bomb. If anything, the government of President Asif Ali Zardari was even more worried than the Americans about Mehsud's intentions. If a dirty bomb was to explode in one of the world's major cities in the coming weeks, officials reasoned, it was more likely to happen in Karachi or Peshawar than in New York or London.

The only bright spot for Islamabad was the Obama administration's newfound interest in Baitullah Mehsud. The Taliban leader was officially blamed for the assassination of the country's former prime minister, Benazir Bhutto, on December 27, 2007, and in the months since then he had declared war on Pakistan's government. Mehsud had targeted Pakistani police and military barracks with suicide bombings, and he had famously cut off the heads of captured army recruits. Pakistan's generals were preparing to expand their military offensive against Taliban strongholds, and they were engaging in fierce clashes in villages along the border. Yet the CIA and its robot planes—so controversial in Pakistan—had done little to help. U.S. officials had long viewed the Mehsud clan as a local problem for the Pakistanis and were reluctant to agitate yet another militant faction that might cross into Afghanistan to attack U.S. troops.

The dirty bomb threat changed everything. Now the Obama administration was privately talking about targeting Mehsud, and Pakistani officials, for once, were wholeheartedly embracing the idea of a U.S. missile strike on their soil.

"Go after him," one Pakistani security official pleaded to one of the U.S. officials in Jones's delegation.

In Langley, meanwhile, the search by Elizabeth Hanson and her fellow targeters was beginning to bear fruit, as daily cables from Kabul and Islamabad brought fresh reports on the movements of Taliban commanders close to Mehsud. Some in the CIA had developed a theory about the origins of the Taliban's mysterious devices: They were part of an al-Qaeda project that had been disrupted by the relentless Predator strikes on the terrorist leaders. An al-Qaeda bomb maker named Khalid Habib had been aspiring to build a dirty bomb before his plans were cut short in October 2008, when a missile slammed into his car in northwestern Pakistan. Habib's closest ally and the presumed heir to his bomb-making projects was Osama al-Kini, the al-Qaeda commander who died in the Predator strike on New Year's Day. Had al-Qaeda bequeathed its dirty bomb factory to Baitullah Mehsud?

The CIA had long worried about collusion between al-Qaeda and

Pakistan's loose confederation of militant groups, and now Hanson and her team were seeing increasing examples of it. In their natural state, many of the local extremist groups were rivals who fell regularly into spasms of bloody intertribal feuding. But lately, squeezed by encroaching Pakistani troops from the south and the constant threat of death from CIA missiles, the militants were consulting and cooperating in ways that could make them far more dangerous.

Hanson was skimming classified cables for the names of Mehsud lieutenants in late June, when Pakistani informants reported that a kind of pan-jihadist strategy session had taken place near Baitullah Mehsud's ancestral home of Makeen, in South Waziristan. The eleven-member guest list included a top al-Qaeda emissary, Abu Yahya al-Libi, as well as Sirajuddin Haqqani, the charismatic young commander who presided over the powerful Haqqani network, and Baitullah Mehsud himself. The reputed purpose of the gathering was to persuade the Taliban leader to negotiate a truce with Pakistan; Haqqani and al-Qaeda leaders were watching the army's advance through South Waziristan and worried that their territory might be next.

Hanson jotted some notes and leaned back to think.

Mehsud, al-Qaeda, and the Haqqanis, sipping tea and planning strategy. The groups had maintained informal contacts for years. But this was something more.

James L. Jones was wrapping up his meetings in Islamabad on June 23, when the CIA caught a break in its search for Baitullah Mehsud and the weapon he was feared to be hiding: A midlevel commander in Mehsud's organization was spotted in Taliban country. A plan was quickly hatched to strike Baitullah Mehsud when he attended the man's funeral. True, the commander, a trusted aide named Khwaz Wali Mehsud, happened to be very much alive as the plan took shape. But he would not be for long.

Before sunrise on June 23 a lone Predator drone circled high over tiny Lataka, a mountain hamlet in Taliban country, forty miles northeast of the provincial capital of Wana. Two missiles sliced through the humid predawn air, racing ahead of their own sound waves, sensors locked onto a mud-brick building on the village out-skirts. Anyone watching from the street would have seen only a small impact flash and then an eruption of rock, dust, and smoke as the house burst apart from the inside. Neighbors clambering over broken walls and singed furniture and bed mats found the mangled bodies of five Taliban fighters and their leader, Khwaz Wali Mehsud.

It was a significant hit, but it was only the prelude to what CIA officials hoped would be a much bigger score.

The Mehsuds, like other Pashtun tribesmen who live along the Afghanistan-Pakistan border, attach great significance to funerals, which often surpass weddings as social occasions. The passing of a prominent member requires a show of respect from his relatives, and often large crowds of mourners gather around the body to wail and chant prayers. Village elders and other prominent citizens then fall in line to escort the shrouded corpse to the gravesite.

As the smoke cleared in tiny Lataka, spy agencies watched and listened when Mehsud notables began pouring into the village to recover the bodies and organize a hasty burial. Among the names gleaned from phone intercepts was Qari Hussain Mehsud, Baitullah Mehsud's top deputy and heir apparent. Qari Hussain was among the most ideological of the Mehsud clan, a man with deep hatred for Pakistan's secular government and a vision for a broader alliance between the Pakistan Taliban and other jihadist movements. He had founded suicide bomber camps for young boys and was behind several deadly attacks in Pakistan and Afghanistan.

The second big name on the guest list was a surprise: Mullah Sangeen Zadran, a military commander in the Haqqani network. Sangeen was a top deputy to Sirajuddin Haqqani, Jalaluddin's son, and a man with a bounty on his head. The Pentagon had targeted him twice during raids inside Afghanistan, but he had slipped away both times. Now his presence at a Mehsud clan funeral reinforced U.S. fears of a deepening alliance between the Mehsuds and the Haqqanis that would surely benefit al-Qaeda as well.

Among Pashtuns, burials frequently occur within hours of a

person's death, so on this day the CIA immediately dispatched its drones to Makeen, the town nearest to Lataka and the presumed setting for Khwaz Wali Mehsud's funeral. Agency officials in Khost and Langley watched on flat-screen TVs as cars arrived and mourners gathered, the men in long tunics and the women in burkas and veils. They watched as the shrouded body was carried through the streets and as prayers were chanted at the graveside. They listened as the officiating mullah urged the crowd to disperse quickly because the low-pitched humming of the *machays* or bees—the Pashto name for the pilotless planes—was drawing nearer.

Muhammad Saeed Khan, a thirty-five-year-old Pashtun tribesman, was leaving the gathering when the first two missiles hit almost simultaneously.

"It created a havoc—there was smoke and dust everywhere," Khan told a Pakistani journalist afterward from his hospital bed. "Injured people were crying and asking for help. They fired the third missile after a minute, and I fell on the ground."

Pakistani news reports initially listed both Qari Hussain Mehsud and Sangeen Zadran, the Haqqani commander, as having been killed in the strike, and agency officials strained to hear if Baitullah Mehsud had been killed as well.

It took another two days before the truth was known. Both Qari Hussain Mehsud and Sangeen Zadran survived the attack, as they gleefully informed local broadcasters in interviews.

Baitullah Mehsud, if he attended the funeral at all, had slipped away before the missiles flew.

7

THE JIHADIST

Amman, Jordan—July 2009

Humam al-Balawi arrived alone in northwestern Pakistan on March 19 with his two battered suitcases, and the vastness of the country swallowed him up. The CIA's paid informants watched him pass through customs at Peshawar and spotted him again at the crowded bus terminal where he boarded a coach for the frontier city of Bannu. But then he vanished, disappearing into the blackness of one of the harshest and most isolated places on earth.

In Amman, Ali bin Zeid checked his in-box day after day for news. The Jordanian intelligence officer had set up a special e-mail account to be used only by his new informant, whom bin Zeid had code-named Panzer after the legendary German battle tank. Balawi had been cautioned to limit his e-mails in case he was being watched, but days had passed with no contact at all. Was the informant sick? Had he gotten lost? A possible explanation, bin Zeid knew, was that he had been killed. Any traveler from pro-Western Jordan would be viewed by the Taliban as a likely spy. Balawi's Arabic and English skills would do little to help him out of a jam in Pashto-speaking Taliban country. Balawi had known it, too.

I'm afraid I will die in Pakistan, Balawi had blurted out at one of their last meetings before leaving Amman. *I will be killed, and there will be no one to look after my family.*

Bin Zeid had been reassuring, but now he was consumed with worry and guilt. He began to prepare for the possibility that the Balawi experiment would utterly fail. It had happened before.

Then, one morning in late March, bin Zeid was sitting at his computer, sorting through the day's e-mail, when he spotted an unusual item forwarded from one of his little-used accounts. The subject line was a series of code words, but there was no mistaking the sender.

The text was also in code, a few short phrases the two men had agreed upon as a way of verifying identity at the first contact. The translation was roughly this: *It's Balawi. I'm here.*

In a series of notes that followed, Balawi reported that he was getting along tolerably well in his first assignment as a spy. He was living in the South Waziristan market town of Wana, using the cash the Mukhabarat had given him as start-up money. Like most of the larger towns, Wana had a public call house with computer terminals, which Balawi would use to communicate with Amman. He had a list of contacts, including Pakistani jihadists he had met online when he wrote under the name Abu Dujana al-Khorasani. The plan was for Balawi to approach the Taliban's emissaries in Wana to ask for their help in setting up itinerant medical clinics in tribal villages. Balawi would pose as a devout physician looking to perform jihad by treating the Taliban's sick and wounded. If it worked, Balawi would have the perfect cover to roam freely through Taliban country, gathering information for reports that he would send to bin Zeid from his home base in Wana.

Bin Zeid sent his new recruit encouraging replies. You're doing important work, he wrote. He tried to appeal to the physician's patriotism, thanking him for his sacrifices on behalf of his country and king. "You have made us proud," bin Zeid said.

Balawi also tapped out a note to his wife. Before his departure he had confided to Defne that he was traveling not to Turkey, as he had told his family, but to Pakistan. *I want to study medicine there,* he told her. The story made little sense, but Defne knew not to question it. Now Balawi's wife and girls were living with her parents in Turkey, where she had gone that spring at the behest of her father-in-law to search for her husband. After a few weeks she had finally told the elder Balawi the truth: Humam was in Pakistan. The Mukhabarat had sent him there.

The old man was incredulous. "How could Humam be in Pakistan?" he asked. "He can't find his way around a traffic circle." Later he began pressing Defne to return to her in-laws' apartment in Jordan, the proper place for a married woman whose husband was away. But Humam would have none of it.

Stay in Turkey and I will come to you there, he wrote. He promised to send money for an apartment and furniture and offered suggestions on finding a good place. Eventually they would live there together, he said.

The pep talks from bin Zeid seemed to work. Balawi continued his e-mail updates throughout April and early May, making cryptic references to low-level Taliban contacts he had made. Then, in mid-May, he made a startling announcement: He informed bin Zeid that he had accepted an invitation to move in with some members of the Tehrik-i-Taliban, the largest of the insurgent groups based in the province of South Waziristan. The Taliban needed Balawi's medical skills, and the group had offered to allow the physician to participate in one of its training camps.

I will be busy and I will be closely watched, he wrote to bin Zeid. *You may not hear from me for a while.*

It seemed rash to bin Zeid—very possibly, Balawi was being lured into a trap—but already it was too late to argue. Bin Zeid's next e-mails to Balawi went unanswered. The final weeks of May passed, then all of June. Now it was July, and there had not been a word from the informant in two months.

Bin Zeid discussed the developments with Darren LaBonte, the CIA officer from Amman, who was now officially partnered with bin Zeid as the American case officer for Balawi. The long silence certainly was bad news, they agreed. Maybe Balawi was dead, or perhaps he had crossed the line and joined the Taliban, either voluntarily or by force.

The idea of sending the untrained, untested Balawi to Pakistan had been a gamble from the beginning, bin Zeid knew. It was one of dozens of long shots and what-ifs that were being flung at an incredibly complex problem: getting inside the inner circle of al-Qaeda. Eventually, given enough time and the CIA's deep pockets, one of them was sure to stick.

The recorder's light flicked on. Humam Khalil al-Balawi shifted in his seat and waited for the question from his Taliban interviewer.

"Abu Dujana is a personality known for articles and contributions posted on jihadist forums on the Internet. We would like the kind reader to know more about him. Who is he, then?"

Balawi regarded the reporter, an Arabic-speaking Pashtun writing for a midsummer edition of the online Taliban magazine *Vanguards of Khorasan*. It was exactly the right question. *Who was he, really?*

Balawi began with the basics, lightly fudged. "Your little brother comes from the Arabian Peninsula, may Allah liberate it," he said. "I am a little over thirty years old, married and I have two little daughters."

It was a surreal moment for a man who had worked hard to conceal so much about himself, from his Internet alter ego to his decision to travel to Pakistan. Now he was submitting to the jihadist equivalent of a celebrity interview, revealing to the world at large that he—or the part of him that was Abu Dujana al-Khorasani—had quit the writing business to perform jihad. There were real risks to going public; every word in the article would be scrutinized, by intelligence officers from the CIA and Jordan's Mukhabarat, of course, and also by al-Qaeda. At this moment everyone was watching, and no one on either side was sure what to make of Balawi.

The topic turned to Abu Dujana's Internet columns, and Balawi was able to breezily recount the circumstances behind his first online essay about al-Qaeda's defeat in the Iraqi city of Fallujah. He talked about other writers he admired. He threw in a hearty denunciation of the "Hagana dogs, the Jews," who had covertly hacked their way into jihadist Web sites, including the former al-Hesbah site for which he had once served as moderator. The cyberattacks had "closed forums and destroyed links to jihadist publications," he complained.

But again, he was asked about himself. *What changed in you after you stepped into the land of jihad?*

"You should rather ask, what did *not* change in me?" Balawi said. "I was reborn here."

That much was true. What was less certain at this time was whether Balawi would survive infancy in his alien new world. Balawi had indeed received an invitation to board with the region's most powerful Taliban group. It had come from the leader of the group, a short, paunchy man with an outlandish black beard and a sadistic sense of humor. His name was Baitullah Mehsud, and he was, at the moment, the most wanted man in all of South Asia.

Baitullah could barely read and spoke little Arabic and thus could scarcely appreciate the Jordanian's writerly gifts. But Baitullah was a man who lived according to his instincts, and they had pronounced the young physician trustworthy after their first meeting. The two had a mutual acquaintance—one of Baitullah's Arab supporters knew Balawi from his days as a Web site moderator and had vouched for him—and the Taliban commander had been impressed by Balawi's tale of being pressed into service by Jordan's intelligence agency. Balawi's training as a physician held immense appeal to Baitullah, who was afflicted with diabetes and leg ailments and desperately short of medical care for his sick and wounded fighters. Any lingering doubts were resolved when Balawi pulled out a large wad of bills, travel money given to him by the Mukhabarat.

But not everyone was ready to believe in Balawi. In the Mehsud camp, Baitullah's opinions were often contested by his own kinsmen, particularly his cousin Qari Hussain Mehsud. Just six months earlier, Qari had beheaded a kidnapped Polish geologist in a grisly, videotaped execution, in defiance of Baitullah's orders. The killing had strained relations between the cousins for months. Now Qari was eyeing the Jordanian suspiciously.

Outside the Mehsud clan, other groups also were openly suspicious of Balawi. Certain that he was a spy, Sirajuddin Haqqani joined al-Qaeda commanders in refusing to meet Balawi or even be in the same building with him. If Baitullah Mehsud were to suddenly disappear, Balawi might well share the same fate as the Polish geologist.

That is, if the Americans didn't kill him first. The unrelenting threat of death from a missile strike had begun to gnaw at Balawi, just as it did others in the tribal belt. The low buzzing of the CIA drones was nearly constant now, and it so unnerved Balawi that he often had trouble sleeping. There had been eight Predator strikes in North or South Waziristan since early June, including two in the village, Makeen, where Balawi and a small entourage of Mehsud fighters had been bedding in different houses, moving every few days for security. They traveled in groups of two or three and avoided cars when possible.

Feeling safer outdoors, Balawi sometimes moved his pallet into the courtyard. He stared into a black sky thick with humidity and unseen threats, the interviewer's question still flicking at his addled brain: *Who are you?*

The seed had been planted by Balawi himself. *I could go to FATA*, he told Ali bin Zeid one day. FATA is the Federally Administered Tribal Areas, the strip of mountainous country in northwestern Pakistan along the border with Afghanistan. The very name is a synonym for rugged, ungovernable, backward, extreme. It is al-Qaeda country. And Balawi was saying he had contacts there.

Bin Zeid was listening.

It had happened in February, during one of their dinners in Amman. The two had spent several evenings together, and the conversations had become relaxed. Doctor and spy had even found a few common interests, such as a mutual dislike for Jordan's Muslim Brotherhood, the formerly radical Sunni Islamic movement that had cut a deal with the monarchy that allowed it to become a legitimate political party. Balawi had attended a few of the Brotherhood's mansaf dinners, named after the rice and lamb dish that is a national favorite in Jordan and a popular choice at fund-raising banquets.

"The people of mansaf," bin Zeid said mockingly. "They eat mansaf and talk about jihad without actually doing anything."

Perhaps sensing an interest, bin Zeid also began to slowly pull back the curtain on the world of the Mukhabarat. The spy service's reach is vast, he said, and many of its greatest achievements have never been publicly acknowledged. Bin Zeid explained how he himself had set up sting operations in which volunteers for holy war in Iraq were lured to a pickup point near the border, only to find the Mukhabarat waiting for them, he said.

Balawi respectfully nodded his approval.

It was also true, bin Zeid continued, that Jordan had supplied the evidence that led to the fatal missile attack against Abu Musab al-Zarqawi, leader of al-Qaeda in Iraq. And the Mukhabarat had netted much bigger prey. He claimed that a Jordanian spy had been behind one of the greatest and most mysterious assassinations of a terrorist figure in decades, the 2008 slaying of former Hezbollah security chief Imad Mughniyeh. The man who was dubbed Abu Dokhan—the "father of smoke"—because of his uncanny ability to elude capture had been killed by a bomb hidden in the headrest of his car in Damascus. Initial speculation had pointed to a rival Hezbollah faction or Syrian agents. But U.S. terrorism experts came to suspect Israel's Mossad spy agency, despite Israel's strong denials, simply because the hit had been so exquisitely planned and executed. Mughniyeh's name had been on numerous most wanted lists, including that of the FBI, which blamed the Lebanon-born militant for separate bombings in 1983 of the marines' barracks in Beirut and the U.S. Embassy there. The latter strike had killed more than sixty people, including eight CIA employees. It was the deadliest single event in the history of the U.S. intelligence agency. And it was the Mukhabarat, bin Zeid said, that had exacted vengeance.

There was yet another surprise. One of the most enduring mysteries since the founding of the modern jihadist movement was who had killed Abdullah Azzam, the revered Palestinian cleric who helped lead the anti-Soviet insurgency in Afghanistan in the 1980s.

Azzam had been a mentor and teacher to Osama bin Laden, but in his later years he had clashed with bin Laden's followers over the terrorist group's willingness to spill Muslim blood to advance their cause. His death in 1989 by a remote-control bomb in Peshawar, Pakistan, was the Muslim world's equivalent of the John F. Kennedy assassination, drawing legions of conspiracy theorists, who variously linked the slaying to the Soviets, Israelis, Americans, Pakistanis, Afghans, and even bin Laden himself. Now bin Zeid said flatly that Azzam's death too had been the work of the Mukhabarat. He even offered the name of the assassin: bin Zeid's own boss, Ali Burjak, the "Red Devil."

"If you go and kill any leader of the mujahideen, you'll become the top man in Jordan, like my chief," bin Zeid had said.

It was now clear what bin Zeid was looking for, and Balawi, after some thinking, decided to float his idea. *I could go to FATA*, he offered.

The proposal sparked furious discussions at the Mukhabarat and at the Amman counterterrorism center run jointly with the CIA. Balawi was no agent, that was clear; he had no training, spoke no Pashto, and could hardly be considered reliable after a few nights in detention and a handful of dinners and coffees with bin Zeid. On the other hand, there was little to lose.

A quick consensus was reached on the key points. For the cost of only a few thousand dollars, Balawi could be set loose in Pakistan with a serviceable cover story. Fortunately for him, he already possessed assets that would accord him instant credibility in Taliban country, including a medical degree and an Internet persona. He would essentially work on spec, earning significant rewards only in the unlikely event that he could deliver someone important. He would not be given fancy communication gadgets or anything that might expose him as a spy if he were discovered. If he were killed—the chances were judged to be high—few outside Balawi's own family would notice or care.

Questions were raised about why Balawi would even consider leaving his home and job for such a dangerous assignment. To judge from his behavior in his meetings with bin Zeid, the answer seemed obvious: money. In reports summarizing Balawi's views about his possible assignment, the physician appeared to vacillate between deep concern over his safety and endless curiosity about the size of his reward.

With the CIA now fully on board, the logistics of Balawi's journey came together with remarkable speed. Balawi would need an expedited Pakistani visa, so a letter inviting the Jordanian physician to a diabetes conference in Pakistan was drafted. E-mail accounts were created and tested. Code words were forged and memorized.

Balawi would also have a new code-name. No longer Panzer—the handle bin Zeid had chosen—he would now be known by his CIA name, Wolf.

A critical decision that fell to the CIA was whether to inform Pakistan, a U.S. ally, of the plan to insert an undercover operative into its sovereign territory. Langley quickly rejected the idea. Top CIA officials were convinced that Pakistan's Inter-Services Intelligence agency harbored agents sympathetic to Jalaluddin Haqqani, a Pashtun warlord who had been backed by Islamabad during the 1980s and was now a supporter of the Afghan insurgency. Balawi could be betrayed and killed before he had time to unpack his bags.

The final step was airline tickets. An open-ended return flight was purchased and hand-delivered by bin Zeid, along with a fat envelope stuffed with dollars.

Months later some U.S. intelligence officials still marveled over how quickly the plan came together and also over the eagerness with which agency veterans bought into the notion that the untrained Balawi could survive in a lawless FATA, let alone penetrate a dangerous terrorist network. Such a thing had never happened, not like this. By luck of timing, Balawi had turned up on the Mukhabarat's doorstep with his unique set of assets—a physician with impeccable jihadist credentials, seemingly willing to put his life on the line—at the precise moment the CIA and a new U.S. administration were scrambling to find new methods and agents for a ramped-up global hunt for Osama bin Laden.

"Balawi dangled that he could go," said one recently retired agency official privy to internal conversations about the Jordanian. "And he happened to match with a beautiful priority."

Sleep eluded Humam Khalil al-Balawi. The day had been insanely hot, and the temperature was still in the nineties well after sundown. Worse, as he lay still in the dark, the humming of drones grew even louder, like a mosquito he could never swat away.

Balawi's home through midsummer was in one of the Mehsud clan's walled compounds in Makeen, a small town of loosely clustered mud-brick houses and shops surrounded by scrubby hills. At bedtime he had taken his mat into the outer courtyard and unrolled it near one of the guard posts to try to sleep. In the dim light he could make out a familiar form, a paralyzed man whom the fighters called Ahmad. The Pashtun man had lost his legs to disease, but Ahmad insisted on taking his turn at guard duty and refused to be relieved when his shift ended. He sat in his wheelchair with his rifle in his lap until sunrise. Humam could hear the man praying softly and occasionally sobbing. It was an impressive display of devotion that was, in true Taliban fashion, carried to a pointless extreme.

The same was true for Baitullah Mehsud himself. There were little things, like his behavior during group dinners. Baitullah would make a dramatic display of personally dishing out the choicest cuts of meat to his dinner guests until there was nothing left for himself but bones and fat. The performance made Balawi so uncomfortable that he made excuses to avoid eating with his host.

Baitullah Mehsud also appeared to have bought into the myth of his own invincibility. Two years after becoming chief of the Pakistan Taliban, he had grown fond of media attention, and he enjoyed staging news conferences, allowing the cameras full view of the head that was said to be worth more than five million dollars in bounty payments. Between staged events he would engage in long interviews over an open phone line, talking and laughing with journalists, seemingly oblivious of the possibility that his phone signal might be a beacon guiding a CIA missile to his compound. His swagger extended to absurd boasts about how his small band of illiterate, ill-equipped mountain fighters were poised to defeat not only Islamabad but also the great powers of the West.

"We pray to God to give us the ability to destroy the White House, New York and London," he told a television interviewer. "And we have trust in God. Very soon, we will be witnessing jihad's miracles."

Baitullah's insistence on his own supremacy in all things—military strategy as well as more mundane matters such as the divvying up of profits from contraband smuggling—sometimes sparked violent clashes with other Mehsuds. The diminutive commander also seemed to delight in agitating the Haqqanis and other militant groups by picking gratuitous fights with the Pakistani army and intelligence service, practically daring Islamabad to come after him, as eventually it did. Once, after surrounding and capturing an entire garrison of 250 Pakistani soldiers and paramilitary troops, Baitullah proceeded to cut off the heads of three of his prisoners as the opening gambit in a negotiated prisoner swap.

It was a far cry from the idealized holy war that Balawi had championed in his blog. Baitullah Mehsud was neither a revolutionary nor a prophet. He was a thug with a massively inflated ego, a murderer who enjoyed killing other Muslims. He presided over a town that was dirty, backward, and mean, where girls barely older than Balawi's daughter Leila were condemned to lives of little or no formal education and no appreciable rights, in a region where a newborn is three times more likely to die in his first year of life than a child born in Balawi's native Jordan.

For the moment, though, Baitullah Mehsud was the best friend Balawi had. The two men could barely communicate except in fragments of Arabic or Pashto. But Baitullah had become convinced of the Jordanian's sincerity. He had devised a singularly cruel test to prove it.

The plan, according to a Pakistani Taliban official familiar with the details, called for Balawi to use his open channel to the CIA to order a missile attack on Baitullah Mehsud—only the real target would be a decoy, not the Taliban leader himself. Balawi was to send word that Baitullah would be traveling in a district called Ladha in a specific car, a Toyota hatchback model that local tribesmen have dubbed Ghwagai or "the cow." Inside, posing as Baitullah, would be one of his trusted drivers. All other details about the car and its route would precisely match the description given to the CIA by Balawi.

It worked exactly as planned, according to a version of events related by two Taliban officials. A missile flattened the car, killing the man who had posed as the Mehsud leader. The incident was never reported by local news media and never confirmed by the CIA. But it became instant legend among Baitullah's men.

Mehsud later claimed that the driver knew of the plan and consented to sacrifice himself to help his boss and assist Balawi's efforts to prove his worth to the CIA. To outsiders it might seem an extravagant waste of a life. But the Taliban chief brought his own calculus to such decisions. Every American missile that lit up the sky over Pakistan, he said, was like a recruiting poster, driving more angry young men and boys into his camps.

"Every drone strike," he would say, "brings me three or four new suicide bombers."

On August 5, Baitullah Mehsud and a small group of trusted guards moved their quarters under cover of darkness to Zanghara, a tiny town a few miles east of the Taliban stronghold of Makeen. At the edge of the village was a large, high-walled compound well known to him. It was the home of his father-in-law, Malik Ikramuddin, and the young girl who had recently become his second wife. Now thirty-five and the father of four girls from another marriage, Mehsud had decided to put serious effort into producing a male heir.

Unknown to the Pakistani, his every move was being recorded. Two sets of mechanical eyes—a Predator drone and a smaller one hovering at close range—had trailed him to Zanghara and watched him enter the mud-brick farmhouse where he was staying. One of the drones maneuvered to get a clear view into the second-floor room where Mehsud was staying. In Langley, Virginia, six thousand miles away, a series of urgent messages pulsed through the corridors of the executive wing: The target's identity had been confirmed. It would be a clean shot.

But suddenly Mehsud was moving again, padding around the upper floors of the house in his white shalwar kameez. The Predator's pilot and weapons operator eased off on their controls and watched their screens. They would have to wait.

It was a brutally hot night, and Mehsud was restless. His diabetes made him constantly thirsty, and his legs were swollen and achy. Shortly after midnight he opened a small door and, trailed by a second robed figure carrying medical equipment, climbed out onto the roof. A full moon bathed the rooftop in light and illuminated Mehsud's bearded form as distinctly as if he were onstage. There was a small mattress on the roof, and Mehsud walked over to it and flopped down, belly first. The second figure knelt next to him and began to set up what appeared to be an intravenous drip. The CIA's analysts quickly concluded that the other person was a doctor. Could it be Balawi? It didn't matter. The Predator team armed their Hellfires a second time.

The missile launch awaited only final approval from the CIA director, but now there was a hitch. Leon Panetta had authorized a strike on a second-floor bedroom, but Baitullah Mehsud was lying on the roof on the building. The change was not insignificant: Panetta had insisted on maximum precautions to prevent the deaths of innocents, particularly women and children. What if the missile caused the entire building to collapse? Panetta would have to sign off on the change, or not. And he would have to decide quickly or risk letting the opportunity slip away.

At that precise moment Panetta was not in his CIA office but in downtown Washington, attending a meeting of the National Security Council at the White House. A little before 4:00 P.M. Washington time, he excused himself from the meeting and walked into the hallway to take an urgent call. He frowned as he listened, visibly worried. For several minutes he paced the floor with his cell phone to his ear, asking questions and going over details and options. By some accounts there were dozens of people staying in the same house as Mehsud, including mothers with children.

"Is that thing going to collapse?" Panetta asked. "What's in there? Are there women and family members around?"

On the other end of the line, his chief of staff, Jeremy Bash, and a senior counterterrorism adviser passed along updates. It was a tricky shot, from twenty-three thousand feet away, but the agency would use a smaller, less destructive missile, Panetta was told. The targeting would be extraordinarily precise. And the damage would be minimal.

Panetta gave his consent.

It was now 1:00 A.M. in the Pakistani village. Baitullah Mehsud, leader of the Pakistani Taliban and chief protector of the Jordanian physician Humam al-Balawi, now lay on his back, resting as the IV machine dripped fluid into his veins. At his feet, a pair of young hands, belonging not to a doctor, as the CIA supposed, but to his new wife, were massaging his swollen legs. Barely aware of the buzzing of a distant drone, oblivious of the faint hissing of the missile as it cleaved the night air, he took a deep breath and looked up at the stars.

The rocket struck Mehsud where he lay, penetrating just below the chest and cutting him in two. A small charge of high explosives detonated, hurling his wife backward and gouging a small crater in the bricks and plaster at the spot where she had knelt. The small blast reverberated against the nearby hills, and then silence.

Overhead, the drones continued to hover for several minutes, camera still whirring. A report was hastily prepared and relayed to Panetta at the White House.

Two confirmed dead, no other deaths or serious injuries. Building still stands.

8

PRESSURE

Langley, Virginia—August 2009

On August 11, nearly a week after the CIA's missile strike, a Taliban spokesman phoned Pakistani journalists to denounce "ridiculous" rumors about the death of Baitullah Mehsud. The Taliban leader was "alive, safe and sound," he said, adding that the world would soon see proof.

By that date Leon Panetta had already seen all the proof he could stomach. The missile impact that killed Mehsud had been captured on video and replayed, in its grisly entirety, on the giant monitor in Panetta's own office at Langley. As if that were not enough, a second video surfaced, showing the Taliban commander's body as his comrades prepared to bury him. The CIA's counterterrorism team looked into the face of the man whose death they had ordered, pale and serene now in his crude wooden coffin, his head resting on a pillow strewn with marigolds. The hand of an unseen mourner stroked the corpse's face, brushing against the dozen or more fresh scars that pocked the skin around his eyes and forehead.

Panetta had little time to dwell on the images. That week his staff was caught up in the drafting of a proposal that he would deliver in person to the White House in the coming days. The CIA had unfinished business in Pakistan's tribal belt, and Panetta would make a personal appeal to the president for help. Of the many secret plans he would approve as CIA director, none was more likely to change the course of the country's war against al-Qaeda than this one.

The successful targeting of Mehsud had only served to under-score the urgent nature of the work that still lay ahead. For one thing, Mehsud's "devices" remained unaccounted for. All summer, as the CIA searched for the Taliban leader, thousands of Pakistani troops backed by helicopter gunships swept the Taliban's valley strongholds, picking off the forts and hideouts one by one. By the time the campaign ended, the Pakistanis were sitting on a moun-tain of small arms and enough explosives to supply a madrassa full of suicide bombers. But they found no trace of a dirty bomb. The radiation detectors never sounded at all. The CIA's counterterrorism chiefs puzzled for weeks over the meaning of the missing devices. Many Taliban survivors had fled into neighboring North Waziristan to take shelter with that province's dominant militant group, the Haqqani network. Had they taken their bombs with them? Had it all been some kind of trick? On this, the classified reports were silent. There was no further talk of devices in the agency's intercepts, and back in Washington, Obama administration officials made no mention of the dirty bomb scare. Publicly, it was as though the threat had never existed.

More ominously, Baitullah Mehsud's Taliban faction had quickly regrouped and was veering off onto a dangerous new course. The missile strike on August 5 had created a temporary leadership vacuum and touched off several bloody rounds of street fighting among Mehsud's would-be successors, but now Baitullah's charis-matic cousin, the recklessly ambitious Hakimullah Mehsud, was firmly in charge. While Baitullah Mehsud had contented himself with waging attacks against Pakistani soldiers and police, his cousin was more virulently anti-American and also more willing to commit his forces into alliances with al-Qaeda and other militant groups attacking American troops in Afghanistan. Greater numbers of Mehsud fighters were signing up with al-Qaeda's Shadow Army, a paramilitary force led by a Libyan commander, Abdullah Said al

Libi, that wore its own distinctive uniform and carried out lightning raids on military targets on both sides of the border. These
were al-Qaeda's new shock troops, and they were drawing funds and
recruits from as far away as Saudi Arabia and Kashmir.

This was Panetta's dilemma. The CIA's missiles were finding
their marks, but it wasn't enough. Slain commanders were being
quickly replaced, often with younger leaders with more extreme
views and international ambitions. Al-Qaeda was adapting, com-
manding a widening network of committed followers from the
region's patchwork of militant tribal groups. Meanwhile the terrorist group's most senior leaders, including Osama bin Laden and
his operational commander, Ayman al-Zawahiri, were coordinating
strategy from secure hiding places. Something more was needed to
flush them out.

In the late summer and early fall Panetta and his team final-
ized the detailed plan the director would present to the president
and his National Security Council, which was in the middle of a
months-long review of its Afghanistan strategy. Panetta had a long
wish list, but the lead item was the most critical one: more robot
planes—lots of them. Not just Predators, but the newer, more powerful Reaper aircraft, along with operators and hardware to support them. Panetta wanted to dramatically increase the pressure on
al-Qaeda, not only with increased firepower but also with blanket
surveillance, enough human and mechanical eyes watching the
tribal region around the clock to detect the movement of even small
groups of fighters. It would be "the most aggressive operation in the
agency's history," Panetta later said, and its chief aim would be to
find and destroy the graybeards who were the root cause of all the
trouble.

"The leadership of al-Qaeda—from bin Laden down to the top
twenty—these guys are located in a place that is our primary target,"
Panetta said. "And we're the point of the spear."

When it was time to make his case, Panetta made the trip to the
White House to deliver his pitch to President Obama in person.

"Mr. President," he began, "in order to really accomplish our mission, these are the things I need." He proceeded to describe al-Qaeda's resilience in the tribal region and his plan for ratcheting up the pressure, denying the terrorists even the smallest space to hide or regroup.

Obama looked at Panetta thoughtfully for a moment and turned to his aides.

"We're going to do what Leon wants," he said.

The discussion was over.

It would take months to deploy the new orbits, as the systems of unmanned aircraft and operators were called, but the agency proceeded immediately to put pieces of the new plan into place. CIA targeters would be needed not only in Langley but also nearer to the front line, to coordinate a highly specific search for senior al-Qaeda leaders.

The limits of the new strategy were understood. The Predator was an impressive machine, but air power and advanced robotics could accomplish only so much against a widely dispersed enemy that hid among the local population in Pakistan's tribal region. The same kinds of technology had helped turn the tide against Iraq's insurgents, but there was an important distinction: In U.S.-occupied Iraq, U.S. Special Forces commandos had free rein to go anywhere in the country. They worked in tandem with the drones and could rapidly act on new intelligence during any time of day or night, inserting small teams on the ground to kill or capture. No such possibilities existed in Pakistan.

There was yet another problem. To eliminate al-Qaeda's generals, the CIA first had to find them. Nine years after Osama bin Laden's terrorist attacks on New York and Washington, U.S. intelligence officials had no idea where he was.

It was even worse than the public knew. In the years since September 11, several U.S. officials suggested in interviews that the CIA knew roughly where Osama bin Laden was hiding. Those claims had been wishful thinking, at best. The last credible report of a bin Laden sighting came in 2002, shortly after the Saudi terrorist fled from his Tora Bora stronghold on the Afghanistan border into Pakistan. Since then there had been nothing: no near misses, no tangible leads, not even a single substantive tip. Defense Secretary Robert Gates, in a moment of candor, acknowledged in a 2009 television interview that "it has been years" since the bin Laden case had been active.

"We don't know for a fact where Osama bin Laden is," Gates said. "If we did, we'd go get him."

Occasionally, leads emerged that would revive interest in the hunt. One of the most promising involved an al-Qaeda courier reputed to deliver messages between the terrorist group's operational commanders and bin Laden, who studiously avoided telephones and electronic messages. Nearly all the CIA's targeters, including Jennifer Matthews and Elizabeth Hanson, had been caught up in the search for the courier in some way. After two years of hard work and lucky breaks, the agency finally deduced the man's name in 2007; yet two years later, it had no idea where to find him, or whether he was even alive.

The failure to find bin Laden was the fly in the ointment, the big black asterisk that overshadowed what had been the greatest tactical success in the CIA's history: the 2001 overthrow of the Taliban and the routing of al-Qaeda in Afghanistan. Even as New York's twin towers still smoldered, the agency had led an offensive so overwhelming that only a few hundred foot soldiers and a handful of senior leaders managed to slip away, leaving thousands of others dead or in prison camps.

The Taliban's defeat had been engineered by a small group of CIA officers who had been spoiling for a chance to go after bin Laden since long before he dispatched his teams of hijackers to crash airliners into buildings in New York and Washington. With their input, within hours of the September 11, 2001, attacks, the CIA director George Tenet had a plan on President Bush's desk that would allow the White House to immediately go on the attack against al-Qaeda in Afghanistan, rather than wait for the Pentagon to organize a conventional military campaign. In a meeting with the president on September 13, J. Cofer Black, then the director of the CIA's Counterterrorism Center, described how a force of CIA-led commando teams and friendly Afghan Northern Alliance fighters could defeat the planners of the September 11 attacks in a matter of weeks.

"When we're through with them they will have flies walking across their eyeballs," Black famously said.

Bush approved, and Operation Jawbreaker was launched. Just three months later, in December 2001, the Taliban government toppled, and the remnants of the Taliban army were being pursued through southern and eastern Afghanistan. Osama bin Laden and a rump force of a few hundred loyalists attempted a last stand in the mountain fortress of Tora Bora on the Pakistani border.

Then, as Pentagon officials debated whether to send in American troops to finish the job, the terrorist leader escaped, reportedly after paying bribes to an Afghan warlord. He slipped through the lines of pro-U.S. Afghan fighters and sought refuge in Jalalabad and in villages in the eastern provinces of Kunar and Khost. He stayed briefly as a guest of Jalaluddin Haqqani, an Afghan warlord and former comrade from the civil war against the Soviets, before eventually disappearing again in the Pakistani hills.

Al-Qaeda's No. 2 leader fled on horseback into Pakistan along a different route. In the coming years, occasional sightings of Ayman al-Zawahiri sparked furious activity and a failed attempt to capture or kill him. Bin Laden appeared only on video, his beard longer and grayer and his usual camouflage fatigues replaced by robes and an Arab-style kaffiyeh. Officially, the search for him continued, but in reality there were no clues or leads to chase.

The CIA's Alec Station, which had been established initially to search for bin Laden, gradually lost its targeters to other units that were hunting for lesser al-Qaeda figures and Taliban warlords. In 2005 it was shut down for good.

Panetta's new Predators would not arrive in Afghanistan until nearly the end of the year. In the meantime, the agency would send scores of new officers to the Kabul station, including some of its best targeters. One of them was Elizabeth Hanson.

The thirty-year-old chief targeter was coming off an extraordinary run, having worked on more than a dozen high-profile cases that ended in Hellfire explosions in Pakistan's tribal belt. She had helped the CIA locate some of the biggest players in the jihadist world, from Osama al-Kini to Baitullah Mehsud. Now she was being dispatched to Afghanistan as part of a renewed push to find the biggest names of all.

She arrived in Kabul in August to a pungent stew of odors, dust, and broiling heat, her mother's admonitions still ringing in her ears. The elder Hanson, also named Elizabeth, had been unhappy when her daughter joined the CIA, and she had been horrified by her decision to move to such a dangerous place as Afghanistan. She tried for weeks to talk her out of it and continued to fret long after it was clear that the decision was final.

"Don't you think you should at least try to learn karate before you go over there?" the mother asked one day before the departure.

"Mom," she replied, "if the time comes when you find that you need karate, the game is already over."

That was typical Elizabeth—Bitsy or Monkie to her family—frustratingly stubborn, but with a wry twist that made it impossible for anyone to stay angry with her. Mrs. Hanson would have no choice but to let her daughter go, but she would insist on a call home nearly every day, and she would keep a handset strapped to her body at all hours, in case there was bad news.

The truth was, Hanson's mother had seen this day coming for a long time. Once, as a little girl of about four years, Bitsy had plopped into her chair at the family dinner table and announced, in very mature English, that she "wanted to try everything in life, and learn everything there is to learn." With that, she picked up a crystal goblet of ice water and bit into it so sharply that it shattered.

"The glass broke in her mouth," her mother remembered. "But it didn't faze her."

Years later she joined the CIA for the same reason, prizing romance and adventure above the easy money she could have earned with her private school education and economics degree. She was a girl's girl who adored children and appreciated nice clothes and a good manicure, yet she would leap at any chance to get her hands dirty, whether from rock climbing and bungee jumping, or from shooting grenade launchers and slogging through the mud at the CIA's training academy. She was a self-professed nerd who read physics textbooks in her spare time, yet was so naturally funny that her friends encouraged her, quite seriously, to become a stand-up comic. The career might have pleased her mother more but for the fact that her taste in humor was, as Mrs. Hanson explained, "not very ladylike."

Volunteering for duty in Afghanistan was in keeping with Hanson's adventurous side, and she was thrilled at the chance to go, her friends say. There were serious risks in living even in the relatively safe Afghan capital, a place where suicide bombers occasionally rammed into military convoys and where gunmen sometimes shot their way into five-star hotels. Hanson would work and live in the CIA station inside the ultrasecure U.S. Embassy, but her job sometimes required meetings with informants outside the steel-plated gates. Hanson was again a targeter, but now she would be leading a focused effort to find and kill the top al-Qaeda and Taliban leaders who were driving the Afghan insurgency and plotting terrorist attacks against the West—including bin Laden and Zawahiri.

Her mother never pressed Hanson for details of her work, but she knew the essentials, and she never fully understood how her daughter was able to adjust mentally to work that involved the killing of other human beings, even terrorists. Sometimes she asked her daughter about it.

Elizabeth Hanson leaned to the left politically, and "she hated war," her mother said. And yet she seemed to have no doubts about where she belonged.

"Whether you approved of the war or not made no difference," the elder Hanson said, recalling her daughter's words. "You don't run away from a fight, and you always have to take care of the people who are over there, fighting your war."

In her daughter's words, she said, it would usually boil down to this: "It's just what you have to do."

Hanson quickly settled into the daily rhythm of her new job. Her living quarters consisted of a tiny dorm room with a shared bath, and there was precious little to do in the way of socializing, so she worked. Fourteen-hour days, seven-day workweeks. Dinner and lunch at her desk. Gym breaks in the afternoon. She would put in a full day before Langley was awake, and another full day while the Counterterrorism Center's senior officers were at their desks, asking questions and demanding updates.

Hanson's targets were closer now, just a half hour's chopper ride to the east, hiding in the steep valleys of Kunar and Khost and in the Pakistani tribal lands beyond. Baitullah Mehsud was gone, but his Taliban minions were still there. So were the Haqqanis and the Shadow Army paramilitary troops loyal to al-Qaeda. Somewhere among the mountain villages, Sheikh Saeed al-Masri was plotting his next move, perhaps in consultation with Ayman al-Zawahiri or even Osama bin Laden himself.

If they could be found, Elizabeth Hanson would find them.

9

CHIEF

Khost, Afghanistan—September 19, 2009

At 4:58 A.M., two hours before sunrise, Jennifer Matthews was roused from sleep by a loud bang. It sounded close—it was hard to tell in the dark, and she was new to such things—and it was strong enough to rattle the picture frames in her tiny hooch. Instinctively she rolled out of bed, grabbed her flak jacket and helmet, and walked out the door toward the shelter. *Rocket attack.*

Outside, other figures stumbled along the same path, and some exchanged a grim greeting. The dark sky was still chalky with stars, with no trace of the new moon that would mark the end of the month-long Ramadan fast later that evening. Somewhere in town, a muezzin was sounding the predawn call to prayer, his lilting baritone rising and fading against the squawks and beeps of the base's emergency loudspeakers.

Matthews felt the heaviness of the air, still warm even at that hour. The airfield lights glowed yellow through a dusty fog, casting a feeble light over the parched terrain beyond the fence. Farther up the valley, clusters of tiny lights from the army's Salerno base shimmered like distant constellations.

It was a thrilling sight and oddly serene. The Haqqani fighters who lobbed occasional mortar rounds at the base rarely hit anything, so the perfunctory huddle in the concrete shelter was mostly an annoyance and a chance to catch up on gossip. But Matthews, barely twenty-four hours into her new job as Khost base chief, found even the little things fascinating. It was perhaps a strange admission, coming from a woman who a week earlier had been a suburban mom working in a sleek office building in northern Virginia, but she loved being in Afghanistan.

"It is exhilarating," she told one close agency friend back home. Her Afghan assignment was going to take up a year of her life, and she would be absent from her three children for most of that time. She would miss twelve months' worth of ball games and bedtime kisses, stomachaches and school projects, recitals and family dinners. And she would miss Christmas. But Matthews had volunteered for the posting, and she was now determined to extract every possible advantage from the experience. And to the extent she could, she would enjoy every bit of it, even the middle-of-the-night visits to the bomb shelter.

This one was mercifully short, as there were no other explosions. A chopper crew circling the base with a searchlight found the strewn body parts and quickly pieced together the story. A lone man had crept up the main approach to the base in the moonless blackness and attempted to bury an IED, or improvised explosive device, near a dip in the road where the morning convoys would pass in a few hours. But the bomb had exploded prematurely, leaving pieces of the man scattered across the highway. An almost identical incident had occurred near the same spot a few months earlier, only it ended with two would-be bombers lying dead, one of them a schoolteacher.

In an odd way, such attacks validated Matthews's belief in the low risk of living in such a dangerous place. She would be safe at Khost, she told worried relatives and friends, because she would stay inside the wire. Local jihadist groups would fling themselves against the walls at regular intervals, but they never quite amounted to a serious threat.

"She told me, 'I would never allow myself to be put in danger, because of my kids,'" said a CIA colleague who met with Matthews a few weeks before she went overseas. "I think she honestly believed it."

Matthews had already concluded that life in a war zone wasn't so bad. Her first glimpse of her temporary Afghan home was from the heaving side of a Black Hawk helicopter making the thirty-minute run from Kabul. The city and CIA base were perched on a high plateau surrounded by dun-colored hills, and the terrain reminded her of parts of the American Southwest. "I kept expecting to see the Marlboro Man show up," she quipped to one of her e-mail pals back in Virginia.

The land had a kind of austere beauty best appreciated from the air. To the north, and visible from the base on a clear day, were the snowcapped White Mountains—home to the infamous al-Qaeda fortress Tora Bora, from which Osama bin Laden had escaped in 2001. The invisible line separating Afghanistan from Pakistan ran along another line of low hills just twenty miles to the east. The territory in between appeared almost lush, by Afghan standards, with irrigated fields and a scattering of trees, in contrast with the relentless brown of much of the country during the hot months.

Khost, home to 160,000 mostly ethnic Pashtuns, had survived a four-year military siege by Soviet forces during the 1980s, yet was remarkably intact. Instead of ravaged, the city appeared merely poor, a maze of dirty, mud-brick houses and shops with only a single noteworthy public structure, an elegant turquoise-domed mosque built by the patriarch of the Haqqani clan, Jalaluddin Haqqani. Bordering the city to the east was the concrete sprawl of Khost Airfield and the base itself, an American island isolated from the host country by concentric rings of HESCO barriers—the ubiquitous sandbags on steroids present at all U.S. military installations in Afghanistan—and concertina wire. A few crumbling relics from the Soviet occupation still stood; they included a squat two-story control tower built by the Russians that now served as a lookout post and the dozen or so wrecked 1980s-vintage aircraft that lined one side of the runway. Most of the newer buildings were prefabricated military structures, such as cargo containers converted into improvised barracks. All things natural and man-made—buildings, streets, houses, vehicles, uniforms—were muted shades of beige and brown, dulled further by an omnipresent coating of dust.

Life inside the wire came with not only a presumption of safety but better than average amenities. The mess hall served up surprisingly good food, including lobster or crab legs on Fridays. The main rec room's satellite receiver beamed in live baseball and football and the newest Hollywood releases. A separate CIA lounge drew crowds of off-duty officers with its private stock of wine and ice-cold beer. The base gym gleamed with the latest fitness equipment, from elliptical machines to racks of Olympic barbell plates.

Matthews was a runner, and she quickly took up the habit of lacing up her sneakers just after dawn for a lap around the airfield with an eclectic group of CIA and military officers that called itself the Khost Running Club. After her workout she returned to her trailerlike quarters and one of the greatest perquisites accorded to her, the ranking officer on base: a private bathroom. Matthews had bargained hard for the extra privacy, perhaps the most coveted luxury of all.

The commute from her room to her CIA office was only a few steps, instead of the two hours of interstate and Beltway traffic she faced back home. But the new role that awaited her there would be her toughest adjustment by far. The subject matter, al-Qaeda and the Taliban insurgency, she knew well. She had also managed people before. But now she commanded American and Afghan men and women in a place where the bombs and bullets were real. For the first time in her career, the hard choices she faced on the job carried profound consequences for the people working for her.

Matthews answered to her bosses in Langley, just as before, but now she sparred with a new set of partners who thought differently and had priorities separate from those of the CIA. They were the soldiers: Pentagon and NATO brass in Kabul, field commanders in and around Khost, and, most immediately, the Special Forces teams that operated out of the base. The commandos were military rock stars, supremely confident in their skills and used to being treated as elites. They formed natural alliances with their Special Forces brethren within the CIA's ranks, including several of the paramilitary officers from the CIA's Special Activities Division, as well as the base's security detail, which included retired Green Berets and Navy SEALs now working for Blackwater. Some were disdainful of the CIA generally, mocking the newcomers as "children" or eggheaded "Clowns in Action." It wasn't just that the CIA lacked military skills; many of them also had little grasp of the local language and culture and rarely left the base to venture outside, military officers said.

The dislike was mutual. In private, the case officers and analysts complained about the gun toters as "knuckle-draggers" and "hot-house flowers" with egos to match their inflated biceps. Both views were stereotypes, but Matthews was hypersensitive to male skepticism about her ability to do a job. She had battled against it for her entire career.

The CIA still was very much a man's world when Jennifer Matthews signed up on January 3, 1989. Three other women joined the agency the same day, and the foursome quickly concluded that they needed to stick together—"the only women in a sea of men," one member of the quartet later recalled.

By chance, they shared a similar look: four white women in their mid-twenties, of roughly the same height and build, with brown hair and size 4 clothes. When they traveled together as a pack, as they often did, they turned heads in Langley's buttoned-down corridors. The four lunched together in the cafeteria, took group vacations, and even planned one another's weddings. Matthews felt obliged to serve as leader because she was the oldest by a few weeks. She also was the most ambitious. When the new recruits were asked during orientation about their future plans, Matthews answered without hesitation: "I'm going to be the DCI"—director of the Central Intelligence Agency.

That kind of unabashed ambition, and a belief that she could conquer anything through willpower and hard work, was a lifelong trademark. As a young girl, the middle of three children born to a press operator and a nurse in a working-class suburb of Harrisburg, Pennsylvania, she bored into her books while her girlfriends chased boys and partied. She grew up with a strong feminist streak and a belief in a divine will that ultimately shapes all human destiny. Her social world as a child and teenager revolved around a small Christian fundamentalist congregation that embraced both patriotism and a literal interpretation of the Bible. Her theology evolved as she grew older, but she considered herself an evangelical Christian for the rest of her life.

After high school she attended a small Baptist university in western Ohio called Cedarville, a school that advertises its commitment to teaching a creationist approach to science. There she studied broadcasting and met a fellow cross-country runner whom she later married, a religiously devout chemistry student named Gary Anderson. Both later attended nearby Miami University of Ohio, where Matthews earned a master's degree in political science. She worked briefly as a paralegal before deciding, with encouragement from a relative who served in the intelligence community, to try for a job at the CIA.

Very few women had been permitted to join the elite fraternity of case officers in those days, so Matthews and her three new CIA friends took positions that traditionally were open to women. Matthews became an imagery analyst and spent many hours poring over satellite photos of suspected chemical weapons factories in Libya. A natural writer, she later became a reports officer, a job that entailed translating raw intelligence from the field into concise prose.

Even there, Matthews was driven by a perceived need to outshine the men around her just to be accepted, remembered a female colleague who was part of her close circle of friends.

"We worked long, hard hours. We went the extra mile. And we routinely outran our male counterparts," said the friend, who, like

Matthews, eventually became an undercover operative with a protected identity.

Matthews briefly followed her husband to Geneva, where he
worked for a Swiss company. But afterward the couple settled into a
suburban Washington lifestyle that was organized largely to support
her career. Because they worked in different cities—Matthews in
the Washington suburbs, her husband in Richmond—they bought
a house roughly in the middle, near Fredericksburg, Virginia, and
logged more than a hundred miles a day in their commutes. But
Matthews kept her maiden name, and when children arrived, the
couple employed nannies so she could quickly return to the office.
Friends say she adored her three children, but her brain was wired
for work. Staying at home would have been as alien to her as growing fins and living in the ocean.

"She was very much a feminist in that way, yet she also was
extremely traditional in her views about marriage and family," said
the agency friend. "There was a dichotomy about her that allowed
her to separate different parts of her life. It's part of what made her
a good analyst."

Matthews rejoined the agency after returning from Switzerland
in 1996, but with entirely new aspirations. She shifted from the
agency's analytical division to the Directorate of Operations, the
side of the CIA that runs clandestine missions overseas. The new
job would require weeks of physically rigorous training at the CIA
boot camp known as the Farm. Eventually she would also have
to give up her right to her own name, becoming an officer "under
cover." Like Valerie Plame, her soon-to-be-famous colleague in the
operations division, her very identity was a government secret.

Matthews truly hit her stride at the CIA when she joined a small
unit within the directorate's counterterrorism division known inter-
nally as Alec Station. It consisted of a mix of officers from different
backgrounds, all devoted to the study of a little-known Islamic terrorist group that called itself the Base, or al-Qaeda. When she first
joined in 1996, the unit was regarded as a CIA backwater. Terrorist
groups were a second-rate threat, and al-Qaeda was a bit player com-

pared with the better-funded Hezbollah and Hamas. But things began to change in 1998 after al-Qaeda simultaneously bombed two U.S. embassies in Kenya and Tanzania, killing more than 220 people. The attacks catapulted bin Laden to a spot on the FBI's ten most wanted list. Suddenly Alec Station and its analysts were in demand.

As a group the officers became so al-Qaeda obsessed that they jokingly referred to themselves as the Manson Family. The hard part was convincing official Washington that Osama bin Laden was a threat to the U.S. homeland. Led by Matthews's boss, a blunt-spoken analyst named Michael Scheuer, they eventually won the backing of senior CIA leaders, including Director George Tenet, and Cofer Black, who headed the Counterterrorism Center. The officers in the late 1990s drew up contingency plans for killing bin Laden and driving his terrorist allies out of Afghanistan, using friendly Afghan fighters and the agency's newly acquired unmanned aerial vehicle, the Predator. But the Clinton administration passed on a chance to assassinate bin Laden in 1999, and the newly elected Bush administration deflected Tenet's urgent requests for action and ultimately postponed any significant policy discussions about al-Qaeda until September 4, 2001. Seven days later al-Qaeda–trained hijackers crashed commercial jetliners into the World Trade Center and the Pentagon.

The morning of the attack was a normal workday at Langley, and many CIA employees were just arriving at the office as the first plane hit the World Trade Center's North Tower at 8:46 A.M. When the second tower was struck seventeen minutes later, there was an audible gasp of recognition: *This is the work of al-Qaeda.*

Cofer Black, the CIA's counterterrorism director, assuming that CIA headquarters was likely on the terrorists' attack list, ordered most of the staff out of the building. He and the Alec Station analysts stayed behind and got to work. Some did not see their families again for days.

"We're at war now, a different kind of war than we've ever fought before," Black told the counterterrorism team as he prepared to issue marching orders. "We're all going to have to do our part. And not all of us are going to make it back."

Matthews's close friends say her experiences during those weeks forever changed her. Before September 11 she had worked long hours with her Alec Station colleagues, trying to uncover the al-Qaeda plot they believed was in the works, but after the terrorist attacks she slept in a chair in her office and didn't go home for days. Pregnant with her third child at the time, she became physically exhausted and eventually suffered a miscarriage, a misfortune that she suspected was due to the stress of her job. Yet she continued to work, telling friends repeatedly that she believed that a new attack was imminent, and only the CIA had the resources to stop it. Where al-Qaeda was concerned, Matthews had "drunk the Kool-Aid," a CIA friend said.

Matthews was one of the first officers to be assigned the title of targeter, then a newly minted job in the agency's counterterrorism division, and she soon acquired a high-profile case: She was to lead the agency's search for an al-Qaeda logistics planner who went by the nom de guerre Abu Zubaida. Zubaida, a Palestinian whose real name is Zayn al-Abidin Muhammad Hussein, ran a jihadist camp near Khost before September 11, and over the years he had facilitated the training or travel arrangements for scores of al-Qaeda militants in Afghanistan. Matthews believed that Zubaida knew details about a planned second wave of al-Qaeda attacks against the United States, and she convinced her CIA superiors to let her assemble a team of newly hired intelligence officers to coordinate a global search for him.

Matthews set up shop in a small conference room that was soon jammed with computers and bodies. Her team worked elbow to elbow for weeks until, in March 2002, they caught a break: They traced Zubaida to a safe house in the Pakistani city of Faisalabad. On March 28, Pakistani and American intelligence officers raided the house and captured the man after a firefight that left him gravely wounded. He was the first significant al-Qaeda operative to be nabbed by the CIA.

Within days of his capture, Zubaida handed his American interrogators an intelligence breakthrough, revealing the identity of the principal architect of the September 11 attacks: Khalid Sheikh Mohammed. Later, when Zubaida stopped cooperating with his interrogators, the Bush administration authorized the use of "enhanced interrogation techniques," including waterboarding, to force him to talk. Among the witnesses to these sessions was Matthews, who was flown to Thailand to help guide the teams of CIA interrogators in questioning the new captive. Years later the case became the center of a roiling controversy. Human rights groups, congressional committees, and even former Bush administration officials questioned every facet of the CIA's handling of Zubaida, who came to symbolize the debate over the agency's use of secret prisons outside normal legal constraints, as well as interrogation practices that the International Committee of the Red Cross condemned as torture. Later evidence suggested that Zubaida was never truly an al-Qaeda leader, but rather a logistics man with limited knowledge of the terrorist group's strategy and plans. Still, Matthews would be admired within the counterterrorism division as the officer primarily responsible for the takedown of the agency's first high-value terrorist captive and the man who led the CIA to the mastermind of the September 11 attacks.

By the middle of the decade Matthews was in management, directing the Counterterrorism Center's teams of reports officers. She also forged alliances with a cadre of other tough women who were ascending into the division's leadership ranks a few career jumps ahead of her. One of her new mentors was a notoriously sharp-tempered redhead who had played a key role in many of the agency's most aggressive—and controversial—operations, from "enhanced interrogation" to a classified program known as rendition, in which suspected terrorists were abducted overseas by CIA operatives and flown to a third country to be interrogated and, in some cases, tortured. The two women shared an infatuation with tough guy actor Tommy Lee Jones, and they were fond of quoting a particularly apt line from his 2007 film *No Coun-*

try for Old Men: "You can't stop what's comin'. It ain't all waiting on you."

As she moved up the hierarchy, Matthews was sometimes accused of being abrasive, stubborn, and impatient. Nothing riled her more than the suggestion that she as a woman was not adequate to a task—any task. In Langley several male colleagues began to refer to her by an unflattering nickname, Ruth, short for ruthless.

There, and later at Khost, she would feel obliged to prove herself time and again, fighting a never-ending battle for respect in a world that had long been dominated by men.

"You're telling boys how to do their business," said a CIA Afghan hand who counseled Matthews before she left for Khost. "Typically the answer is, 'Missy, you don't know what it's like.'"

It was true that the Khost Matthews knew was nothing like the Khost of a few years before. Long before the base was safe enough for the likes of analysts and targeters, Khost belonged to America's original black ops force, the paramilitary officers of the CIA's Special Activities Division. Recruited mostly from the ranks of Green Berets, Navy SEALs, and other elite military units, the CIA's SAD officers had been the country's premier force since the 1950s for clandestine missions outside the writ of conventional troops, such as sabotage, guerrilla warfare, and targeted killings. Teams of SAD officers and Special Forces commandos spearheaded the assault against al-Qaeda in Afghanistan in 2001 that drove the Taliban government out of power. About a dozen of them set up camp in the eastern city of Khost that winter to begin cleaning up lingering pockets of Taliban resistance, and SAD officers had stayed there ever since.

In those final days of 2001, when Matthews and her team in Langley watched in anguish as Osama bin Laden slipped away into Pakistan, the Khost SAD team formed at an air base in the Pakistani city of Jacobabad and choppered across the mountains to take control of the airfield. They very nearly met with disaster in their first minutes on the ground.

They arrived in Khost at 2:00 A.M. on a bitterly cold morning, carrying light weapons and gear, along with a small trunkful of cash and a pledge of assistance from a local commander who opposed the Taliban. The local commander was waiting for them, as promised. But so were dozens of fighters from rival clans. Turbaned gunmen glowered at one another in a tense standoff with the Americans in the middle.

In the darkness, the U.S. team could see that several Afghans on different sides had pulled out grenades. They were prepared to fight to the death, as the CIA officers later learned, to decide who would get to play host and receive the bulk of American money and modern weapons.

"One of the factions knew we were coming, and then all the others found out," said one American officer who was present. "It was early in the morning, and no one had had their tea. So the grenades came out."

One of the CIA officers quickly stepped up and began lavishing praise on the Afghans for their hospitality and bravery. Uncle Sam's pockets are deep, the man assured the group, a rough-looking assemblage of bandoliers and craggy, bearded faces that reminded some of the Americans of the cantina bar scene in *Star Wars*. The fighters drifted off, the crisis temporarily defused. Relieved, the weary officers proceeded to pick their way through the town in the darkness, with some of them bunking down at an abandoned elementary school that would serve as temporary outpost.

It was a poor choice for a fort. The school building was on a major thoroughfare and nearly impossible to defend against suicide bombers or rocket attacks. Nearby houses and trees offered hideouts for snipers. There was no running water or electricity. The town itself was dirty and sinister, overrun by armed gangs from as many as seven different clans, whose allegiances seemed to shift by the day. Random gunfire at odd hours kept the men on edge, never completely sure if the shots portended an attack or if it was just another Afghan wedding celebration.

The darkest moment came on January 4, 2002. After a meeting with elders in a nearby village, a gun-toting Afghan suddenly opened fire on the Khost team. One of the CIA paramilitary officers collapsed, struck by a bullet that pierced his chest through a gap in his body armor. Also hit was an energetic Green Beret sergeant named Nathan Chapman, a communications specialist and Desert Storm veteran who had been detailed to the CIA team at Khost. Chapman, thirty-one, had been shot through his thigh, and his wound was deemed less serious than that of the CIA officer.

Within minutes the two wounded men were in the air on their way back to Khost, where the CIA officer with the chest wound was eventually stabilized. Chapman meanwhile was rapidly losing blood from what turned out to be a severed femoral artery. By the time the helicopter touched down in Khost, the young soldier was dead. He was the first American GI from any service to die in combat in Afghanistan.

Soon afterward the CIA moved its headquarters to the grounds of the airfield outside town. Though abandoned for years, it offered ample space for sleeping and working, including a fully intact control tower with a roof that provided sweeping fields of fire for a machine gunner. The runway was salvageable, if littered with broken and bombed-out aircraft from the time of the Soviet occupation. The Americans got to work shoveling dirt into HESCO barriers to begin the fortification of what was to become the first CIA base in Afghanistan outside Kabul.

Someone suggested a name for the new facility: Forward Operating Base Chapman, after the Special Forces officer killed a few days earlier. It became the official name for the base, though most of the CIA inhabitants referred to it by its shorter handle, Khost.

The first order of business was deciding how to deal with the region's largest militant group. Local warlord Jalaluddin Haqqani had spent years on the CIA's payroll when he served as an Afghan rebel commander during the war against the Soviets, and he now controlled thousands of fighters along the Afghanistan-Pakistan border. He had nominally allied himself with the Taliban after that group's rise to power in the 1990s. But Haqqani was a free agent, more interested in perpetuating his own smuggling empire and protection rackets than in theology or conquest.

Haqqani also was loyal to his friends, including his former comrade-in-arms Osama bin Laden. The two men had cemented their reputations in the 1980s fighting the Soviets in the mountains around Khost, a region that repeatedly proved impervious to Russian assaults. Bin Laden, the son of a wealthy construction magnate, used Saudi money and engineering connections to help the mujahideen guerrillas build a complex of tunnels and cave fortresses in the hills. Haqqani became a legendary military commander, personally leading his fighters into improbable David and Goliath victories against Soviet commandos and helicopter gunships. The Soviets occupied and expanded the airfield at Khost mainly in a failed attempt to bomb Haqqani and his allies out of their mountain redoubts.

Thus, when SAD teams and pro-U.S. Afghan forces closed in on bin Laden in late 2001, the al-Qaeda leader sought the protection of the tall, bushy-bearded warlord who had fought with him against the Soviets. Haqqani offered his friend sanctuary in a house outside Khost until it was safe to cross back into Pakistan to rejoin his followers.

Haqqani remained behind. He had been sanguine about the Taliban's defeat and was prepared to switch loyalties, as he had done so often in the past. Pakistani officials who had dealt with him for decades strongly urged the Americans to accommodate him and perhaps even give him a token role in the new Afghan government.

But in Washington, Bush officials in the Defense Department were not in a mood to bargain. Haqqani had abetted the escape of Osama bin Laden and might still know his whereabouts. Two rounds of secret talks were held with Haqqani's emissaries, in Islamabad and then in the United Arab Emirates, according to a former senior U.S. official intimately familiar with the events. But at both meetings, the official said, the U.S. side offered the same terms: unconditional surrender, including Haqqani's personal acquiescence to donning an orange jumpsuit and joining the other detainees at the newly opened U.S. prison camp at Guantánamo Bay, Cuba. After a reasonable interval—presumably after Haqqani had told military interrogators everything he knew about bin Laden—he would be allowed to return home.

Haqqani's refusal to accept such an offer was a given, the former intelligence official said.

"I personally always believed that Haqqani was someone we could have worked with," the official said. "But at that time, no one was looking over the horizon, to where we might be in five years. For the policy folks, it was just 'screw these little brown people.' "

Haqqani did refuse. Jalaluddin Haqqani had bedeviled the Russians over nearly a decade of guerrilla warfare in the 1980s. Now, at age fifty-one, he would go to war against the Americans. In time the so-called Haqqani network, led by Haqqani's son Sirajuddin, became one of the greatest threats to U.S. forces in all of Afghanistan, and it was Haqqani's fighters who now woke Matthews and her colleagues at all hours, firing rockets at the walls of the base at Khost.

In the years that followed bin Laden's escape, some CIA paramilitary teams continued to operate as before, working out of small compounds where they lived and fought alongside Afghan soldiers. But the old SAD base at Khost expanded, bulked up, and assumed new responsibilities, mostly in support of Pentagon objectives. The hunt for Osama bin Laden shifted to Pakistan and relied largely on robot planes. And for the first time CIA reports officers, targeters, and analysts from Langley were routinely deployed to frontline bases to help with the collection and interpretation of intelligence, mingling with and sometimes directing the men with the guns.

Langley embarked on a program of cross-training for the two very different types of officers. SAD officers were drilled in classic intelligence-gathering techniques, while Afghanistan-bound civilian officers were required to take a three-week "overseas preparation course" to learn basic war zone survival. In the latter program, officers worked on their shooting skills, learned battlefield first aid, and practiced driving through roadblocks and ambushes. It was a start, but even some of the trainers acknowledged the program's inadequacy.

"It's just rudimentary, baseline, box-checking training," said one career officer who taught one of the courses. "It's familiarization, as opposed to proficiency."

A decade earlier the same course had lasted twenty-one weeks and included extensive instruction on bombs and explosives, as well as lessons in team building, navigation, and even parachuting. But the longer program was dropped because it was judged to be expensive and time-consuming for an agency that needed to deploy operatives to the field quickly. Some of the skills taught in the longer course—parachuting, for example—were deemed irrelevant in an age in which so much of the business of spying depends on computer networks, satellites, and robotics.

"After September 11, the question was asked, 'Do we need to teach these hard skill sets to everyone?' And the answer was no," said the retired officer who taught the overseas course. "You can simply subcontract those parts of the job to others." The hard skill sets were the special domain of the soldiers and the paramilitary elites. The "meat eaters," as some called themselves, were still needed at Khost. But they would no longer be in charge.

In the command center at Khost, with Baitullah Mehsud now confirmed dead, Matthews could focus her attention on the mission she had always regarded as the highest priority: locating and killing bin Laden, along with his deputy, Ayman al-Zawahiri, and their senior commanders.

Matthews had quickly come to appreciate the extraordinary assets that the base brought to the hunt. Foremost among them were the Counterterrorism Pursuit Teams, a new force of CIA-funded Afghan commandos trained by the SAD. There were three thousand of these soldiers in the eastern half of Afghanistan, a mix of Pakistani- and Afghan-born ethnic Pashtuns who could slip across the border in local costume to kill or capture suspected terrorists or collect information. The intelligence they gathered was shared with the base's contingent of American case officers and funneled, along with the usual phone and Internet chatter, into the CIA's giant databases, to be teased and sifted by targeters—Elizabeth Hanson and others like her. Active leads about specific terrorists could be quickly transformed into hard geographic coordinates for the CIA's growing fleet of Predators.

After eight years of practice, the cogs and wheels turned smoothly most of the time. And lately the men and women in charge of the CIA's complex machine had seen new evidence of progress. After more than a year of relentless missile strikes, al-Qaeda's leadership in Afghanistan appeared to be in complete disarray, an assessment based on intercepted conversations between the group's demoralized operatives. Bin Laden had gone so deeply into hiding that he was effectively absent. Though Zawahiri still guided strategy, command of day-to-day operations had fallen to a handful of lieutenants, chiefly the man known as Sheikh Saeed al-Masri, the Egyptian who had filled the void after the death of Osama al-Kini. But CIA intercepts showed that al-Masri was a highly unpopular leader, tyrannical, manipulative, and controlling. Al-Qaeda fighters whose conversations were monitored complained bitterly about the group's presumed acting leader.

And the best news of all had come not from Pakistan but from Amman. The Jordanian intelligence service had recruited a star informant who had been dropped into the tribal region with CIA help. The new agent, a Jordanian, had disappeared for several months but had just resurfaced with breathtaking new information. In the course of a few months he had somehow managed to penetrate first the Pakistani Taliban and then, by all accounts, al-Qaeda itself. At senior staff meetings back in Langley, top CIA managers were now speaking in hushed tones about a "golden source."

A golden source, operating just across the hills in Pakistan, perhaps fifty miles from the small office where Jennifer Matthews now sat. She skimmed the daily cables and waited with increasing anticipation to see what would happen next.

10

THE DOUBLE AGENT

Langley, Virginia—September–October 2009

See attached.

Humam al-Balawi's first big score as a spy, the one that would surely cement his reputation as the decade's greatest, arrived at CIA headquarters on a late August morning as a jumble of computer code attached to an e-mail. The agency's data forensics specialists had been warned, and they set upon it like an army of sushi chefs. They sliced and filleted, separating larger chunks of data into bits and bytes and then reassembling them again.

Several days of scrutiny later the agency's initial impression stood: The file was authentic. And it was nothing short of miraculous.

Nearly a month after Mehsud's death, Balawi had seemed to vanish from the earth. There had been no e-mail, phone call, or even intercepted Taliban transmission to explain what had happened to him. Then he suddenly resurfaced in late summer in a short message to bin Zeid. He was back, and he had a gift, he wrote, one that bin Zeid would find to be worth the wait.

The gift was a small image file, a few seconds of low-quality video taken by a handheld camera, the type that can be purchased at any electronics store for a few hundred dollars. The video depicted a small gathering of men in traditional Pashtun dress talking in a dimly lit room. In the foreground was a young man, seen mostly in silhouette, until a sideways turn clearly revealed him to be Balawi. Seated near him was a slim, dark-bearded man in his early forties who was doing most of the talking. His face was instantly recognizable to the agency's counterterrorism experts, even though no American officer had seen the man in eight years. His name was Atiyah Adb al-Rahman, and he was one of the closest associates of al-Qaeda leader Osama bin Laden known to be alive.

Al-Rahman, a Libyan and an Islamic scholar, had been a top aide to bin Laden since the 1980s, and the two had escaped together into Pakistan after the Tora Bora debacle in late 2001. Afterward he was believed to have fled to Iran, but he emerged again in 2006 as one of al-Qaeda's top strategic thinkers and spiritual advisers. It was al-Rahman who had tried unsuccessfully to rein in Abu Musab al-Zarqawi, the leader of al-Qaeda in Iraq, when his sadistic attacks against Shia Muslims began to shift the tide of Iraqi public opinion against al-Qaeda. There had been no confirmed sightings of al-Rahman in years; yet here he was, holding forth on video, with a CIA informant seated at his feet.

The images left jaws agape and unleashed a torrent of questions. Yet this much was undeniably true: The Jordanian physician Humam al-Balawi had been in the same room with one of al-Qaeda's top commanders. He had managed to capture the encounter on videotape. And he had delivered the evidence to the very doorstep of the CIA.

In the eight years since the start of the war against al-Qaeda, no one had ever gotten so close.

Three times a week Leon Panetta opened his seventh-floor office for a gathering of the CIA's top counterterrorism officials. His deputy, Steve Kappes, attended, along with the directors of the agency's National Clandestine Service and Counterterrorism Center and a phalanx of aides and briefers. Squeezed around Panetta's mahogany table, beneath the tattered American flag that had once flown above the World Trade Center, they sipped coffee from china cups and discussed the latest events in Pakistan. One afternoon in early September, the group gathered to pore over an extraordinary transmission from an obscure agent known as Wolf.

There were still photos and a blow-by-blow description of a video—at the time, still undergoing evaluation by technical teams—that showed a presumed CIA informant conversing with one of al-Qaeda's senior advisers. The agency's senior managers were bursting with questions. Where did the agent come from? How did he get such amazing access? No one was yet sure what to make of it, except that it was extraordinarily good news.

Two snippets of information about Balawi were particularly intriguing to Panetta. One was the fact that the informant had managed to get his nose under al-Qaeda's tent with such speed. The time frames for running agents in this region are always very long, the CIA director thought. This one is going from asset to target incredibly fast.

The other surprise was how little the agency seemed to know about the operative in the video.

"Nobody from the CIA has really had any person-to-person contact with him," Panetta marveled.

There were plausible explanations for all of it. The informant was one of the Mukhabarat's recruits, and he was already in Pakistan before any American officers could take a look at him. As for his access, it was simple: Balawi was a doctor. Al-Qaeda desperately needed doctors.

Balawi was talented, no doubt. Exactly how good was something the agency needed to find out, and with all possible speed.

"You have lifted our heads," Ali bin Zeid wrote to Balawi one morning in one of his regular missives from Amman. "You have lifted our heads in front of the Americans."

Bin Zeid was receiving verbal high-fives from his Jordanian colleagues over the stunning performance of his star recruit, and he wanted to pass the compliments along. Balawi had surprised every-one, bin Zeid most of all. How had he managed it? What else could he provide?

The encouragement seemed to work. In the weeks after Balawi resurfaced, as the dry northerly winds of autumn swept away the last traces of summer's heat, his e-mails crackled with interesting tidbits. He described jihadist fighters he met, passed along rumors, and sketched out the complex web of relations among local militant groups.

More intriguingly, he began to serve up graphically detailed descriptions of the damage wrought by CIA missile strikes, down to conditions of the corpses and body parts pulled from the shat-tered cars and flattened houses. He wrote about the frustration and rage among Taliban and al-Qaeda leaders, all of whom now lived in dread of the buzzing *machays*.

Balawi could rarely be precise about locations—he was still a stranger to the area and spoke little Pashto—but his reports helped the agency's Predator teams narrow their search for targets. Some agency officials concluded that as many as five Taliban soldiers were killed as a result of Balawi's detailed accounts. After a missile strike, the informant would e-mail bin Zeid with his on-the-scene accounts of death and mayhem, along with words of encouragement. *You're on the right track now*, he would say.

CIA analysts in Amman and Langley studied the messages with increasing fascination. The agency collected its own bomb damage assessments, usually based on video taken by Predators lingering in the area after a strike. Its reports matched Balawi's with striking accuracy. The Jordanian was clearly present at the targeted sites, presumably giving medical aid, because his reporting was unfail-ingly spot-on.

Technically Balawi was communicating only with bin Zeid, who had been assigned to the case full-time. But increasingly CIA offi-cials discovered that they could ask questions and get rapid answers. Balawi was displaying the hallmarks of a true double agent, despite his utter lack of training.

The CIA had recruited a handful of successful double agents

during the Cold War, most famously the Soviet military intelligence colonel Oleg Penkovsky, code-named Agent Hero. It was Penkovsky who alerted the Kennedy administration in 1962 to secret, Soviet-built missile launch sites in Fidel Castro's Cuba, a tip that started the Cuban missile crisis. Penkovsky was himself betrayed by a Soviet double agent and executed in 1963.

More recently the CIA had used informants, most of them recruited by the spy networks of friendly governments, to dismantle terrorist groups. Secret agents were instrumental in defeating Abu Musab al-Zarqawi's terrorist cell in Iraq, as well as the al-Qaeda–allied Indonesian terrorist ring known as Jemaah Islamiyah. In the latter case, the group's leader, Riduan Isamuddin, better known by his nom de guerre, Hambali, was ratted out by an informant and captured in a joint operation by the CIA and Thai police near Bangkok in 2003. His organization in tatters, Hambali was shuffled among CIA secret prisons before finally landing at the U.S. detention camp at Guantánamo Bay, Cuba.

Could Balawi become the greatest double agent of them all?

The other intelligence officer assigned full-time to the Balawi case wasn't so sure. CIA case officer Darren LaBonte was wary by nature. He also was extremely protective of bin Zeid, a man he had known for only nine months but regarded as a close friend or perhaps even a younger brother. Though the two men were seasoned intelligence officers of roughly the same age, LaBonte was taller by half a head and battle hardened from multiple tours of Afghanistan. The two traveled together on joint assignments as far as Southeast Asia and Eastern Europe, sharing information and coordinating tactics in a way that mirrored the close ties between their two countries. But as they worked, LaBonte secretly kept watch, worrying about his friend's vulnerability to kidnapping, assassination, or even mistreatment by the Mukhabarat, with its rivalries and inscrutable internal politics.

"He needs me," he explained to an associate in Amman. "I have to be there for Ali."

LaBonte had initially moved to the Middle East from South Asia to cool off. The former Army Ranger had been running covert missions as a CIA paramilitary officer in violent eastern Afghanistan for nearly two years, a job that fitted him as easily as the hard-knuckled military gloves he liked to wear during firefights. But in early 2009, when the CIA offered a new position in relatively tranquil Jordan, LaBonte decided to take it. At thirty-four, he was now a family man. Besides, he had been getting signals lately that it was time to ease off on the adrenaline.

The first sign was the rocket-propelled grenade that came within a whisker of creasing his face. LaBonte had been deep inside Taliban country at the time, near an Afghan border town called Asadabad, when an insurgent pointed a launching tube directly at him. The projectile whooshed past within easy arm's reach, so close that LaBonte could feel the rush of wind and smell the propellant. He was still shaky when he called his wife over Skype hours later, just to hear her voice.

A second message arrived on the day his daughter, Raina, was born. LaBonte had flown all night from Afghanistan to make it home for the delivery, and he arrived at Washington's Dulles Airport to discover that his wife, Racheal, was already in labor. He jumped into his father's waiting car, and the pair cut and swerved through sixty-five miles of traffic to the Annapolis, Maryland, hospital where the doctors were trying their best to slow the clock. The car roared up to the hospital door, and LaBonte leaped out and blew past orderlies and wheelchairs in a sprint to the maternity ward. The nurses draped a gown over the sweaty, unwashed father-to-be and led him into the delivery room just in time to see his first child brought into the world.

Just over a year later LaBonte put the body armor and night-vision goggles away and said good-bye to Afghanistan, perhaps forever. His new posting, the CIA's largest counterterrorism hub in the Middle East, was hardly sleepy, but the Jordanian capital was stable enough to accommodate officers' families. For the first time in years, LaBonte could look forward to evenings at home with his wife, and Racheal could be spared the constant worrying that her husband had been wounded in an ambush or blown up by a roadside bomb.

But Amman was no rest stop. By March 2009, three months after the move, the contours of LaBonte's new role were finally clear. As he had hoped, he now hunted even bigger quarry, international terrorists, rather than the Taliban hirelings he had often chased in the Afghan hills. Soon he was busier than ever, routinely working late into the evening and traveling abroad for secret meetings with a whirligig of turncoats, hustlers, and informants.

He and bin Zeid had become a remarkable team. Bin Zeid brought a deep knowledge of Arab culture and years of experience investigating jihadist networks throughout the Middle East. LaBonte was a combat veteran expert at all the practical skills essential to covert work, from stakeouts to kicking in doors.

LaBonte's call sign among his Ranger comrades had been Spartan. It was a name that particularly suited LaBonte, a man who was forever being compared to action heroes. Relatives playfully called him Captain America because of his earnest patriotism and the way he unabashedly spoke about wanting to protect his country. His agency friends joked about his "spidey sense," his uncanny knack for sniffing out danger like Spider-Man.

He even looked the part. Six feet tall and broad-shouldered, LaBonte was two hundred pounds of rugged good looks and muscle, a born athlete who was said to bench-press four hundred pounds and run a marathon after barely bothering to train for it. He radiated a kind of unforced confidence that made him a natural leader, first as a standout baseball player and later as a martial arts champion, an Army Ranger, and an FBI cadet. He liked being in charge because he liked playing the role of older brother or protector.

"He was the sheepdog who protects the sheep," said one close friend from his army days. "It's how he saw himself."

Finding the job that suited his protective instincts was a years-long struggle. LaBonte's strong pitching arm earned him an invitation to play minor-league baseball for the Cleveland Indians, but he turned down the offer, explaining to family members that a professional sports career would distract him from more important goals he had set for his life. He found himself increasingly drawn to the military but rejected a chance to go to officers' school. Instead he decided to test his mettle against the punishing physical standards of one of the army's Special Forces units, the elite Seventy-fifth Ranger Regiment. He quickly earned his Ranger's tab and later a prestigious position as a member of the regimental color guard.

The army also introduced him to a pretty dance student named Racheal. In March 1999, LaBonte found himself in need of a date for the year's big formal event, the Ranger Ball. At the last minute—just hours before the first dance—a mutual friend persuaded Racheal to help one of his army buddies out of a jam.

"Is he cute?" Racheal asked.

"He looks a little like Daniel Day-Lewis," said the friend, referring to the actor best known at the time for portraying Hawkeye in the film *The Last of the Mohicans*, "but without the long hair."

As Racheal said later, the tall young Ranger who arrived at her door that evening in his dress uniform was more than just handsome.

"I knew in the first minute that this was someone important in my life," she said of her future husband. "From that point on, life would be different."

The two married the following year, and by 2001 Darren LaBonte was out of the army and serving as a SWAT team officer for the Libertyville Police Department in Chicago's northern suburbs. He was working the graveyard shift, chasing rowdy teenagers and feeling restless, when the day came that was to change his life forever.

He had just gotten home from work on the morning of September 11 when the TV news anchor broke in with reports that a plane had crashed into one of the World Trade Center's twin towers. LaBonte watched for a moment mesmerized, then phoned his mother, who lived in another suburb a few minutes away.

"You need to turn on the news," he said.

Like many Americans that morning, Camille LaBonte assumed at first that the crash was accidental. But her son was convinced that something more sinister had occurred.

Humam al-Balawi was a straight-A student destined for a medical career when he posed for this photograph in his senior year
of high school. *(Associated Press)*

Balawi, armed with a toy gun, plays pretend terrorist with
his eldest daughter in this family photograph posted years
later by Balawi's wife on a jihadist Web site. *(Courtesy of SITE
Intelligence Group)*

Humam al-Balawi's father, Khalil, was a school administrator, teacher of Arabic literature, and father of ten children. When he was a boy, his family were forced to leave their home in what is now Israel after the partition of Palestine in 1948. They settled in Jordan, becoming part of a Palestinian refugee community that grew to nearly two million people. (*Joby Warrick*)

Balawi's Turkish wife, Defne Bayrak, was a journalist for a conservative Istanbul newspaper when the two met in an online chat room. A fluent Arabic speaker, she translated a biography of Osama bin Laden into Turkish. (*Courtesy of CNN*)

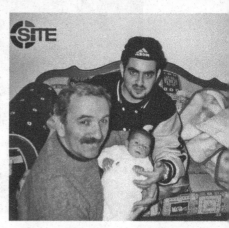

Balawi relaxes with his newborn eldest daughter and father-in-law in this family snapshot. The family enjoyed a comfortable, middle-class lifestyle and wore Western clothes while Balawi worked as a physician in the Jordanian capital. (*Courtesy of SITE Intelligence Group*)

Balawi turned down more lucrative medical opportunities to work in this United Nations medical clinic in a Palestinian refugee camp on the outskirts of Amman. While tending to refugee women and children, he developed a secret identity as a jihadist blogger, writing anti-Israel and anti-Western screeds that eventually attracted the attention of Jordan's intelligence service. (*Joby Warrick*)

Ali bin Zeid, a captain in Jordan's General Intelligence Department, commonly known as the Mukhabarat, was a cousin to Jordan's king. He went on off-roading excursions to relieve the pressure of counterterrorism work. Bin Zeid took charge of the Balawi case and believed he saw potential in the young doctor to become a double agent for the West. *(Courtesy of Fida Dawani)*

Former Army Ranger Darren LaBonte fought the Taliban in Afghanistan as a CIA paramilitary officer before moving to Jordan to work on counterterrorism cases. He became the CIA's American case officer for Balawi. *(Courtesy of the LaBonte family)*

Osama bin Laden (left) went deep into hiding after 2002, becoming so isolated that his influence over al-Qaeda's decisions diminished. His top deputy, Egyptian-born Ayman al-Zawahiri, narrowly avoided a CIA attempt on his life in 2006, and afterward taunted President George W. Bush in a videotaped diatribe, saying, "Bush, do you know where I am?" *(Courtesy of SITE Intelligence Group)*

And they will not rest
until they avenge him

Sheikh Saeed al-Masri, al-Qaeda's long-time financial chief, rose to take charge of the terrorist group's day-to-day operations. He gradually came to see an opportunity in the young Jordanian doctor who turned up in Pakistan's tribal belt in the spring of 2009. *(Courtesy of SITE Intelligence Group)*

Jennifer Matthews helped lead the CIA's search for al-Qaeda terrorists in Washington and London, and by early 2009 she was in line for her first command posting in a war zone. She had been in Afghanistan only three months when CIA officials put her in charge of the agency's first meeting with Balawi. *(Courtesy of David Matthews)*

Elizabeth Hanson was barely thirty and already a seasoned CIA "targeter" when she was dispatched to Kabul to help the CIA track down senior al-Qaeda operatives. She helped put the agency's unmanned Predator aircraft on the trail of Taliban and al-Qaeda leaders in Pakistan. *(Courtesy of the Hanson family)*

The CIA relied on its fleet of Predators to strike terrorists in places where U.S. troops couldn't go. The pilotless planes can hover for hours to conduct surveillance and can fire laser-guided missiles at targets with unparalleled accuracy. The Predators have killed hundreds of suspected terrorists in Pakistan in dozens of strikes since 2008. *(U.S. Air Force photo by Lieutenant Colonel Leslie Pratt)*

Michael V. Hayden, who became the Bush administration's third CIA director in 2006, saw signs that al-Qaeda's strength was increasing in Pakistan's tribal belt in 2007. He pressed the Bush administration to ramp up lethal Predator strikes in an effort to prevent another September 11–style terrorist attack against the West. *(Courtesy of Nikki Khan/*The Washington Post)

The leader of the Taliban alliance in Pakistan, Baitullah Mehsud, became the focus of a massive U.S.-Pakistani search in 2009 after intelligence linked him to a possible dirty-bomb plot. A CIA missile struck him on August 5, 2009, on the roof of his father-in-law's house in northwestern Pakistan. *(Courtesy of SITE Intelligence Group)*

After the killing of his cousin Baitullah, the charismatic Hakimullah Mehsud (middle) took the reins of Pakistan's Taliban alliance and talked openly of targeting the American heartland. Initially suspicious of Balawi, he came to regard the Jordanian physician as an instrument for exacting revenge on the CIA. *(Courtesy of SITE Intelligence Group)*

The town of Khost lies on Afghanistan's eastern fringe in territory long controlled by the Haqqani network, allies to the Taliban and al-Qaeda. The city's greatest landmark, a blue-domed mosque, was built by the clan's patriarch, Jalaluddin Haqqani, a friend of Osama bin Laden. *(Joby Warrick)*

The first Americans to arrive in Khost after the fall of the Taliban were a CIA-led team of Special Forces troops and paramilitary officers. They established Forward Operating Base Chapman, now known to most officers simply as Khost, at an airfield outside of town. It became a key outpost for gathering intelligence in eastern Afghanistan and in the Taliban heartland just across the border. *(Courtesy of Charles McComes)*

Jeremy Wise, thirty-five, fought in Iraq as a Navy SEAL before leaving the armed services in 2009. Newly married with a young son, he received an offer to work for the security contractor Xe Services LLC, formerly known as Blackwater. Wise traveled to Khost in mid-December 2009 for his first deployment protecting CIA operatives in Afghanistan. *(Courtesy of Dana Wise)*

At forty-six, Dane Paresi was one of the oldest and most battle hardened of the Americans at Khost. As a Green Beret, he had won a Bronze Star for his role in destroying a column of al-Qaeda and Taliban fighters in eastern Afghanistan. Paresi also had recently joined Blackwater in hopes of building up a nest egg for retirement. *(Courtesy of Mindy Lou Paresi)*

Harold Brown Jr., thirty-seven, was a one-time army intelligence specialist who worked in private industry before returning to government to work for the CIA. At Khost, his first overseas posting, he was invited to help evaluate the Jordanian informant, Balawi, who claimed to have connections to al-Qaeda's inner circle. *(Courtesy of Janet Brown)*

Scott Roberson, thirty-eight, busted drug dealers as an Atlanta police officer and protected U.S. dignitaries in war-torn Iraq before joining the CIA in 2009. He became the head of security at Khost and sparred with CIA managers over how to handle security for the planned meeting with Balawi. *(Courtesy of the Roberson family)*

Atiyah Abd al-Rahman, a senior al-Qaeda leader in Pakistan, appeared with Balawi in a fabricated video designed to convince the CIA that the Jordanian doctor had penetrated the terrorist group's inner circle. *(Courtesy of SITE Intelligence Group)*

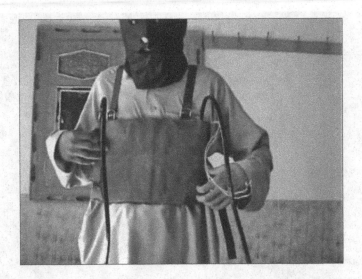

An unknown Jihadist models the suicide vest made especially for Balawi's mission at Khost. Far more powerful than typical suicide bombs, it contained several pounds of military C4 explosive concealed inside a pouch. *(Confidential source)*

Humam al-Balawi posed for several "martyrdom" videotapes before beginning his mission. In this video, he showed off the detonator he would use to set off a suicide bomb strapped to his chest. "Don't think that just by pressing a button and killing mujahideen, you are safe," he said, referring to the CIA and its Predator attacks. *(Courtesy of SITE Intelligence Group)*

In another martyrdom tape, Balawi (right) appears seated with Hakimullah Mehsud, his host in Pakistan. "His conscience did not allow him to spy on Muslim brothers for the infidels," Mehsud said of Balawi. *(Courtesy of SITE Intelligence Group)*

The CIA's Darren LaBonte (left) and the Mukhabarat's Ali bin Zeid posed for a snapshot at Khost on the day before Balawi's arrival. The two were partners on terrorism cases in Jordan and became close friends before they teamed up for the Balawi case. *(Courtesy of the LaBonte family)*

Jordanian agent Humam al-Balawi entered the CIA base through this gate and was waved by without a search. CIA operatives often insisted that high-level informants have no contact with Afghan guards at the base, for fear that their identity might be compromised. *(U.S. government source)*

The meeting was set to take place inside the CIA's heavily guarded compound within the Khost base. Balawi was driven past three guard stations before pulling up outside the building where he was to meet with bin Zeid and the Americans. He was greeted by a group of sixteen intelligence operatives anxious to debrief him. *(Courtesy of Tim Brown/Global Security.org and GeoEye)*

CIA director Leon Panetta (left, front) vowed to strike back against the al-Qaeda leaders responsible for killing the seven officers at Khost. In June 2010 he presided over a ceremony adding new stars on the CIA's Memorial Wall for the slain officers and contractors. *(Courtesy of CIA Public Affairs)*

Under Panetta's direction, the CIA targeted Hakimullah Mehsud and al-Qaeda's No. 3, al-Masri, in a series of missile strikes in the spring and summer. Panetta acknowledged that "systemic" problems had contributed to the CIA's deadliest day in a quarter century. *(Courtesy of Bill O'Leary/*The Washington Post*)*

Ethan Wise embraces the flag that draped the coffin of his father, fallen security guard Jeremy Wise. *(Courtesy of Katrina Clay)*

"That wasn't dumb. That was intentional," he said.

He drove to his parents' house and arrived in time to see the second plane hit the south tower. He and his mother then watched in disbelief as one tower collapsed, and then the other. When Camille turned to her son, he was crying.

Within weeks, LaBonte was privately taking Arabic lessons while sorting through his options for landing a meaningful role in the fight against terrorism that was just getting under way. He considered, and then rejected, the idea of reenlisting in the army; it was unlikely that he would end up in the job or unit that he wanted, he reasoned. Instead he decided to sign up with the U.S. Marshals Service, a law enforcement arm of the Justice Department that tracks down fugitives and protects federal courts. His Ranger experience landed him a coveted spot on the marshals' special operations team, yet it quickly became clear to LaBonte that the job was not the one he was looking for. Instead of searching for suspected terrorists, he was spending his days tracking down drug dealers.

LaBonte then applied simultaneously for positions at the FBI and CIA. The FBI called back first, so he enrolled in the bureau's academy in Quantico, Virginia. He won commendations as a cadet for leadership and shooting skills, and after graduation he landed a prime spot in the bureau's New York office, working for an organized crime unit investigating the city's Mafia families. Still, he burned for something more.

At last, in 2006, the CIA came through with the offer he had been waiting for. The intelligence agency saw in LaBonte a combination of skills that were most in demand five years into the global war against al-Qaeda: the tactical abilities of a Special Forces soldier, combined with the resourcefulness of a classic CIA case officer. LaBonte was among a handful of CIA recruits who would be trained for both jobs. He catapulted to the front of the waiting list for the agency's training school, the former Defense Department reservation in southern Virginia known as the "Farm." Months later he was on his way to Iraq and then to Afghanistan.

This job felt right, at last. His comrades and commanders were impressed by the enthusiasm of the young ex-Ranger who was always the first to volunteer for difficult assignments and the last to complain about the hardships the group endured. Though less experienced than some of the older combat veterans, he distinguished himself for his clearheadedness and sharp instincts during firefights. One officer who fought next to him in Afghanistan was struck by LaBonte's "total confidence in who and what he was.

"He was living his calling, without pretense or guile, brag or boast," the former comrade said. "Darren believed his predestined role was to serve as a professional warrior, a protector for those less able to protect themselves."

Such qualities were on display one summer night when LaBonte led a two-man surveillance mission in Kunar Province. The men were walking alongside a river when a sudden noise alerted them to an approaching Taliban patrol. The Americans froze and hugged the riverbank as the insurgents filed into view, then paused in a clearing a few yards from their hiding place. A dozen fighters arrived, then two dozen, and still more. At last the group swelled to more than one hundred Taliban fighters, all armed with assault rifles and rocket-propelled grenades and obviously staging for some kind of attack. They lingered for several minutes, so close that the two Americans could hear their conversations. If any one of them had wandered a few feet toward the river, the pair would almost certainly have been discovered.

The other man was new to the CIA base and had never been in such a scrape. LaBonte kept a hand on his shoulder and whispered words of encouragement.

"Don't worry, everything is going to be OK," he said.

Eventually the insurgents moved on, and the two men scurried back to their base—but only after relaying the Taliban group's coordinates to the nearest NATO dispatcher.

As the months passed, though, LaBonte slowly lost some of his early optimism about the tide of battle against al-Qaeda. By the time he arrived in Jordan, he was convinced that bin Laden and his followers were winning the ideological struggle, appealing to ever larger numbers of young Muslims who could serve as fodder in the next wave of suicidal strikes against the West. He brooded about the attacks that were surely coming and worried about how to safeguard those he cared about most.

That list was topped by his wife and baby daughter, now with him in a Middle Eastern country in which American officials had been targeted for assassination. It also included bin Zeid, who he feared, was being swept along by the collective enthusiasm for Balawi, a double agent whose achievements already bordered on the implausible.

"This guy is too good to be true," LaBonte flatly told an ex-military friend in late autumn.

Among most of the intelligence community, though, Balawi fever was real and about to get much worse.

11

DANGLE

Humam al-Balawi's breakthrough as a spy was one hundred megabytes of flash and sizzle, titillating and wholly unexpected. But his next big score would blow everyone away.

It arrived, again by e-mail to his handler, bin Zeid, this time in the form of a simple typed message. Balawi, the doctor, had a new patient. His name was Ayman al-Zawahiri. The Jordanian had made direct contact with the deputy commander of al-Qaeda, second only to Osama bin Laden himself.

As Balawi described the events, he had been as surprised as anyone. One day he was told that Zawahiri was experiencing problems, and then suddenly the bearded, bespectacled terrorist leader was standing in front of him, asking him for medical treatment. Zawahiri, himself a doctor, was suffering from a range of complications related to diabetes, and he needed advice and, he hoped, some medicine. It was not so easy for Zawahiri, a wanted man with a twenty-five-million-dollar bounty on his head, to write his own prescriptions.

Balawi happily consented, and within minutes he was alone with Zawahiri, checking the vital signs of the man who had helped dream up the terrorist attacks of September 11, 2001.

In his e-mail, Balawi supplied a summary of Zawahiri's physical condition as well as his medical history, providing details that perfectly matched records the CIA had obtained years earlier from intelligence officials in Egypt, Zawahiri's home country. Most important, Balawi revealed that he had scheduled a follow-up visit with his patient. He would be seeing Zawahiri again in a few weeks.

From Kabul to Amman to Langley, marble buildings seemed to shift on their foundations. The last time the CIA had caught a whiff of Zawahiri was in 2006, when the agency bombed a house in southwestern Pakistan on the basis of faulty intelligence that suggested he was eating dinner there; there had been no verified sighting of Zawahiri by a Westerner or government informant since 2002.

Now, everyone with a top secret clearance wanted to know about the "golden source" who had been in the terrorist's presence.

Even the White House would have to know.

Leon Panetta met with members of the Obama administration's national security team to apprise them of the stunning developments. The CIA director himself served as chief briefer, and among those seated around the table were the national security adviser, James L. Jones; Dennis C. Blair, the director of national intelligence; and Rahm Emanuel, Panetta's old friend and White House chief of staff. Afterward Panetta would repeat the briefing in a private audience with the president of the United States.

"There are indications that he [Balawi] might have access to Zawahiri," Panetta announced, his tone deliberately low-key. The next step, he said, was to meet with the informant and train him for an important new role.

"If we can meet with him and give him the right technology, we have a chance to go after Zawahiri," Panetta said.

The reaction was instantaneous and dramatic. How quickly can we make this happen? NSC officials wanted to know.

"Everyone was very enthusiastic," said one of the security officials present at the briefing, with considerable understatement, "that for the first time in a long time, we had a chance of going after Number Two."

If Balawi had offered up bin Laden himself, it could hardly have evoked more excitement. After so many years deep in hiding, al-Qaeda's reclusive founder was merely a figurehead. It was Zawahiri, together with his old friend Sheikh Saeed al-Masri, who now steered al-Qaeda's ship. The two Egyptians decided strategy for the group, raised money, and planned operations. If al-Qaeda were to unleash another September 11–style attack on the United States, it would almost certainly be Zawahiri's handiwork.

The physician, fifty-eight now and scarred, physically and mentally, from years in Egyptian prisons, was the al-Qaeda version of a mad scientist, a man who was forever scheming up sensational ways to kill large numbers of people, using chemicals or viruses or even nuclear weapons, if he could get them. He was also al-Qaeda's great escape artist, ever managing to elude death or capture by slipping away just as the trap was being sprung. Once, before September 11, 2001, he traveled to the United States without being noticed, raising money for terrorist causes under a fake name and departing, still undetected. After the plane attacks the CIA came close to killing him on three different occasions, but each time he walked away unharmed. The older counterterrorism hands at Langley who had battled with him over the years respected his capabilities and loathed everything he stood for.

Zawahiri had been on the CIA's watch list since the mid-1980s, long before anyone had heard of bin Laden, and over the years the agency witnessed his rise from Egyptian revolutionary to international terrorist. He was the intellectual force behind many of al-Qaeda's grandest ambitions, including its fledgling efforts to acquire nuclear and biological weapons. It was Zawahiri who decreed that al-Qaeda must take on the "far enemy"—the United States—before it could defeat its principal target, the "near enemy," the pro-Western Arab regimes that stood in the way of the group's dream of uniting all Muslims under a global Islamic caliphate.

"To kill Americans and their allies—civilian and military—is an individual duty for every Muslim who can do it in every country in which it is possible to do it," Zawahiri wrote in a 1998 manifesto.

As documented in the CIA's case files, Zawahiri's early life bore striking similarities to Balawi's. Both were born to educated, middle-class parents from religiously tolerant communities, and both were drawn simultaneously to medical studies and radical Islamist ideology. Zawahiri, who grew up in a well-to-do Cairo suburb, was the son of a well-known professor of pharmacology, and his maternal grandfather was a president of Cairo University. As an earnest, bookish teenager Zawahiri was introduced to the writings of Sayyid Qutb, an Egyptian author and intellectual who became one of the founders of modern Islamic extremism. Qutb's execution by Egyptian authorities inspired the young Zawahiri to organize a group of like-minded friends into a secret society he called al-Jihad, or the Jihad Group. He continued his studies and eventually earned a medical degree, but all the while he looked ahead to a day when his al-Jihad would seek to overthrow Egypt's secular government.

As a new doctor, Zawahiri spent time volunteering in refugee camps along the Afghanistan-Pakistan border. There, while patching up the wounds of anti-Soviet mujahideen fighters, he first crossed paths with a charismatic young Saudi, bin Laden, who had also come to Afghanistan to support the ragtag rebels in their struggle against the Communist superpower. Not long afterward, upon returning to Egypt, Zawahiri and his small cell joined with other antigovernment factions in a series of plots to assassinate Egyptian leaders, culminating in the fatal attack on Egyptian president Anwar Sadat on October 6, 1981, as he sat in a reviewing stand to watch a military parade. Zawahiri was imprisoned for allegedly participating in the conspiracy to silence one of the Arab world's most moderate and pro-Western leaders. He later claimed in a memoir that he was tortured by Egyptian security officials.

The experience left Zawahiri even more determined to undermine secular Arab governments and their financial underpinnings through spectacular acts of terrorism. His signature attack during his pre–al-Qaeda years was a savage 1997 assault on foreign tourists at Egypt's famous Luxor ruins, in which gunmen systematically slaughtered sixty-two people, including Japanese tourists, a five-year-old British child, and four Egyptian tour guides.

Ordinary Egyptians, previously accustomed to thinking of al-Jihad as engaged in a grassroots struggle against corrupt and autocratic rulers, were repelled by the wanton slaughter, and support for Zawahiri and his Jihad Group evaporated. Soon afterward Zawahiri told followers that operations inside Egypt were no longer possible, and the battle was shifting to Israel and its chief ally, the United States. In 1998 the Jihad Group officially merged with bin Laden's larger and better-financed al-Qaeda.

The newly expanded terrorist group immediately set out to make a splash with attacks on U.S. interests. First on the list were the U.S. embassies in the capitals of Kenya and Tanzania, which were bombed in 1998 in coordinated attacks that killed hundreds of people.

Three years later, working from al-Qaeda's new base in Afghanistan, Zawahiri helped oversee the planning of the September 11 attacks. His primary mission, however, was to plan follow-on waves of terrorist strikes that would continue for months and years to come. He personally took command of an ambitious biological weapons program, establishing a laboratory in Afghanistan and dispatching disciples to search for sympathetic scientists.

U.S. intelligence officials believe that Zawahiri's efforts to launch a large-scale anthrax attack might have succeeded had he not run out of time. Within weeks of the collapse of New York's World Trade Center towers, the U.S.-backed military campaign that drove al-Qaeda and its Taliban allies out of power in Afghanistan forced Zawahiri to abandon his bioweapons lab and flee the country. U.S. forces were to discover the lab, along with Zawahiri's detailed instructions to his aides to acquire a highly lethal strain of the bacterium that causes anthrax.

By 2002 Zawahiri, like bin Laden, was in hiding in Pakistan, with a twenty-five-million-dollar bounty on his head. But unlike bin Laden, he continued to personally direct numerous terrorist operations, including an alleged 2003 plot to attack New York

City's subway system using chemical weapons. Zawahiri himself called off the attack for reasons that remain unclear.

Because of his willingness to insert himself into terrorist operations, CIA officials clung to hopes that Zawahiri eventually would make a mistake, yet each time the agency's targeters managed to locate him, he slipped out of their grasp.

The last attempt was in January 2006, when CIA informants learned of a gathering of al-Qaeda leaders in Damadola, a town in the northern Pakistani province of Bajaur. Zawahiri was known to have visited the same province two years earlier, and agency officials were highly confident when they dispatched a Predator aircraft to orbit a mud compound a few miles outside the town. CIA missiles destroyed the building, killing eighteen people, including several al-Qaeda figures, but not Zawahiri. Pakistani intelligence officials said afterward that the al-Qaeda deputy changed his mind at the last minute and sent aides to the meeting instead.

Days later Zawahiri appeared in a new video to taunt the White House.

"Bush, do you know where I am?" he said. "I am among the Muslim masses."

The CIA never came close again after that until the morning in November 2009 when a little-known Jordanian physician surfaced with a story about an ailing Zawahiri entrusting himself to his care.

In the days that followed, a single imperative emerged: The CIA must meet Humam al-Balawi.

As CIA officials in Langley prepared a summary for the classified digest known as the President's Daily Brief, the files on Balawi were distressingly thin.

The Jordanians seemed to trust him, but no American had ever met him. He had bombarded Islamic Web sites with violently anti-Western screeds, yet he had flipped after only three days of relatively light interrogation by the Mukhabarat. Nothing in his lifestyle suggested a fondness for material wealth, yet he seemed only too happy to risk his life and sell out his ideological brethren in exchange for U.S. greenbacks.

Nothing about the case made sense. On the other hand, there was the matter of the al-Rahman video and Zawahiri's medical data. In the dozen years since al-Qaeda emerged as a global threat, no one had seen anything like it.

In meetings and in conference calls between Langley and Amman, a series of options for a meeting with Balawi were weighed and rejected. Under one proposal the Jordanian would be flown back to the Middle East for an extensive debriefing. It was an appealing prospect, since Balawi's Mukhabarat and CIA case officers were based in Amman. But it was finally rejected out of fear that Balawi's lengthy absence from Pakistan might raise suspicions among his Taliban sponsors.

An alternative plan called for a secret meeting in a Pakistani city—Islamabad or Karachi, perhaps—but it also was ruled out. The Americans had intentionally kept Pakistan's Inter-Services Intelligence agency in the dark since Balawi's arrival in that country, and no one wanted to risk blowing the Jordanian's cover at such a sensitive moment. Pakistan's major cities were chockablock with ISI agents, and a high-level CIA gathering would almost certainly draw attention.

A safer bet, it was decided, would be to meet Balawi in Afghanistan, presumably in a place near the border that would be easily accessible for Balawi but also discreet and utterly secure. The meeting spot would have to be reachable by car from Pakistan's tribal region, yet also firmly under the CIA's control, with no possibility of detection by Taliban spies.

The CIA commanded at least six bases along the Afghan frontier, but only one of them sat on an asphalt highway that connected directly with Miranshah, the town in North Waziristan, Pakistan, closest to Balawi's last known position. Thus, by accident of geography, the CIA's choice for its much-anticipated first meeting with the Jordanian agent was the agency base known as Khost.

Key details of the proposed meeting, including Balawi's willingness to submit to such a plan, were still far from clear. But from the day the informant invoked Ayman al-Zawahiri's name in an e-mail, the mission to find Balawi and drain him of information became a priority of almost unrivaled importance.

"The upper level of government was crying out for information and wanted answers to keep the country safe," said former U.S. ambassador to the United Nations Thomas Pickering, a career diplomat who co-led a classified, independent investigation of the events. "There were government servants who were intent on getting the job done, and they were prepared to go the last mile to do it."

"Yes, but . . ."

Humam al-Balawi was not making it easy. Jordanian intelligence captain Ali bin Zeid, unsure how Balawi would react, had broached the idea of a meeting somewhat tentatively at first. *Your reports have been most interesting,* bin Zeid wrote in a late-November missive. *Now we'd like to take things up a notch.*

Balawi seemed instantly agreeable to the idea of seeing bin Zeid again. But he put up so many conditions and qualifiers that bin Zeid was left wondering whether the meeting would ever come about.

Yes, but I don't want to meet with anyone except you, he wrote at one point.

Yes, but it's too dangerous to cross the border, he said in a separate note. And, finally: *Yes, we should meet. But I think you should come to me.*

Over several days of exchanged messages, Balawi became increasingly insistent. The ideal meeting place, he declared, was Miranshah, North Waziristan's sprawling market town just across the mountains from Afghanistan. Balawi knew the town and would find a secure place where both he and his Jordanian countryman would be safe. There were cafés and bazaars, shops and mosques, all of them crowded with people. The two Jordanians could meet discreetly without attracting attention, and then Balawi could be on his way again.

Bin Zeid gently pushed back. North Waziristan was too risky, he said. Khost, on the other hand, was a fortified military camp guarded by Special Forces commandos and attack helicopters. Both men would be safer there.

"I'm the one who's taking all the risks over here," Balawi protested. He was sure that Afghan spies at the American base would betray him, and then he'd be finished, killed in the most gruesome of ways. Balawi had seen what the Taliban did to suspected informants. He repeated his plea.

Come to Miranshah, he wrote.

Bin Zeid shared the e-mails with his CIA partner, Darren LaBonte, who was starting to feel queasy. LaBonte was getting hammered with requests for updates from his bosses in Amman and Langley, and his answers so far had not been popular. The two partners talked for hours about Balawi and his e-mails and what it all meant. This was shaping up as the biggest case either man had ever been associated with; yet more than anyone around them, they harbored doubts. The video evidence had been staggeringly impressive, but also perplexing. How was it that Balawi, this frightened mouse of a doctor who weeks earlier had begged to come home, had come up with something so spectacular? Was Balawi a con artist? Was he trying to scam the CIA for more money, as so many bogus informants had done in the past? Perhaps Balawi was everything he seemed, but as the two men hashed it over, they were less than convinced. It was too much, too soon.

Later LaBonte tried to summarize his concerns in an internal memo. The bottom line, he wrote, was that the CIA didn't yet know enough about the Jordanian agent to trust him entirely. He *seemed* real enough, but that wasn't a sound basis for divining the man's intentions.

"We need to go slow on this case," he wrote.

The top CIA officer in Amman was a veteran operative who had served in Pakistan and understood the fickle art of running covert agents better than most. The station chief, whose name is classified, accepted LaBonte's recounting of the key facts of the Balawi case, but he reached an entirely different conclusion: A meeting with Balawi was urgently needed precisely because the CIA knew so little about the informant and his motivations. Yes, there were risks, the station manager said. But if ever there was a moment for risk taking, it was this one.

Let's move forward, he said.

Ali bin Zeid spent the first days of December preparing for what he believed would be a short trip. Winters in eastern Afghanistan are notoriously cold, so bin Zeid called his older brother, Hassan, and asked to borrow his heavy jacket, the one with the thick insulation and the North Face logo. He did some last-minute shopping and buffed up the black Desert Eagle .44 Magnum he liked to take on his business trips.

Then, just days before his planned departure, bin Zeid was summoned unexpectedly to a meeting on the Mukhabarat's executive floor. He entered a conference room to find his immediate supervisor and several other senior officials waiting for him, all dark suits and ties, their faces as dour as buzzards'.

We're sending someone else to Afghanistan to meet with Balawi, one of the officers said. *The mission is simply too risky for someone from the royal family.*

Bin Zeid exploded. "But it's my case," he protested.

He spent much of the day appealing the decision, from one end of the Mukhabarat's headquarters building to the other. He argued and complained, and when neither worked, he threatened.

"I'm going to Afghanistan, even if I have to make my own arrangements to get there," bin Zeid said. Then, eyes narrowed to slits, he dropped the ultimate threat.

"I'm going to Afghanistan," he repeated, "even if I have to go with the Americans."

Bin Zeid had already laid the groundwork for this threat, and sure enough, a call was made from the CIA's Amman station to the Mukhabarat headquarters, officially requesting bin Zeid's presence at Khost. The Jordanian captain was the only one who knew Balawi, the Americans explained, and the informant might balk if he wasn't around.

"We need Ali," the CIA caller said.

The Mukhabarat relented.

Bin Zeid and LaBonte were scheduled to leave for Afghanistan on December 6, but the Jordanian was fully packed a day early. There were tearful good-byes from family members, including bin Zeid's sister-in-law, who had been plagued with feelings of dread since she first learned of the trip.

The men's wives had been unusually anxious as well. Racheal LaBonte was beginning to fret about the Italian vacation the couple had planned for the Christmas holidays, and she now worried that Darren LaBonte wouldn't make it back in time. More important, she had managed to piece together the outlines of the mission from snippets of conversation, enough to know that her husband had grave doubts about the informant he was flying to Afghanistan to meet.

"He could turn out to be a suicide bomber!" she finally blurted out.

Often Darren LaBonte would crack a joke to relieve the tension when his wife expressed such fears about his work. This time he did not.

"You're right, he could be," he said solemnly. Then, taking her hand, he tried to explain his conflicted feelings about the case. This one was worth the risk, he said, and what's more, if it succeeded, it might finally be enough for him. He could even walk away from the terrorist-catching business forever.

"If I don't go, and this case is everything that it's supposed to be, it would be a big mistake," he said. "If it's successful, then I can stop. I can finally say that I've done what I came here to do.

"On the other hand, if I don't go, and something happens . . ."

He paused. Racheal knew he was thinking of bin Zeid.

"Well, I could never forgive myself," he said finally.

The two couples gathered for last farewells at the LaBontes' apartment at 5:00 A.M., just before the two men departed for the airport, and sat for coffee on the balcony. The usual weepy scenes in the terminal attracted too much attention, and besides, this time the wives had planned something different. Both women had been unusually anxious about the trip to Afghanistan, but they decided together to go out of their way not to show it.

The women knew the men shared a fascination with ancient warrior culture, for the armies of Athens and Sparta. In ancient Greece the mothers of Spartan warriors exhorted their sons to bravery with the words that Fida Dawani and Racheal LaBonte now spoke to their departing husbands: "Return with your shields or on them."

But as the two officers gathered their bags, Fida could not restrain herself. She pulled Darren LaBonte aside, her dark eyes imploring.

"Take care of Ali," she said.

The Mukhabarat tried once more to block Ali bin Zeid from meeting with the informant Humam al-Balawi. It happened on December 5, as the Jordanian intelligence captain and his CIA partner, LaBonte, were making final preparations for their journey.

That evening one of the Jordanian spy agency's senior managers phoned an old CIA friend at the Amman station to talk privately about the Balawi case.

We have serious concerns, the Jordanian said before proceeding to lay out two of them.

The first was a matter of historical precedent, he said. The Mukhabarat had been dealing with jihadists of all stripes for many years, and it knew a few things about them, including which ones could be flipped. The low-level types—the thugs and opportunists who glommed on to terrorist movements for personal advantage—could be transformed and might even become useful informants. But radicals and ideologues never truly switched sides. A true believer might lie and deceive, but deep down he could never betray his cause. And Humam al-Balawi had all the markings of a true believer.

It was a compelling argument, coming from a Mukhabarat veteran who had interrogated scores of radical Islamists. The CIA officer listened attentively.

The second concern derived from the Jordanian's observations as the case had unfolded in recent weeks. Wasn't it curious, he asked, that Balawi kept insisting that the meeting take place in Miranshah, rather than inside a fortified base where his security would be assured?

He could be leading you into an ambush, the Jordanian officer warned.

As he summed up his thoughts, the official acknowledged that the Mukhabarat had found nothing damning against Balawi and had no specific reason to doubt that the operative had truly made inroads into al-Qaeda's senior ranks. There were just vague concerns, he explained, including a worry that bin Zeid might not be the right officer for this particular case. Perhaps over time bin Zeid had gotten too close to his recruit and had lost his ability to make dispassionate judgments.

The Jordanian had finished unburdening himself, so the CIA officer thanked him for his insights and bade him good night. Afterward, as he thought about the warning, he focused in particular on one of the phrases the man had used: *bin Zeid might not be the right officer.*

The Mukhabarat, for all its strengths, was known to be constantly roiled by rivalries and turf battles, as different factions sought to gain advantage. Even mild-mannered bin Zeid was reported to have numerous enemies among senior officers who feared that the king's cousin would use his royal heritage and CIA connections to secure a plum position.

The warning suddenly made sense. The Jordanians were worried all right: They were afraid that Ali bin Zeid would soon become their boss, the CIA officer reasoned. He filed the contact away mentally and mentioned it to no one outside of Amman.

The next morning, under a slate gray sky, bin Zeid and LaBonte boarded a plane at Amman's Queen Alia International Airport and departed for Afghanistan.

12

REHEARSAL

Just after sunset on Christmas Day, Jennifer Matthews plopped down in front of her computer and switched on the small Web camera clipped to the top of the screen. It had been a rough day, and though she didn't know it yet, things were about to get worse. At that hour a Northwest Airlines flight from Amsterdam was closing in on Detroit, carrying a young Nigerian passenger who had hidden eighty grams of military explosive in his clothes. The Nigerian's attempt to blast the plane from the sky would ring alarm bells at CIA stations around the world and keep counterterrorism officers busy through the night. Yet back home in snow-covered Fredericksburg, Virginia, it was still blissfully quiet, and Matthews's kids would be waiting to open their Christmas presents. She would join them via Skype.

She clicked "home" and waited for the connection. In a few seconds a small video panel appeared, and Matthews was looking at the twinkling lights of a Christmas tree in her own family room.

"Hi, Mommy," came the chorus of greetings from her three children.

Matthews's husband had set up the video connection so the kids could see their mother during their regular chats while she was overseas. The couple had planned in advance to celebrate Christmas morning this way, with Matthews's parents joining the gathering to spend the holiday with their daughter's likeness on the video screen. They would all try to make the day as normal as possible.

Matthews caught up with the family news, and then everyone unwrapped presents, first the kids, then their mother, who opened gifts that had been sent to her in Afghanistan weeks earlier. After that was done and the small talk had waned, Matthews's youngest child, a six-year-old boy, piped up with a question. "Mommy, can you show us your gun?"

Everyone laughed, but Matthews dutifully complied. She picked up the rifle she kept in her hooch and then unholstered her pistol as well. Her questioner beamed. Not many of his friends' moms had their own assault rifles.

The conversation halted when an aide rapped on the door to announce that dinner was ready in the mess hall. It was a special holiday meal, and Matthews as base chief would be expected to attend. After a few good-byes and blown kisses, Matthews was back at work in Afghanistan. She grabbed her heavy coat and flak jacket and headed to the dining room.

The day in Khost had been overcast and raw, adding to the gloomy pall that had settled over the base in the past two weeks. Until December life for Khost's new base chief had seemed manageable and predictable and even somewhat ordinary. She had adjusted to the long hours and settled into roles that had initially seemed foreign to her. She went for a run almost every day and was losing weight. She was beginning to appreciate how quickly a year could pass at a busy base like Khost.

Then Humam al-Balawi came along.

Matthews had become aware of the Jordanian informant in the early fall, but until recently neither she nor Khost had had anything to do with him. Balawi was Amman's recruit, and he was being managed by Langley and the CIA's Islamabad station. But now it had been decided that Balawi would come to Khost and Matthews would play host.

Normally such an opportunity would be thrilling for a new base chief looking to cement her reputation. But after weeks of waiting and endless quarreling about arrangements—with her staff, with Langley, and, indirectly, with the informant himself—her enthusiasm was gone.

Multiple outsiders, including CIA chiefs in Langley, Amman, and Kabul, wanted to be in on the Balawi operation. But no one person was clearly in control. Meanwhile Balawi might show up at Khost tomorrow, or the next day, or maybe not at all.

At least the first problem, of control, could be fixed. Matthews had never been shy about asserting herself. Yes, her decisions were being challenged, but if it happened on her base, Jennifer Matthews decided, she would be in charge.

The pressure had been exquisite. Perhaps two dozen people in the world knew about the pending visit by Humam al-Balawi, but one of them happened to reside at 1600 Pennsylvania Avenue in Washington. President Barack Obama, in his second briefing about Jordan's "golden source," had been told of CIA plans to meet with the informant in Afghanistan. He knew that the man would be scrutinized and vetted by an agency team and then armed for his mission against one of America's most determined adversaries, al-Qaeda's No. 2 leader, Ayman al-Zawahiri. The president of the United States would be awaiting news of the extraordinary events at Khost.

As the person in charge of the details of Balawi's visit, Matthews sat down at her computer one wintry afternoon to create the most important ops plan of her life. She had to devise a way to transport Balawi to Afghanistan, win his cooperation, provide training, and send him home again without being missed or noticed. In two decades of CIA work, nothing she had written had come close to this. Many weeks later agency veterans studied Matthews's plan and marveled at its elegant simplicity.

Timing would be critical. As Matthews figured it, the CIA had about nine hours, just barely longer than a Washington workday, to accomplish all of it. The first hurdle was the extraction from Pakistan. Balawi could find his way to the border town of Ghulam Khan, but he would need help crossing the border and the Taliban-infested mountains beyond. Helicopters were out of the question, and sending SAD officers or other Americans would be too risky, she decided. They would draw attention to the informant, and if they were stopped, they would likely be kidnapped or killed. A trusted Afghan would be sent to the border instead.

Balawi would need a cover story—a plausible reason to be away from his Taliban hosts for several hours—and the CIA came up with a clever one. As Zawahiri's new doctor he needed to go to Miranshah to find medicine for his famous patient. The agency would provide Balawi with a package to take home with him: pills and salves to relieve the old diabetic's poor circulation and skin problems.

The next hurdle was getting Balawi in and out of the base without compromising his identity. The chief worry, Matthews knew, was the front gate. There could well be Taliban spies among the Afghan soldiers who manned the outer perimeter, and there almost certainly were some among the local civilians who congregated near the gate to apply for work or seek medical care. At Khost, the CIA had always whisked key informants through the main gate without an ID check so their faces would not be seen. An agent as valuable as Balawi would merit even greater precautions.

Finally, there was the meeting itself. Matthews envisioned an all-hands event. Langley needed to know whether Balawi was real or just a talented con artist, so Matthews would call in her experienced case officers to ask questions and study the agent's body language. Balawi presumably would know details about a great many terrorist operatives other than Zawahiri, so Matthews needed her best al-Qaeda and Taliban experts with her to take advantage of what might well be the agency's only chance to interview an al-Qaeda double agent. Most important, if the Jordanian were indeed ready to lead the CIA to Zawahiri, he would need special training and perhaps tools. Technicians would show him how to send secret signals to communicate where and when a strike should take place. The agency had numerous gadgets in its tool kit, including a cell phone that could take and send digital photographs that appear ordinary in every way, except that they are encoded with hidden geographic coordinates. The image, once deciphered, would reveal exactly where on earth it was taken.

There was another critical ingredient, and Matthews gave it considerable thought. The CIA was asking Balawi, more than ever, to risk his very life. The agency would have to do everything it could to keep him happy and motivated. Matthews had listened carefully to the Jordanian intelligence officer, Ali bin Zeid, when he described the informant's moodiness and fragile ego. Balawi came from a culture that demanded social courtesies in business dealings, and after ten months of dangerous work in Pakistan, he felt entitled to some respect, bin Zeid explained. Matthews would make certain that he got it. There would be Arab-style formality, including an extensive reception with introductions, handshakes, and exchanged pleasantries. Balawi would be offered medical care and food. And as a personal gesture intended to cement the friendship, he would be surprised with a birthday cake. It was a sheet cake with chocolate frosting, made by the base's own chefs.

"He has to be made to feel welcomed," she repeatedly told her subordinates.

Matthews reviewed what she had written. Including the security detail and Balawi himself, there would be sixteen people at the meeting, and possibly more. It was an unusual plan, but then, Balawi was a highly unusual agent. What he offered was far beyond the kind of typical Taliban gossip that gets whispered in a café or alley. Balawi promised payback for September 11 and a hundred other infamous crimes. Very possibly, he could point the way to the destruction of al-Qaeda itself.

When she finished, Matthews reviewed the essence of her plan with Langley and solicited opinions. Some of the details invited haggling, and the CIA announced it would send two officers from Kabul, the deputy station chief and Elizabeth Hanson, to help manage the meeting. But top CIA managers were in full agreement on the key points. Balawi must be protected at all cost, shielded from harm and from prying eyes. *He should be treated with the respect accorded a trusted asset*, Matthews was told.

Was he trustworthy? In calmer times, before the agency was simultaneously managing intelligence collection for two wars, the CIA would assign a specialist to monitor each double agent and foreign spy for evidence of possible duplicity. Screening for spies was the domain of the agency's counterintelligence division, masters of the science of rooting out double agents and other intelligence threats. But there was precious little time for screening once the Iraq War began and the sheer number of informants overwhelmed any effort to track them all. Unreliable or difficult operatives were simply dismissed and replaced. There would be no formal counterintelligence review for Balawi, an operative who had been recruited by a friendly intelligence service and had already been deployed as a spy before American officers had had a chance to size him up.

Many weeks later, counterintelligence officers who knew about the case told CIA investigators they had found Balawi's behavior suspicious. Like the Mukhabarat officer in Amman, they worried that events in Pakistan were coming together too quickly, too easily.

None of these concerns, however, reached Matthews, who in late December won approval for her careful, well-written plan that revolved around a single objective: keeping Humam al-Balawi safe.

Darren LaBonte surveyed the throng that gathered outside the CIA's debriefing center and shook his head. It was rehearsal day, a practice run for the meeting with the still-absent Jordanian informant, and everything seemed wrong.

"This is a gaggle," he scoffed, using his pet term for useless bureaucratic gatherings. "It's a clown show."

The ex-Ranger, now two weeks into his Khost stay, was standing with Ali bin Zeid and thirteen other officers on a gravel lot, reviewing how they would welcome Humam al-Balawi, should the elusive Jordanian decide to show up. A ragged receiving line of men and women in jeans and military surplus clothing stretched along the front of the building where the meeting was to take place, while Jennifer Matthews went over their parts. The building, a gray, concrete structure with a metal awning supported by steel pillars, was at the far end of the CIA's minifortress inside the base, a few yards from a guard tower that looked out over Khost City. After two tedious weeks in the CIA compound, LaBonte knew the place well.

He regarded the woman in charge of the drill. He liked Matthews, but as he explained to a close friend in a late-night Skype call during Christmas week, her my-way-or-the-highway management style quickly grated on him.

"They butted heads constantly over Balawi," said the friend, describing LaBonte's portrayal of events. "He was the case officer so it was his case. But he didn't like how it was being handled."

LaBonte's chief complaint: too many people. Fourteen intelligence operatives and a driver were about a dozen too many, by his way of thinking. Both LaBonte and bin Zeid had worked with numerous undercover agents in Afghanistan and the Middle East, and in their world, informant meetings were almost always small. One officer would drive to the pickup point while his partner would sit in the backseat to pat down the agent for wires or weapons. At Khost the officers from Amman were barred from leaving the base—the risk of kidnapping was judged to be too great—but still, LaBonte believed in small meetings for security's sake. Even the most trusted informant was usually kept in the dark about the agency's operations and was never allowed to know the names or faces of CIA operatives other than his handlers. That was for everyone's protection: The less the informant knew, the less he could give up if he was caught by the other side and threatened with torture or execution.

Logistics aside, LaBonte had a bad feeling about where things were heading, a sense of foreboding that he mentioned both to bin Zeid and to the friend he spoke to on Skype. Whether it was just anxiousness spilling over from two weeks of uncertainty and boredom or something more—his famous "spidey sense," perhaps—was unclear.

"Both he and Ali [bin Zeid] were feeling skeptical," the friend said. "They were not aloof to the fact that this guy could be bogus, and maybe just looking for money. There were no red flags, and nothing that suggested the guy had flipped. But who sits next to Zawahiri and then takes part in an operation to kill him?"

Others, including several of the heavily armed men in charge of keeping the CIA officers safe, had similar misgivings. During the practice run, security chief Scott Roberson and Matthews clashed sharply in an incident later described to CIA investigators.

Roberson, though also new to the base, had spent much of the decade protecting top U.S. government officials in Baghdad, honing his instincts during the worst years, when insurgents were staging hundreds of attacks a day. On the day of the rehearsal, several officers witnessed Roberson and Matthews stepping away from the group for a heated argument conducted in hushed tones. Afterward, witnesses said, Roberson walked to where security guard Dane Paresi was standing and shrugged. Whatever the nature of the dispute, it seemed to those watching to be settled.

Around this time, Paresi, the former Green Beret, complained to colleagues at Blackwater about the security arrangements. And ex-SEAL Jeremy Wise, just two weeks into his assignment at Khost, e-mailed a SEAL friend on December 21 hinting that he had had differences with the agency's civilian managers in the lead-up to an important operation. "Sometimes it's your job to say something— 'Sir, I don't think you should do that. It's not a good idea,' " he wrote.

After days of such conflict, LaBonte finally decided to appeal to his CIA supervisors in Jordan. He sat down to type out an e-mail to the Amman station chief, copying several of the station's other managers, warning that the Balawi case was in danger of veering off the rails.

There are three problems, he wrote, according to an officer who read the note. Then he listed them.

There are too many people involved.
We're moving too quickly.
We're giving up too much control by letting Balawi dictate events.
The e-mail created a stir in Amman. The station chief read the

contents carefully, but decided not to intervene. The case was too important and must proceed, he told colleagues.

Whether CIA managers in Langley saw the note before Balawi's arrival is unclear. It was never forwarded to Matthews, who in any case knew LaBonte's concerns by heart.

Later, as final arrangements for Balawi's visit were being made, Khost's security chief offered a word of advice to a colleague who was planning to go to the meeting to see the informant who had generated such excitement.

Roberson cautioned the officer, *Stay far away from this*.

The passing of Christmas only deepened the misery bin Zeid and LaBonte were feeling. When they arrived at Khost, the two Amman officers had planned on a short visit and a quick meeting, but now they were in their third week on the base with little to do and no Balawi in sight.

LaBonte's efforts to alter the arrangements for the meeting had failed. Matthews was in charge at Khost, and both Kabul and Langley were solidly behind her. There had been small concessions on security. Matthews agreed that Balawi would be searched immediately when he entered the CIA's inner sanctum inside the base, while the other officers stood a respectful fifty feet away. But there was to be no compromise on the meeting's location and no retreat from the view that a debriefing of such importance demanded a large and diverse team. LaBonte was beginning to wonder if it mattered: Balawi was still insisting on a meeting in Pakistan that everyone knew would never happen. There was now a real chance that the meeting would be scrubbed, and the entire mission deemed a failure.

Adding to the gloom, both men were feeling homesick. LaBonte was already a week late to join his family at the Tuscan vacation home he had personally picked out over the Internet. Instead he was sleeping on a cot in a smelly guesthouse with strange men. Bin Zeid, meanwhile, was going stir-crazy from weeks of close confinement. Fearing that a Jordanian royal would make an all-too-tempting target for any Afghan soldiers who might be secret Taliban sympathizers, the CIA had restricted him to a small area of the base.

Bin Zeid had given the CIA officers a rare moment of levity when he nearly burned down one of the compound's bathhouses. A confirmed germophobe, he had tried to sterilize a toilet by dousing the seat with a chemical cleaner. When he lit a match, the small fireball that erupted nearly singed his eyebrows.

Others on the base sought to extract whatever small bits of pleasure they could salvage from the occasion of Christmas. There were toasts in the CIA's lounge, one of the rare places to buy a beer in the otherwise bone-dry constellation of U.S.-run installations in Afghanistan. Care packages of Christmas cookies and cakes were opened and shared. Wise, the former Navy SEAL and Blackwater guard, showed off an illustrated Christmas list his young son Ethan had colored and sent by e-mail.

Three days later the last of the Christmas treats had been eaten, and all expectations for a meeting with Balawi had dried up. LaBonte used bin Zeid's cell phone to share the news with his wife: The business in Afghanistan was over, and he would be on his way to Italy as soon as he could book the flight.

The announcement quickly proved premature. Within hours of the call, bin Zeid finally received the e-mail with the news everyone had been waiting for. Humam al-Balawi had agreed to come to Khost after all. He would be at the base the next day.

LaBonte decided against calling his family again. He didn't want to disappoint them, and besides, Balawi's change of heart meant only a slight delay in his departure. He could still be in Italy by New Year's Eve.

Balawi's imminent arrival also meant that Elizabeth Hanson would soon be on her way back to Kabul. She called her mother in Rockford, Illinois, to tell her so.

Hanson always tried to sound upbeat in conversations with her mom to keep her from worrying. She had told her mother that an important meeting was coming up but said little else about it.

But on this evening, with Balawi at last on his way, Hanson was not her usual breezy self. She ended the conversation with words her mother had not heard her utter since childhood. "Pray for me," Hanson said. "Just say a prayer that it goes well."

13

THE TRIPLE AGENT

Datta Khel, North Waziristan—December 2009

The Pashtun tribesman known as al-Qaeda's tailor lived in a house near the village of Datta Khel in North Waziristan, where he made a living making suicide vests. One morning in mid-December he sat at his antique sewing machine to fill yet another order, this one very different from the vests he usually made.

The man was celebrated for his ingeniously simple designs that were both reliable and cheap, two key selling points for a terrorist organization that waged suicide bombings on an industrial scale. He started with a sturdy cotton vest, often surplus military gear from the local bazaar, and attached thick straps so it could be secured snugly against the torso. He added fabric pouches and stuffed them with packets of white acetone peroxide powder, an explosive popular in Pakistan's tribal region because it can be cooked up at home using common ingredients. Next came the shrapnel layer, which consisted of hundreds of nails or other bits of metal glued to sheets of thick, adhesive-backed paper or cloth. Finally, he inserted blasting caps in the powder and attached them to wires that ran to a small nine-volt battery and a cheap detonator switch. The latter item he sewed into a separate pouch that closed with a zipper. That, he explained, was to prevent excitable young martyrs-to-be from blowing themselves up too quickly. An extra second or two of fumbling with the zipper would remind the bomber to move in closer to his target to ensure the maximum possible carnage.

The vest's tight constraints and the positioning of the explosive pouches would channel the energy of the blast outward, toward whoever stood directly in front of him. Some of that energy wave would inevitably roll upward, ripping the bomber's body apart at its weakest point, between the neck bones and lower jaw. It accounts for the curious phenomenon in which suicide bombers' heads are severed clean at the moment of detonation and are later found in a state of perfect preservation several yards away from the torso's shredded remains. When waves of suicide bombers attacked Israeli commuter buses and cafés during the Palestinian uprising in the early 2000s, police discovered that they could often distinguish the dead bomber from his victims by finding the corpse that was minus its head.

On this day a group of young Pakistani recruits, some of them tapped as future suicide bombers, gathered to admire the vest maker as he worked. One of them took photos with his cell phone as the man reached into his explosives chest and pulled out a surprise: not the usual bags of powder, but doughy sticks of a far more powerful military explosive called C4. He kneaded the sticks to flatten them and began to pack them into a row of thirteen fabric pouches he had sewn into the outside of the vest. Next he dipped a paintbrush into a bucket of industrial adhesive and slathered the white goo over a large square of sturdy cotton. The man then patiently studded the sheet with metal bits, piece by piece and row by row, alternating marble-size steel ball bearings with nails and scrap and, finally, some shiny twisted pieces that would have been recognizable to any American who happened to be in the room: children's jacks.

Among the spectators, there had been lively discussions about the man who would likely wear the special vest. Most speculation centered on the young foreigner whom the recruits called Abu Leila, using the Arab practice of referring to adult men by the name of their oldest child and the word *Abu*, or "father of." But Leila's father wasn't nearly so certain. When he left for Pakistan, Humam al-Balawi imagined himself a mujahideen, a holy warrior, fighting and maybe even dying in a righteous struggle against the enemies of God. What he hadn't pictured for himself was a suicide vest. The one in the tailor's shop in Datta Khel was still coming together, row after metal-studded row, but there was still time. In the coming days Balawi tried his best to make sure that the vest ended up belonging to someone else. Anyone but him.

Nothing had turned out as Balawi expected.

The death of Baitullah Mehsud had seemed like the end of the line and maybe the end of his life. The diminutive Mehsud had been Balawi's host and principal defender when other Taliban leaders and even his own aides eyed the physician warily. Now that he was gone, the suspicions returned. Perhaps it had been the Jordanian who had directed the missiles against Taliban commanders, including Baitullah Mehsud himself.

Fortunately for Balawi, there were plenty of other possible suspects. Fifteen months of relentless Predator strikes had given rise to outlandish theories about how the CIA's missiles found their targets with such precision. Much of the speculation centered on an "invisible ink" sprayed on automobiles with syringes or on mysterious microchips, called *ghamay* or "ring stones" by some Pakistanis, that served as homing beacons for missiles and could supposedly be hidden inside cigarettes or even disguised as ordinary stones. Many a tribesman had been executed by the Taliban on suspicion of planting the devices around the homes of prominent fighters.

But the search for spies was interrupted when Baitullah Mehsud's followers began skirmishing over who would replace the dead Taliban leader. One of the disputes turned into a gun battle that very nearly killed Hakimullah Mehsud, Baitullah's charismatic younger cousin and the presumed front-runner in the leadership contest. The wounded Hakimullah needed a doctor, and Balawi's skills likely saved the young man's life and perhaps his own.

Barely thirty, Hakimullah was tall and handsome, a shaggy Che Guevara to Baitullah's diminutive Karl Marx, but the men shared the same impetuousness, and both took a liking to the Jordanian physician. Hakimullah had been affected deeply by his cousin's death, and the moral obligation of *badal*, the Pashtun tribal tradition of blood vengeance, fell on his shoulders as the new chief. Balawi possessed useful abilities, apparently including the means to plant messages inside the CIA. Could he help avenge Baitullah's death?

For the moment, Hakimullah decided, Balawi could use military training. The Mehsud clan ran training camps for jihadist recruits, and soon the doctor was on his way to a dusty camp in a North Waziristan village called Issori, with a few dozen other young men who aspired to fight for the Taliban.

Now Balawi's days started at 5:30 A.M. and continued through the midday with calisthenics, target practice, and obstacle courses. In the afternoons the trainees studied bomb making, including the mechanics of suicide vests and roadside bombs. The group broke for meals and for mandatory daily prayers at the mosque and gathered in the evenings for discussions of theology and tactics. The local Pashtun youths in their teens and twenties who made up the bulk of the class eagerly welcomed the older Arab doctor who was said to be the famous essayist Abu Dujana al-Khorasani. But the camp's physically taxing regimen showed up Balawi's shortcomings in embarrassing ways. When the course ended, he still struggled with the basics of firing the AK-47 assault rifle, consistently allowing the barrel to jerk upward with the recoil so his shots flew well high of the target.

The worst moment occurred during a practice session for one of the Taliban's favorite tactics, a vehicle ambush involving a pair of motorcycle assassins. Balawi had never driven a motorcycle, yet he found himself roaring along a dirt road, trying to simultaneously cling to the handlebars and to a weapon. Balawi lost control of his bike in the soft dirt and slammed into the second motorcycle, knocking both vehicles to the ground. Balawi felt a painful pop in his lower right leg and then the scrape of gravel against his face and arm as he skidded across the road. He lay still for a moment, mentally assessing the damage. The fibula bone in his left leg was broken. The injury to his reputation, no doubt, was even worse. What good was a jihadist who had no aptitude for fighting?

Unbeknownst to Balawi, he had been watched and studied for months by men who saw potential in him. Finally, in the weeks after Baitullah Mehsud's death, al-Qaeda made its move.

Balawi was invited to meet with a midlevel commander named Abdullah Said al-Libi, an operations chief for al-Qaeda in Pakistan. Soon afterward, the Libyan native made room for the physician in his compound, and Balawi moved in for a short stay. The Jordanian gradually was introduced to others within the small circle of al-Qaeda leaders in North Waziristan. Balawi drank tea with Atiyah Abd al-Rahman, the group's religious adviser and diplomat. Finally he was introduced to the man who, for all practical purposes, was the chief tactical commander for all of al-Qaeda. In the leadership charts back in Langley, the man known as Sheikh Saeed al-Masri was ranked as the terrorist group's No. 3. In reality, al-Masri called the shots while al-Qaeda's top two communicated only rarely, through trusted messengers.

Al-Masri squinted at Balawi through a pair of narrow, oddly feminine glasses. The cagey old warrior was fifty-three but looked ancient, his long face weathered and deeply creased and his unkempt beard flecked with gray. On his forehead, just below his white turban, was a thumb-shaped bruise, a legacy of years of pressing his head against the floor during daily prayers.

The sheikh was not one for small talk. As a young radical growing up in Cairo, the man born as Mustafa Ahmed Abu al-Yazid had been imprisoned and tortured, along with Ayman al-Zawahiri, for conspiring to kill Egyptian president Anwar Sadat. He had joined Zawahiri's Egyptian terrorist cell, and been present at the merger with al-Qaeda. He had survived numerous attempts on his life, including a close call in 2006, when CIA missiles struck a house in northern Pakistan where Zawahiri was believed to be a guest.

Now nearing the end of his third decade as a wanted terrorist, he was scrupulously attentive to his own safety and utterly indifferent to that of others. The CIA's classified profile, drawn from informants and intercepted communications, was a portrait of an insecure cynic who was hypercontrolling, manipulative, cunning, and deeply disliked by his subordinates. He surrounded himself with machine gun–toting guards, while goading his followers to self-sacrifice with his trademark warning: "If you do not march forth, Allah will punish you with a painful torment."

As al-Masri contemplated Balawi, he pondered the opportunity before him. Al-Qaeda's leadership had lost more than a dozen senior managers and hundreds of fighters in less than a year. Here, perhaps, was a way to strike back. The cost to the terrorist group, if any, would be minimal: one obscure Jordanian doctor who would not be missed.

As they talked, a tentative plan began to take flesh, focusing on the person of Ali bin Zeid, Balawi's Jordanian handler. As a symbolic target bin Zeid was close to perfect. He was an officer with Jordan's Mukhabarat intelligence service, an organization that had inflicted more wounds on al-Qaeda than any single organization other than the CIA itself. He was working closely with the American spy agency, and he was blood kin to Jordan's modern monarch, King Abdullah II, an Arab who had made peace with Israel and thus, in al-Qaeda's eyes, was one of the Muslim world's leading apostates. If they could manage to kill him, the jihadists could strike an unforgettable blow against a mortal enemy. Even better, if they could capture bin Zeid, they could humiliate him and his government before the entire world. He could be tried before an al-Qaeda judge, then convicted, sentenced, and executed in a spectacle broadcast over the Web for all to see.

Al-Masri had the bait for such a trap: Humam al-Balawi. All that remained was for the doctor to somehow convince bin Zeid to come to Pakistan. Here al-Qaeda could help. Al-Masri and the other jihadist veterans were students of the Western intelligence agencies and paid close attention to the CIA's pronouncements in the Western news media. Some in the group had been interrogated in U.S. detention camps, including the prison at Guantánamo Bay.

They knew the kinds of details that the Americans would find most enticing.

Thus began the al-Qaeda–led campaign to transform Balawi into the indispensable agent. It would happen in stages. The informant would start with a grabber, something that would instantly command the CIA's attention. It would have to be solid and credible, yet not so outrageous as to raise suspicions. It would have to be something the technology-obsessed Americans would immediately appreciate.

The video was al-Masri's fiendishly clever idea. Al-Qaeda's propaganda arm already had a crude production studio with cameras and mixing software. Now it would supply the actors, al-Rahman and a handful of terrorist leaders and Balawi, all appearing as themselves.

The shooting took place in late August. Al-Rahman and Balawi took their places and pretended to engage in conversation as the camera rolled. The scene was blocked so that the video footage would have the appearance of an amateur's casual recording of an ordinary gathering. Afterward the production team extracted a short digital snippet. All that remained was for the Jordanian to attach the file to an e-mail and wait.

The first stage was to be followed by a series of small enticements, spread out over weeks to keep the Western analysts interested and eager. Balawi would appear to help the CIA in its quest to find targets, offering advice here and authentic detail there, appearing to move ever closer to, but never quite achieving, a big score. Al-Qaeda would wait for the aftershocks from the al-Rahman video to die down before unveiling the ultimate dangle. Al-Masri knew how hungry the Americans were for information about bin Laden and Zawahiri. The No. 2 leader, despite his secretiveness, could plausibly want to meet with Balawi because of his health problems. Al-Qaeda would supply the details of an imagined medical visit that would ring true to the CIA's analysts, down to the last scar and tooth filling.

Each piece of bait was eagerly snapped up. Whether the Jordanian and American intelligence agencies were entirely convinced was impossible to tell from Pakistan, but Balawi now commanded their rapt attention. Bin Zeid praised his most successful recruit in a November e-mail that Balawi shared with his hosts. "You have lifted our heads in front of the Americans!" bin Zeid had gushed.

Balawi was thrilled to be part of it. The storied American spy agency had ensnared so many jihadists with its technology, money, and clever tricks. Now it appeared to have fallen victim to al-Qaeda's clever ruse, one surely as clever as any dreamed up in the West.

"All praise is due to God, the bait fell in the right spot," Balawi said, "and they went head over heels with excitement."

Humam al-Balawi's handlers were surely interested, but they were not foolhardy. The Jordanian physician was dealt one disappointment after another as his intended target refused to leap into al-Qaeda's trap.

The initial scheme centered on a meeting in Peshawar, the ancient Pashtun capital and now a metropolis of one and a half million people in northwestern Pakistan. Balawi would insist on meeting bin Zeid alone, and at the right moment al-Qaeda operatives would burst in with guns and the Mukhabarat officer would be kidnapped—or "arrested," as Balawi would say. The CIA would almost certainly be watching, and its agents would try to interfere, so there was a Plan B. If the kidnappers were trapped or cornered in their escape, they would execute their hostage as their final act.

Bin Zeid was initially receptive to a Peshawar meeting, since CIA officials knew the city well and had many operatives there. It was the CIA's Islamabad office that nixed the plan. There were too many risks, including the high likelihood that Pakistan's spy agency would learn of the meeting and possibly compromise Balawi's identity.

After Peshawar, the North Waziristan hub city of Miranshah was the militants' obvious next choice. Al-Qaeda's close allies, the Haqqani network, practically owned the town, and the Mehsud-led

Taliban alliance now operated out of villages in the outskirts. Bin Zeid could disappear inside the town's maze of mud walls, alleys, and bazaars before the CIA knew what had happened.

When bin Zeid said no to Miranshah, Balawi kept asking. He offered variations on the plan, and he tried to lay on the guilt. "I'm the one taking all the risks," he repeated.

Balawi's insistence was starting to grate, but veteran CIA officers chalked it up to the agent's greenness. The informant clearly was afraid, and he hadn't yet grasped the limits of the CIA's reach. If given any choice at all, the Americans would never consent to having such an important meeting in a place like Miranshah, a town where the agency's absolute control over conditions was far from guaranteed.

Only one location made sense for the meeting, bin Zeid wrote. It was the American base at Khost, just across the border and over the mountains from Miranshah. Balawi could travel there quickly and return to Pakistan before anyone missed him. Khost offered complete security and protection from accidental discovery by Taliban spies.

For his part, Balawi wasn't interested in the CIA base. As he well knew, going to Khost would be akin to breaking into a prison. There would no chance for an ambush or kidnapping, and no al-Qaeda fighters waiting for the command to attack. Even if he could somehow smuggle a gun onto the base, he would almost certainly be disarmed or killed before he could squeeze off a single round.

Not possible, he wrote back.

Balawi's invitation to visit a known CIA base did present one intriguing option, one that conceivably could allow him to strike a blow against Jordanian intelligence and possibly the Americans as well. Balawi knew it, and his al-Qaeda hosts were almost certainly thinking about it as well. Unlike the other plans they had discussed, this would be a solo mission and a guaranteed one-way trip. It would also be the longest of long shots. For Balawi to have any chance of succeeding as a suicide bomber, he would have to somehow make it past layer after layer of security, starting with multiple rings of Afghan and American guards, followed by pat-downs, bomb-sniffing dogs, and metal detectors. The best he could realistically hope for would be to take out a few of the low-paid Pashtun wretches who stood sentry outside the base to feed their families.

Balawi's feelings about a possible suicide mission can be deduced from the urgency of his efforts to avoid Khost. Through early December, and continuing for weeks after bin Zeid arrived at the American base, he pelted the Mukhabarat officer with requests to come to him. When it was at last clear that Miranshah was out of the question, he proposed still another option, a meeting outdoors at Ghulam Khan, the checkpoint on the Afghanistan-Pakistan border on the highway that runs from Miranshah to Khost.

The haggling was still under way on December 17, when the CIA unleashed one of its most powerful missile barrages in months in Datta Khel district, not far from the village where the special suicide vest was being made. At least ten missiles hit a compound where several al-Qaeda and Taliban operatives had gathered, killing sixteen of them. It was a costly strike. Among the dead was Abdullah Said al-Libi, the al-Qaeda operations chief with whom Balawi had briefly lived.

The pressure for some kind of response was now becoming exquisite. The old warriors cursed the Americans, cast nervous glances at the drones overhead, and eyed the Jordanian doctor expectantly. An opportunity beckoned—the flimsiest of threads, perhaps, but at least it was something. When, exactly, would Balawi's words taste his blood?

His options dwindling as December neared its end, Balawi's mind raged with the desperation of a condemned man. One evening he sat down to try to write, as though he could somehow exorcise his doubts by putting them on paper. As he started, he was struck by the irony of what he was attempting to do.

"I have often wished to know what is going on in the head of a martyr before the martyrdom-seeking operation," he wrote. "It is now my turn today to fulfill the wishes of others."

He began to list his private fears, pausing to admit deep misgivings about the value of suicide attacks. The problem, he acknowledged, is that one could "only do it once in your life," and there was a real chance that he would fail and squander his life for nothing. Why not instead fight on the front lines? he asked himself. Or why not use his brain to come up with something better, a "bigger operation that hurts the enemies of God"?

Balawi tried to convince himself that "intent" was the only thing that mattered: God would honor his sacrifice, even if he were shot and killed before he could press the detonator switch. The harder question was whether he could go through with it. How would he feel in those final seconds, with only a slight twitch separating him from permanent annihilation?

"Do you not fear to be cowardly at the last moment," he asked himself, "and be unable to press the button?"

On December 28, Humam al-Balawi returned to the public call office to compose a brief note to his countryman Ali bin Zeid. *You win*, he wrote.

I'll meet your driver in Miranshah this afternoon as requested, Balawi continued. *See you tomorrow in Khost.*

Afterward Balawi and two al-Qaeda associates drove to a field to record some video footage of the Jordanian firing a few rounds from an AK-47, the gun jerking upward as bullets kicked up dust spouts in the distance. He put his crutch aside for the photos, so he wouldn't appear injured, but as he walked, he limped badly from his leg injury.

Later that morning Balawi went to his room and tried on the suicide vest. He tightened the straps, and the weight of thirty pounds of explosive and metal cut into his thin shoulders. He put on his kameez shirt and gray patou, the shawl-like blanket that doubles as a cloak and mobile prayer mat, and walked back outside where his friend with the video camera was waiting beside a white hatchback. Balawi looked tired, he had aged visibly in nine months, and his face below his right eye still bore scars from the motorcycle crash.

Balawi sat in the driver's seat as the camera rolled. He had decided that his martyr's message should be in English, to ensure the widest audience if the video made its way to the Internet, and he chose lines intended to project a kind of cinematic, bad-guy toughness, as though he were a Hollywood mobster delivering an ultimatum.

"We will get you, CIA team. *Insha' Allah*—God willing—we will bring you down," he said. "Don't think that just by pressing a button and killing mujahideen, you are safe. *Insha' Allah*, we'll come to you in an unexpected way."

Balawi raised his left hand to reveal what appeared to be a wristwatch beneath his kameez sleeve. "Look, this is for you: It's not a watch, it's a detonator," he said. But the tough-guy routine was falling short. Balawi seemed agitated and bitter, and he turned his head from the camera whenever he finished a thought. His eyes were red as he spit out his last words.

"This is my goal: to kill you, and to kill your Jordanian partner, and *Insha' Allah*, I will go to *al-Firdaws*—paradise," he said. "And you will be sent to hell."

With the final phrase his voice cracked, as though he were straining to fight back tears. Balawi looked away, and the image went dark.

14

NO GOD BUT GOD

Khost, Afghanistan—December 30, 2009

Dane Paresi rose early on December 30 and was instantly mindful of two things. One was the cold—twenty-three degrees at daybreak outside the Blackwater employees' quarters, and not so balmy inside either. Another was food. Paresi's Special Forces call sign was Jackal, a tribute to his legendary appetite and reputation for mooching from his comrades' plates. He had developed a special fondness for the Khost mess hall, which he judged to be superior to most of the dozens of others he had sampled in Afghanistan. By this hour, just after 6:00 A.M., the pancakes would be flying off the griddle, and the aroma of greasy bacon and black coffee would be strong enough to grab an ex–Green Beret by the collar from half a block away.

There was a weightier matter as well, one that tugged at his thoughts as he dressed in the frigid room: The CIA's prized informant was at last on his way to Khost. Paresi had dealt with scores of informants over his career, but never had he seen a case that could simultaneously kick up so much excitement and rancor. Plans for the agent's debriefing had preoccupied the base's senior staff for weeks, and tempers had boiled over. For his part, Paresi was highly skeptical of the security plan the officers had rehearsed, and he had said so, sharing his concerns with both his supervisor back in Virginia and the CIA's security chief at Khost, Scott Roberson. Roberson had independently reached the same conclusion about what he believed was the fundamental problem: too many people, standing too close to an agent who had been living undercover and, by definition, could not be trusted.

Normally, such disagreements would have been considered part of the natural order. In nearly twenty-seven years of army service, including nearly six years of Special Forces work in Afghanistan, Paresi had seen endless skirmishing over tactics. Soldiers clashed and sometimes got mad, but in the end the officers decided, and everyone did his job. Today was looking like another of those days, yet it wasn't. Paresi couldn't yet put a finger on what was different.

Paresi dressed quickly and dug around his hooch for his heavy coat and weapon. Space-wise, the room was just a notch above an army tent, but there were plywood walls for privacy and just enough room for his cot, clothes, and gear, along with the books and journals he brought along to pass the idle hours. The hallway outside his room led to a small lounge with a leather sofa where the contract workers could play cards, read, or just sit with their laptops to skim the headlines and check e-mail. The place smelled vaguely of dogs, a legacy of the many strays that wandered through the base and were sometimes adopted as pets. The newest of the Blackwater arrivals, a Navy SEAL named Jeremy Wise, had taken up with a white, lop-eared mongrel he named Charlie that slept in the guards' quarters and liked chewing on the men's beards when they sat on the sofa. Paresi hardly minded. He loved dogs and missed his, a black-and-white Boston terrier so earnestly loopy Paresi had given it the nickname Retard. Dogs reminded him of home, where he planned to be in February, putting Afghanistan and military work behind him for good.

Dane Paresi had spent his entire adult life saluting. He had wanted to be a soldier since childhood, when he played army in the woods around the Willamette veterans' cemetery near his home in Portland, Oregon. He joined the army on the day after high school graduation, and he later became a paratrooper and served in the

First Iraq War. He left the army briefly but was inevitably drawn back again, this time determined to join the army's elite Special Forces. He sweated off thirty pounds in the grueling tryouts and training courses, but in 1995, at age thirty-two, he earned his Green Beret.

Not long afterward, while window-shopping at a strip mall near the base in Fayetteville, North Carolina, he noticed a pretty brunette eating ice cream inside a Bath & Body Works store and wandered in to try to talk to her. The young woman initially recoiled from the bone-thin man in a Batman T-shirt, white socks, and ugly, oversize glasses—"birth control glasses," she later called them. Her friends nearly phoned security, but within a few minutes the two were laughing and making plans to meet for coffee. The future Mindy Lou Paresi wrote her name and phone number in lipstick on a paper napkin. Eight months later they were married.

Life for the newlyweds was an unending series of separations during Dane Paresi's overseas deployments; he served in Bosnia, Rwanda, and the Philippines, among other hot spots. He happened to be home at the time of the September 11, 2001, terrorist attacks, but both husband and wife instinctively knew that things were about to get worse.

"Got to go to work, babe," he said.

Paresi shipped out to Afghanistan and later to Iraq. He returned home for a few weeks at a time to reconnect with Mindy Lou and the couple's two daughters, Alexandra and Santina. He said little at home about his time overseas, except to complain about the sandstorms and lousy weather and, in private moments, about what he saw as the futility of the U.S. efforts to graft a Western-style democracy onto a corrupt, clannish society where two-thirds of adults cannot read. Mindy Lou learned about his Bronze Star commendation when her husband handed her the official letter from the Pentagon and said, "Read this." It was the army's official account of how Paresi had helped spring a trap on an al-Qaeda convoy that included one of the terrorist group's senior commanders. Sixteen insurgents were killed and another was wounded in the 2002 operation.

Among his peers, Paresi was known for his unflappable calm and his Zen-like insistence on looking after small details. He stormed Taliban hideouts in the dead of night, and went on deep-cover assignments in Afghan garb, infiltrating villages infested with insurgents, sometimes with only one other American beside him.

"These were missions where you knew that no one was coming back for you," said one comrade who fought beside Paresi. "You had to know that the other person was capable and would get you back, dead or alive. That was him. He never got excited, and you knew he always had your back."

Afterward, back at camp, Paresi would find a quiet place to unwind, usually with a book and his pipe and a bottle of water. He never drank alcohol or talked loudly. When he was worried or troubled about something, he paced or found some way to busy himself.

He had just turned forty-five in the fall of 2008 and was in prime condition physically when the Defense Department informed him he was no longer needed. After twenty-six years of service he had been on track for making the rank of sergeant major, but instead of a promotion he received his separation papers. The army, flush with middle-aged master sergeants, gave him thirty days to clear out.

Paresi had dreamed of retiring in the mountains of western Oregon, fishing and growing old with Mindy Lou. But an army pension at his rank could not begin to pay the bills, so he started the search for his first civilian job. Weeks passed, then months. With money running low and few good prospects, he decided to sign up with the security contractor Blackwater for a one-year stint. The job was equally split between instructor assignments at home and security duties overseas, mostly in Afghanistan, where Blackwater had been hired to protect CIA installations and officers. The daily rate for overseas work was seven hundred dollars, enough to enable the Paresis to pay some bills and save for retirement. By late February, less than four months from his arrival in Khost, he would again be on his way home, this time finished with Afghanistan for good.

The housing assignment was certainly better than the dozen or more firebases where he had previously bunked, awful places where

Americans and Afghans slept with their guns, lined up like Crayolas inside smelly group tents, and slipped out at dawn to relieve them-selves by squatting in the open over crude pits. But now he was no longer a Green Beret, or even a soldier, but a highly paid security guard whose employer had been tarnished by multiple scandals in the press, including allegations that its employees killed innocent Iraqi civilians. Practically, though, Paresi's real bosses were CIA offi-cers, most of them younger than he and none of them as experienced in surviving the dangers of Afghanistan. When their decisions exas-perated him, he spoke up, but Paresi also understood his place. He had a family to feed and would do his job, even if he didn't like it.

The breakfast trays had been put away, and there was time to kill before the informant arrived, so Paresi wandered down to the motor pool, as he had been doing off and on for several days. He had been an army mechanic once, and he had learned a few tricks in previ-ous Afghanistan tours about hardening a vehicle against a roadside bomb. He had given up hours of free time there, without pay, just keeping his mind busy. And he would do so again this morning, working alone in the cold on old jalopies the CIA's Afghan agents used for meetings in the countryside.

Paresi's journals, his usual outlet for his thoughts, had not been touched for days, because he couldn't sit still long enough to write. When he called home, his voice sounded different, as though he were distracted or preoccupied. Mindy Lou Paresi knew the tone and became instantly concerned.

"Dane, are you safe?" she asked. She knew his reply before the words were uttered.

"Yeah, babe," is all he would say.

Humam al-Balawi scanned the line of cars and taxis, crutch in hand, looking for his ride. It was midafternoon on December 30 when he finally arrived at Ghulam Khan, the only border crossing between Pakistan's North Waziristan Province and the Islamic Republic of

Afghanistan. Balawi was now more than twenty-four hours late for his meeting at Khost. Would anyone still be waiting for him?

The checkpoint, a cluster of mud-brick buildings on the Pakistani side, was manned by a handful of nervous guards with rifles and one antique machine gun with its barrel pointed toward Afghanistan. Passengers crossing to the Afghan side queued up here for taxis and private cars that would ferry them across the dividing line, a mile farther up the road, and to points as far west as Kabul. The line inched forward as Balawi wavered, watching the guards in their heavy coats as they peered into trunks, checked IDs, and picked through suitcases, looking for drugs or weapons.

Physically Balawi was a wreck. His injured leg still ached, and he had spent a jarring afternoon on the rutted road from Miranshah with thirty pounds of metal and explosives strapped to his chest. Now he waited in line for a border check, clutching a Jordanian passport with a Pakistani visa that had expired seven months earlier, and wearing a bomb under his shirt. The line lurched forward again.

Balawi looked up to see someone waving to him from the cluster of taxis waiting for passengers to Afghanistan. He was tall, well built, and Afghan, to judge from his clothes. When the two were close enough to speak, he greeted Balawi softly in Pashtun-accented English.

He opened the door of a white sedan, and Balawi climbed inside. The car started and edged forward into the queue of westbound vehicles. With a flash of the driver's ID card, the vehicle was waved through. It rumbled along a steep incline for several minutes until at last it passed the boundary marker and was in Afghan territory.

The driver mumbled a few words into his cell phone, and the two men began an hour-long descent from the mountains to the semiarid valley that is home to most of Khost Province's one million inhabitants. The road snaked precariously along steep ridges and switchbacks here, and drivers were forced to swerve or brake to avoid craters gouged by flash floods or bombs.

The Afghan officer sat alone in the front, with his passenger directly behind him. Arghawan was one of the CIA's favorites at

Khost, hardworking and as dependable as the morning sun. Just thirty, with hazel eyes and a neatly trimmed beard, he had been an early graduate of Afghanistan's indigenous Special Forces school and had risen to head the detachment of Afghan guards employed by the CIA to help protect the base. It was a measure of the agency's trust that he was sent alone to pick up such an important source. An American might have begun the debriefing in the car, after a quick pat-down for weapons. But an American would not have been able to slip in and out of Pakistan as easily as a Pashtun speaker from outside Khost.

Just at the point where the hilly terrain finally leveled out, the car veered off the highway into a small village. Arghawan drove slowly along an unpaved street, looking for something, then pulled up next to a red Subaru hatchback that was idling behind a mud wall with a man sitting at the wheel. The two drivers got out of their cars and exchanged words; then Arghawan returned and opened the rear door next to Balawi.

Get out. We're switching cars, he said. *It's a precaution.*

Soon the two men were under way again, moving faster now on flat roads lined on either side by irrigated fields. It was already 4:15 P.M., nearly twenty-six hours after Balawi's scheduled appointment at Khost.

The initial delay had been the Taliban's fault. The CIA had expected Balawi to arrive in the Pakistani town of Miranshah on Tuesday, December 29, and then hire a car to ferry him to the border crossing, where Arghawan would be waiting. But Taliban leader Hakimullah Mehsud seemed determined to extract every possible propaganda benefit from Balawi's martyrdom, so the Jordanian's departure was delayed while the terrorist group's videographers set up one recording session after another. By the time Balawi arrived in Miranshah, it was too late to make the sprint to the border before the checkpoint closed for the night.

Balawi was nearly worn out by the multitude of efforts to document his final thoughts. In the last days of December he had written at least two essays and held forth in at least three lengthy video interviews and a few shorter snippets. In one video, Balawi sat out-doors, sandwiched between a pair of masked gunmen, to talk about the virtues of martyrdom. Another was set up as a standard talk show interview in which Balawi answered questions from an unseen "host." In a third, Balawi sat, somewhat nervously, next to Hakimul-lah Mehsud himself, as the two men proclaimed their intention to avenge the death of the Taliban leader's cousin Baitullah.

In the latter piece, the two men spoke in different languages—Mehsud in Pashto, Balawi in Arabic and English—and barely looked at each other as they sat cross-legged on a mat surrounded by weapons and sticks of C4 explosive. The Taliban leader spoke directly to the camera and praised Balawi as a man who "wants to go on a martyrdom-seeking mission.

"His conscience did not allow him to spy on Muslim brothers for the infidels," Mehsud said. He acknowledged that the CIA's attack planes had inflicted "pain and sadness" and said the Taliban had finally found a way to "infiltrate the American bases through a fidayeen in order to cause them a huge blow that they will remem-ber for a hundred years."

Balawi, wearing military fatigues, looked small and pale as he read from written notes. "We arranged this attack together," he said, "to let the Americans understand that the belief in God, our faith, and the piety that we strive for cannot be exchanged for all the wealth in the world."

The piety that we strive for. From where he sat, Balawi could see Arghawan in the rearview mirror, his eyes trained on the highway, instinctively watching, as all Afghan drivers do, for freshly turned earth that could signal a roadside bomb. The guard was earning a living for his family, but he also was a servant of the Americans. Two days earlier, Balawi had declared that such people were apos-tates and unfit to live—"even their cooks and drivers . . . even he who works in the garden or carwash."

"Killing him is more permissible than killing the American him-self," Balawi had said in one of his video recordings. "These are the hired dogs."

A large airfield had loomed in the distance for several miles, and now Arghawan was pointing to it. *Khost.*

The car had been out of cell phone range for nearly two hours, but with the city outskirts fast approaching, Balawi gestured to the driver to ask for his mobile phone. He dialed a number he had written on a scrap of paper, and in a moment a voice in familiar Arabic came on the line.

"*Salam alekum,*" Ali bin Zeid said. *Peace be with you.*

Balawi apologized for the delay and repeated his concerns about being poked and prodded by Afghan guards who might well be spies. "*You'll treat me like a friend, right?*" he asked.

Bin Zeid was reassuring.

The car was roaring along now, its wheels kicking up clouds of fine dust. Then it slowed at the approach to the main gate. The car passed through a canyon of high walls that narrowed at one end, squeezing traffic into a single lane at the checkpoint. The last few yards were a gauntlet of barriers and razor wire that channeled vehicles into the kill zone of a 50-caliber machine gun. Balawi sat low in his seat, the weight of the heavy vest pressing against his gut, but as bin Zeid had promised, there was no search. Arghawan turned left into the main entrance, and the car barely slowed as it zigzagged around a final series of HESCO barriers and into the open expanse of the Khost airfield.

The car turned left again to travel along the edge of the runway, past the tanker trucks, the dun-colored armored troop carriers, and an odd-looking green helicopter that stood idle on the tarmac, its main rotor blades drooping slightly like the wings of some giant prehistoric bird at rest. To the right were more high walls and barbed wire, and beyond them, the metal roofs of buildings Balawi could not yet see.

Balawi sank back into his seat. For days he had pondered what this moment would be like. In his writings he had imagined the djinn—devils—and their whispered doubts nudging him back from the edge.

"Are you going to perform jihad and get yourself killed, and let your wife remarry and your children become orphans?

"To whom are you leaving your pretty wife? Who will be dutiful to your frail mother?

"How can you abandon your wonderful work?"

There was an opening in the wall, and Arghawan steered the Subaru through a second open checkpoint and then turned left through a third. Balawi was now inside a fortified compound with walls of stacked HESCO barriers ten feet high and topped with razor wire. On the side of the compound opposite from the gate were five newly constructed buildings with metal roofs and a few smaller ones. The next-to-last building in the row had a wide awning. Balawi could see a large cluster of people scattered in a line in front of it. Behind him, the gate to the inner compound was pulled shut.

Arghawan stopped the vehicle in the middle of a gravel lot in front of the building, parallel to the awning but several car lengths away from it. From his spot in the backseat behind the driver, Balawi could finally see the line of people waiting to meet him. There were at least a dozen, including some women. Now he spotted Ali bin Zeid, wearing a camouflage hat and standing next to a larger man in jeans and a baseball cap. The two were at the end of the column of welcomers, but farther to the side and close enough that Balawi could see bin Zeid smiling at him.

Balawi was staring blankly at the group when the car door opened and he was suddenly face-to-face with a bear of a man with a close-cropped beard and piercing blue eyes. One gloved hand reached for Balawi, and the other clutched an assault rifle, its barrel pointed down. Balawi froze. Then, slowly, he began backing away, pushing himself along the seat's edge away from the figure with the gun.

Balawi squeezed the door handle on the opposite side and climbed out of the car, swinging his injured leg onto the gravel lot, and then the good one. Painfully he pulled himself erect, leaning on his metal crutch for support. He was dimly aware of bin Zeid calling out to him, but he would not look up.

When will my words taste my blood?

Balawi began walking in a slow-motion hobble as his right hand felt for the detonator.

Just at the brink, the djinn would pose the most awful questions, he had written.

"Who will take care of your little child? And your elderly father?"

Men were shouting at him now, agitated, guns drawn.

"It is said in the Hadith that he who says, 'There is no God but God alone and praise be to Him,' he is protected by God from Satan on that day," Balawi had written. *"On the day of the martyrdom-seeking operation, the enemy of God will not reach you."*

Now Balawi mouthed the words softly in Arabic. *"La ilaha illa Allah!"* There is no god but God.

Men were shouting loudly now, yelling about his hand, but still Balawi walked. He could hear his own voice growing more distinct.

"La ilaha illa Allah!"

Balawi's path was now blocked. He looked up to see that he was surrounded on two sides by men with guns drawn. The bearded man who had opened the car door had circled around him and was shouting at him from his left, and two other heavily armed officers stood directly in front of Balawi, trapping him against the car with no way forward or back. One of the men, blond and younger than the others, was crouching as though preparing to lunge.

Balawi turned slightly, finger locked on the detonator, and looked across the top of the car. The smiles had vanished, and bin Zeid was starting to move toward him. As he did, the tall man beside him grabbed his shoulder to pull him back.

Balawi closed his eyes. His finger made the slightest twitch.

15

THE MARTYR

In a fraction of a second, Humam al-Balawi disappeared in a flash of unimaginable brightness. The detonator caps sent a pulse of energy through the bars of C4 explosive until they ignited with a force powerful enough to snap steel girders. The heat at the center of the explosion soared briefly to more than four thousand degrees before the molecules themselves were hurled outward on a blast wave traveling at fifteen thousand feet per second.

The wave lifted the car off the ground and slammed into humans like a wall of concrete, blowing out eardrums and collapsing lungs. The three security men closest to the bomber were flung backward, with Dane Paresi thrown against a truck dozens of feet away. A great thunderclap shook the compound, followed by the crunch of hundreds of steel ball bearings ripping through glass, metal, and flesh.

The hail of fragments caused the most grievous damage to human tissue. The car's driver and the five officers with an unobstructed view of the bomber—the three security guards, Darren LaBonte, and Ali bin Zeid—were killed outright. The eleven others standing on the far side of the Subaru were cut down by tiny steel missiles that passed over and under the car and sometimes through it. Shrapnel pierced the compound's metal gate more than two hundred feet away.

All were hit, though the degree of bodily damage was random. Jennifer Matthews fell with grievous wounds, while a man standing near her was largely spared. Elizabeth Hanson, seemingly unharmed, staggered to her feet and ran between two buildings before collapsing to the ground.

The explosion shook buildings at the far end of the base, a half mile distant, and reverberated against the mountains through which Balawi had just passed. Then there was silence, broken only by the thud of falling debris.

Balawi's head, blown skyward at the instant of detonation, bounced against the side of a building and landed in the gravel lot. It was the only recognizable piece of him that remained.

Among the witnesses to the explosion was a CIA medical officer who had been summoned to the Balawi meeting to tend to the agent's leg and other ailments. Knocked briefly unconscious by the blast wave, he recovered to find himself surrounded by carnage and debris.

Though injured himself, he began crawling from body to body, surveying wounds, feeling for pulses, and screaming for assistance. He quickly stumbled upon Jennifer Matthews, moaning and apparently partially conscious with gaping wounds on her neck and one of her legs. Nearby, Elizabeth Hanson, bleeding from a small chest wound, lay motionless on the ground.

More help arrived within seconds as army Special Forces officers, some of them with advanced training in battlefield trauma, sprinted from buildings across the compound at the sound of the explosion, rifles and medical kits at the ready. Their snap assessment was dire in the extreme. The blast victims were so scattered and debris covered that it took minutes to find them all. Six were clearly dead, including the driver, and multiple victims had sustained life-threatening injuries, including penetrating head wounds. The CIA medic checked the badly wounded again as the soldiers applied field dressings and tourniquets. Without immediate surgery, five would die within minutes, he concluded. Matthews and Hanson were among them.

From the airfield across from the compound came the whine of a helicopter's engine roaring to life. A Russian-built MI-17, property of the Afghan army, happened to be at Khost at the time of the bombing and was immediately pressed into service. A world-class battlefield hospital lay just a few miles north of Khost City, in the U.S. base known as Camp Salerno, but the only way to reach it quickly was by chopper. On many an evening, the CIA officers had watched from Khost as specially equipped Black Hawk helicopters rushed American and Afghan casualties to the base from firefights all across eastern Afghanistan. On this night, the incoming wounded would be Khost's own.

Once airborne, the MI-17 could make the dash to Salerno in less than five minutes. It was a lucky break, the CIA medic thought as he helped load the stretchers into aircraft.

But would it be soon enough?

Army surgeon Captain Josh Alley was nearing the end of his shift at the Camp Salerno Combat Support Hospital when the word came of an incident at the CIA base across town.

"Chapman just got a direct mortar hit," one of the medical officers called out as he rushed down the hall. "We're getting an unknown number of casualties."

Alley, a veteran battlefield physician who had served in Iraq, changed into his surgical scrubs and started to wash up as details of the attack began trickling in. The first reports had a mortar round striking the CIA base's gym, news that hit close to home for Alley, who used Salerno's fitness room almost daily. Like its CIA neighbor, the Salerno base was a frequent target of rocket fire.

Minutes later the doctors learned of the suicide bombing and rushed to prepare trauma beds for as many as six patients. A small team of technicians assembled at each station and listened for the rumble of choppers approaching.

The first casualties arrived at dusk. In the landing zone just steps from the hospital, one of the doctors set up a hasty triage, eyeballing wounds and sorting out the priorities by a numbered code. *That's a two. That's a three.* In field hospital parlance, a "two" is a critical, life-threatening wound. A "one" rating means "expectant," or not likely to survive.

Two patients were rolled into the surgical prep area, and Alley was questioning one of them, a man who was badly wounded but conscious, when another doctor called out to him with a more serious case.

"She's got a chest wound," the doctor shouted.

Alley rushed over to look. On the operating table was a young blonde wearing a red tank top and necklace. He judged her to be twenty-five or perhaps younger, and she had no pulse. Alley was used to seeing American soldiers and ordinary Afghans with frightening wounds. He had performed hundreds of hours of what he called meatball surgery, picking shards of shattered bone from legs that had been blown apart by land mines, but this beautiful, intact young girl was a first. Alley found the pea-size opening in Elizabeth Hanson's chest and decided to immediately operate to explore what could be extensive damage within. He cut quickly through bone and muscle and then, with his finger, found the aorta, the main artery leaving the heart. It was flattened and empty. Desperately, he began squeezing and massaging the woman's heart while an assistant inserted a tube into the opening in her chest. The tube filled instantly with bright red blood, a sign of massive internal bleeding.

He had run out of options. A single piece of shrapnel smaller than a marble had shredded the veins and arteries closest to her heart and snuffed out her life.

"Does anyone know her name?" Alley called out. No answer.

There was no time to think. Another patient was brought in, this time an older woman in cargo pants with extensive injuries from shrapnel. Like Hanson, Jennifer Matthews had stopped breathing during the short chopper ride from Khost, but Alley would try to save her.

He assessed quickly. Shrapnel had torn away a large chunk of the woman's neck. One of her legs, just below a field tourniquet, had been nearly stripped of skin and muscle, exposing the bone. A small piece of shrapnel had penetrated her abdomen, and the wound had swollen in a way that suggested internal bleeding. Alley pressed an ultrasound probe against the woman's chest to get a look at her heart. It was motionless.

He couldn't fix this.

The frantic efforts continued for hours without letup. Working in tandem with another surgeon, Alley patched up severed veins and mangled legs. He treated, as best as he could, a young officer who had a piece of shrapnel lodged dangerously in his brain. All the others were stabilized and placed on helicopters for the one-hour flight to the U.S. military's Bagram Air Base near Kabul, where other doctors would take over.

It was late when the last of the wounded had cleared out. Alley went outside and, drenched with sweat from the adrenaline and the eighty-five-degree operating room, sat in the cold for a few minutes. Other bodies, those of fallen CIA officers who had been instantly killed in the explosion, were still arriving, to be brought to Salerno's morgue. Among the remains, he learned, were a few fragments of Humam al-Balawi, collected, he presumed, for DNA testing.

Alley gnawed on a Popsicle to soothe his parched throat. More than 90 percent of the American soldiers who made it alive to his field hospital ended up surviving. At Khost that evening, Alley knew, each of the dozens of factors that were subject to human control had worked perfectly, from the first aid by battlefield medics to the availability of the helicopter to the presence of a first-rate surgical team less than five minutes from the scene of the explosion. Everything had gone right, and it still had not been enough.

He thought again about the two civilian women he had been unable to save. He still didn't know their names. Were they aid workers? Journalists? Each day brought a fresh dose of human suffering to his operating room, and he was used to dealing with it and pushing on. But war was usually men fighting men. This felt different.

More helicopters were heading to the landing zone now. Alley got up and turned to go back to work.

16

FALLEN

Langley, Virginia—December 30, 2009

At the moment of the bombing—it was still early morning in Washington—Michael V. Hayden happened to be in Langley visiting his old office. The former CIA director had been asked to give a policy speech in Pittsburgh, and he wanted to do some research. It was usually quiet at headquarters between Christmas and New Year's, although this week was far from usual. There had been a near disaster on Christmas night when a Nigerian youth named Umar Farouk Abdulmutallab tried to blow up an airliner over Detroit. The case, like so many others lately, made no sense. How does a smart, highly educated kid from a wealthy family decide to kill himself and a couple of hundred strangers with a bomb hidden in his underwear?

Hayden finished his work and decided to check in on some friends on the executive floor. Director Leon Panetta was away for his holiday vacation, and so was Hayden's old deputy, Steve Kappes, so he headed down the hall to say hello to Mike Sulick, the man he had promoted to run the agency's Clandestine Service. At that moment two other managers were walking out of Sulick's office. They looked sick.

"It's really bad," one of them said. "Seven officers are dead."

The men had just broken the news to the most senior officer in the building.

Details were still coming in, and already a feeling akin to shell shock was spreading through the executive floor. Hayden, unsure of what else to do, wandered over to his old office and found Panetta's chief of staff, Jeremy Bash, on the phone with his boss in California, relaying the latest updates.

The first reports had arrived at Panetta's Monterey, California, home just before 5:00 A.M., with a rap on the director's bedroom door by a member of his security detail. One of his aides urgently needed to speak with him on the secure line, Panetta was told.

"I've got terrible news," the woman began. "We've lost seven of our officers in Khost."

"What the hell happened?" Panetta shouted, instantly awake. He heard the words *Jordanian informant* and *suicide bomber* and the outlines of the disaster crystallized in his mind. The double agent. The long-awaited meeting. The chance to get Ayman al-Zawahiri. It had all been a trick.

Panetta pressed for details, but there were few at that hour. He hung up the phone and sat, hoping that it was somehow a bad dream.

As the chief of staff for the Clinton White House he had stood by the president in 1993, when news broke of the bombing of the Alfred P. Murrah Federal Building in Oklahoma City, an attack by American right-wing extremists that killed 168 people. But never had men and women fallen under his direct command.

This is truly war, he thought.

With Bash on the line he began to make phone calls, thinking that the bad news should come first from him. He called Dennis Blair, the director of national intelligence, and Robert M. Gates, the defense secretary. He tapped in the number for Vice President Joe Biden.

Then he called the president.

Barack Obama was on Christmas vacation in Hawaii, but after a moment the CIA director was patched through. *We lost seven officers in Khost*, Panetta began.

"This guy that we thought was going to take us to Zawahiri turned out to be a double agent and blew himself up," he told the president.

The two talked for a few minutes while Panetta summarized the scant facts he had. Obama listened quietly at first, then stopped Panetta repeatedly to press for details. *I want to understand what happened*, he said.

The two talked about what would come next. Family notifications. Services. *The White House should be part of it*, Obama said, thinking out loud. *The families should know that we're with them.*

Please keep me posted, Leon, the president said, finally. *If there's anything at all that I can do . . .*

Back at Langley, Bash had invited Hayden to stay, so he did. Some of the names of the victims were starting to trickle in, and one of them pierced Hayden to his core.

Elizabeth Hanson.

He could still picture her young face from the times she had presented updates on al-Qaeda at senior staff meetings. He remembered her voice from late-night calls from the Counterterrorism Center, when the agency was hot on the trail of some senior commander in Pakistan. She was smart, confident, attractive, a walking recruitment poster for the agency. She exuded the kind of enthusiasm and competence that had made Hayden proud when he served as director.

Hayden sat for a long time in the director's office with Bash and Sulick, talking about the events, the people, wondering what had gone wrong. Finally he said good-bye to the others and let himself out. He walked past the guard station and through the marble entranceway, with its famous engraving of the CIA seal on the floor. He passed the CIA's fallen officer memorial, where dozens of granite stars honor slain intelligence operatives, including many whose names will forever remain secret.

Outside, it was overcast and freezing. Hayden hurried to his vehicle and sat for several minutes in the parking lot. He thought about Hanson and the others and the many families who at this hour did not yet know what lay ahead for them.

Alone in his car in the bitter cold, Michael Hayden wept.

Even before the extent of the losses was known, top CIA officials inaugurated a plan that would guide the agency's response over the coming days. The first immediate step was to seal off Khost entirely, locking down the base itself and cutting communications to the outside world. A few cell phone calls made it to the United States before the access was shut. One of them was from a Special Forces officer who had witnessed the bombing's aftermath and called a CIA friend with the news.

"Your base just got blown up," he said.

The agency imposed a news blackout in an effort to keep details of the attack out of the public spotlight until the senior managers were clear on exactly what had happened and had started the process of notifying the families of the dead and wounded. Within hours, Internet news sites were buzzing about a major explosion at a secret CIA base, but the official response from Langley was silence. At headquarters and in the agency's Amman station, teams were appointed to the grim task of locating wives and parents so they could be told in person.

The CIA had no one reasonably close to Tuscany on December 30, so it fell to the Amman station to deliver the news by phone to Racheal LaBonte. The station chief knew that the LaBonte family was in Italy, expecting Darren to show up at any time. In reality, his wife already sensed that something had gone badly wrong in Afghanistan.

Late in the afternoon she began receiving urgent text messages from Ali bin Zeid's wife, Fida. The Jordanian woman had been watching news reports about an attack of some kind in Afghanistan, and she was worried. Bin Zeid had not phoned when he was supposed to, and now she was having trouble getting through to him. Had Racheal heard from Darren?

Racheal LaBonte figured it was just a problem with phone lines, but to ease both their minds, she punched in the number of the CIA duty officer back in Amman. The voice on the other end sounded a little nervous but was reassuring. There was no news from Khost, good or bad, Racheal was told.

A few hours later, as she put the couple's daughter, Raina, to bed, the fear started to prick her like a thousand little knives. There was a knock on the door. It was the landlord, saying that someone from the U.S. government was trying to reach the family. A phone rang. It was the station chief from Amman.

"Are you sitting down? Is your father-in-law with you?" he was asking.

"Say what you're going to say. I want to hear in person," Racheal demanded.

"I don't know how to tell you this. Darren was killed in a suicide bombing," he began.

Racheal fell to her knees, the phone still pressed against her ear. Darren's parents were hovering over her, asking questions. What happened?

"Darren didn't do anything wrong," the station chief was saying. "He was a hero." Then: "Racheal, are you still there?"

Racheal was lost in a fog so deep it felt as though the events were happening to someone else. "You'll have to tell Dave," she said softly, and handed off the phone. She was dimly aware of her father-in-law, David LaBonte, shouting into the phone in a voice tinged with exasperation and pain.

"What do you mean?" he was shouting. "What are you saying?"

She looked up to see her mother-in-law, Camille, frightened and confused, fearing the worst but not yet knowing. Racheal took her hand to tell her gently that her son would not be coming home.

At the same hour small teams of CIA officers were boarding planes and cars heading to small towns in Virginia, Pennsylvania, and Illinois. Two of Elizabeth Hanson's close friends trekked through a snowstorm to knock on the door of her mother's house in suburban Chicago. Others sat with Janet Brown, whose husband, Harold, had been only a few weeks from completing his Khost assignment and was due to travel home soon; and with Molly Roberson, who was seven months pregnant with a baby girl that she and Scott Roberson had decided to call Piper. A fourth team tracked down Jennifer Matthews's husband and children at a ski resort. Gary Anderson sat with his in-laws, Bill and Lois Matthews, in a hotel in Hershey, Pennsylvania, to learn the details of how his wife had died.

Xe Services LLC, the company better known as Blackwater, sent its representatives to Virginia Beach, and DuPont, Washington, to meet with the wives of security guards Dane Paresi and Jeremy Wise. Dana Wise's visitors showed up at her house as she was putting her son, Ethan, into the family truck for a quick errand. She sent the six-year-old to his room while she sat with the men in her living room. Before they left, she steeled herself for the task of breaking the news to her son.

Ethan was her child from an earlier marriage, but Jeremy had adopted him and loved him as his own. Once, when he was returning home from a long Iraq deployment, he decided to surprise Ethan by showing up at his school. It had been the happiest day in the young boy's life.

Now there would be no more homecomings. With tears welling in her own eyes, Dana Wise scooped up her son and held him as the two sat on his bed surrounded by his toys and stuffed animals. Finally she worked up her nerve.

"Daddy's gone," she said softly.

Mindy Lou Paresi and daughter Santina had been relieved that evening to get a reassuring e-mail from Dane when they landed at Seattle's airport after a holiday visit with family. It had been a rough trip, with endless lines and delays, and they were so exhausted when they arrived home that they left the suitcases packed and went to sleep. At 2:00 A.M. on New Year's Eve, Mindy Lou was awakened by a knock. She looked out from an upstairs window to see three men at her door, one of them a police officer.

"Is Dane OK?" she called down.

"No, ma'am, he's not."

She let the men in, but she didn't believe what they were saying. *You're wrong, I just got a text from him this evening,* she said.

The Blackwater officials were startled, and one of them called the company to check again.

The reply was unambiguous. Dane Paresi was dead.

It would be nearly two days before Mindy Lou Paresi could allow herself to cry. She paced the apartment for hours that morning, folding laundry and making one phone call after another. Later she packed for the trip to Dover, Delaware, where she would meet the plane carrying the bodies from Afghanistan. She took her husband's army uniform and boots out of the closet and put them into a separate bag. Dane would want to be buried in them.

On New Year's Day she went to the airport, holding the bag with Dane's uniform close to her on the car ride and in the airport terminal. At the security checkpoint, one of the attendants asked for the bag to put it through the metal detector. At first, she couldn't bear to part with it. When she finally did, she broke down, sobbing uncontrollably.

Word of the bombing arrived in Jordan in the late evening. It came first to the intelligence service, the Mukhabarat, and then to the palace. An official with the royal court called Ali bin Zeid's brothers and his wife and told them to gather at the family home in Amman.

After everyone was there, a delegation of top government officials assembled in front of the house. It included the king's brother, Prince Ali bin al-Hussein, the prime minister, the Mukhabarat chief, and the commander of the Jordanian armed forces. At 9:30 P.M., they walked in a somber procession to the front door.

The door opened, and for several minutes no one—neither the dignitaries nor the family members—spoke. "Everyone knew," said Ali bin Zeid's brother, Hassan.

Khalil al-Balawi, father of the suicide bomber, got no such visit.

But on the morning of New Year's Eve, the phone rang at both the Balawi house and at the home of Defne Balawi's parents in Istanbul. Both times the caller was a man who spoke in Arabic and did not give his name.

To Khalil al-Balawi, the caller sounded as though he were delivering good news. Humam had killed seven CIA officers in a martyrdom operation in Afghanistan, he said.

"Do not be sad," the man said. "Allah willing, he is in the most exalted heavens."

Khalil al-Balawi was surrounded by family members at the time, but he could not bring himself to mention the call—or perhaps even to believe it—until hours later, when the story had spread through the community that Humam, the doctor who lived in the neighborhood, was behind the suicide bombing that was dominating coverage on the Arabic news channel al-Jazeera. Relatives and family friends began calling, some with condolences and others with messages that sounded more akin to congratulations.

Khalil al-Balawi said little, but at one point he excused himself and went into his bedroom and took out his diary to try to make sense of the thoughts swirling through his brain.

"At the beginning of 2009 he was arrested and detained for three days by the Mukhabarat," the old man wrote. "Then he was released. His father will attest that from that day on, a severe change came over him.

"It is this," he wrote, "that caused me to lose my son."

17

RESOLVE

Langley, Virginia—January 2010

Sheikh Saeed al-Masri had slain a giant, and he was crowing.

"A successful epic," the No. 3 al-Qaeda leader pronounced the suicide bombing in a rare public statement. He praised his star assassin, Humam al-Balawi, the "well-known preacher-writer . . . the migrant and the mujaid" who had penetrated the base of the terrorist group's mortal enemy, the CIA.

Al-Masri's message, posted on jihadist Web sites shortly after the suicide attack, stopped short of directly claiming responsibility, something that the old warrior knew would only increase the risk to himself. But he hinted at his knowledge of the intimate details of the plot, calling it a model of "patience, good planning and management.

"He detonated his fine, astonishing and well-designed explosive device, which was unseen by the eyes of those who do not believe," al-Masri said. Then, addressing the dead bomber directly, he officially absolved Balawi of the doubts about him, questions that had lingered until the very end.

"You won, by the Lord of the Ka'aba, O Abu-Leila, God willing," he said. "You were truthful, and you proved it."

Al-Masri's reaction was restrained in comparison to the Taliban leader Hakimullah Mehsud's. Balawi's former host had gone to the trouble of videotaping the Jordanian before his death, and so he had evidence of his ties to the suicide mission. But in the days after the attack, rival Taliban groups began to assert their own claims. One faction boasted that a disgruntled Afghan soldier was behind the bombing.

Hakimullah was so incensed that he began sending e-mails to Western journalists, using his real name.

"We claim the responsibility for the attack on the CIA in Afghanistan," Hakimullah Mehsud wrote in the e-mails. The bombing was "revenge for the killing of Baitullah Mehsud and the killing of al-Qaeda's Abdullah," an apparent reference to Abdullah Said al-Libi.

The thirty-year-old Taliban leader also began to hint of a bold new phase for the Mehsud clan. The suicide bombing had been his group's biggest operation outside its home base, and it gave a boost to Hakimullah Mehsud's personal clout. He had been a local jihadist with parochial aspirations, but no longer. Like his slain cousin, he began to boast of plans to attack the West, starting with "America, the criminal state," which he blamed for the death of Baitullah Mehsud.

"Our fidaeen have penetrated the terrorist America," Hakimullah Mehsud brashly reported in a videotaped warning. "We will inflict extremely painful blows on the fanatic America."

Balawi had predicted as much in the hours before his death. His sacrifice, he said in one of his final video recordings, was to be the "first of the revenge operations against the Americans and their drone teams, outside the Pakistani borders."

In other words, Khost was only the beginning.

At 8:30 A.M. on January 4 the CIA's senior managers gathered in the director's office for the most solemn Monday staff meeting in nearly a decade. It began with a moment of silence, at Leon Panetta's request. The agency's top counterterrorism officials bowed their heads, some praying while others wept.

The normally loquacious Panetta was subdued, his eyes puffy

from lack of sleep. Soon after the meeting he would depart Langley for Dover Air Force Base in Delaware to meet the military plane carrying the bodies home. He would stand on the tarmac in the bitter cold to watch the flag-draped coffins as they were carried, one by one, from the aircraft. He would huddle with the families in an empty hangar for a brief memorial, the first of many such services scheduled over the coming days.

Panetta had not known exactly when the meeting with Balawi would take place, but he had known how the operation was to unfold, and he had eagerly awaited the results. Now he bore the burden of knowing the names and faces of each of the dead and wounded. He realized he had met several of them in his travels to CIA bases, visits that nearly always included an informal town hall session where ordinary case officers and analysts could ask questions of the CIA director. He had felt proud to lead such smart, capable men and women. Now, in his private conversations with close friends, he agonized that Balawi's treachery had not been spotted earlier. Panetta reread the files about the informant and studied the photos of the red Subaru with its blown-out windows and hundreds of shrapnel holes. He tried to project an aura of calm, but he was deeply frustrated. How could they have let a terrorist slip in like that? he asked repeatedly. "Leon felt accountable," said an administration friend who met with him during the initial days after the attack. "We all did—everyone who knew about the meeting that day."

But when Panetta at last stood up in front of the CIA's division managers at their morning meeting, his voice was firm. After the moment of silence, he told the group to prepare to be exceptionally busy. There would be a full investigation in time, he said, but for the moment the CIA was to focus its energies on the tribal belt of northwestern Pakistan. The loss of seven officers in a day was historic—the worst in twenty-five years—but the agency could not allow the enemy to see even the slightest pause. In fact exactly the opposite would happen, he said.

"When you are at war there are risks that you take, but we are a family—we have to be family," he said. "We now have to pull together to not only deal with the pain of this loss but also to pull together to make sure that we fulfill the mission."

Panetta continued to speak as the agency's veterans sat quietly.

"We hit them hard this past year, and they're going to try to hit us back," he said. "But we have to stay on the offensive."

Indeed, a new offensive had already begun.

On New Year's Eve, hours after the suicide bombing, a lone CIA Predator carried out the first retaliatory strike, hitting a Taliban safe house near the town of Mir Ali in North Waziristan. Among the four killed was a senior Taliban commander named Haji Omar Khan, a close ally of the Mehsud family and a veteran of the civil war against the Soviets.

Less than twenty-four hours later a second strike targeted three Taliban militants in a car a few miles from Mir Ali. Two more Taliban fighters were killed nearby in a third attack on January 3.

And the CIA was just warming up.

On January 6, two days after Panetta's speech to his senior staff, robot planes converged over a training camp in Datta Khel, not far from the house where Humam al-Balawi's suicide vest had been made. The first wave of missiles hit a mud-brick fortress that served as camp headquarters. Then, when insurgents swarmed over the wrecked buildings to look for bodies, a second salvo was launched. When the dust cleared, at least eleven people lay dead, including two Arab men whom Pakistani authorities identified as al-Qaeda operatives.

Another attack—the fifth in nine days—killed five people in a Taliban safe house on January 8. The next day a strike on a training camp in a village near Miranshah killed four more. Among the dead was a Jordanian al-Qaeda operative who had been serving as a bodyguard for Sheikh Saeed al-Masri. If al-Masri was present, he managed to slip away.

And so it continued. By January 19, less than three weeks after the suicide bombing, the CIA had launched eleven separate missile strikes over a small swath of North and South Waziristan, killing at least sixty-two people. It was drone warfare at its most furious:

Never, since the first Predators were launched over Pakistan in 2004, had the pace been so intense.

The barrage was sanctioned all the way to the White House. As top administration officials later described the events, all the Taliban targets had been on the agency's watch list before the suicide attack at Khost. But by the start of the new year, the CIA's fleet of robot planes had grown; new orbits, approved by President Obama in the fall, were now being flown. More important, the agency had won approval to temporarily suspend one of the unwritten rules of its drone campaign. Before the Khost bombing, the CIA had largely avoided carrying out clusters of attacks that might provoke a popular backlash in Pakistan. Now the agency's leaders, and the nation's president, were in no mood to exercise such restraint.

"In the aftermath of Khost, political sensitivities were no longer a reason not to do something," said one Obama administration security official who participated in discussions about the U.S. response to the bombing. "The shackles were unleashed."

The strike that provoked the most excitement at Langley occurred on January 14 in a sparsely populated region called Shaktoi, near the border between the two Waziristans. A CIA aircraft had been flying a slow orbit above a former madrassa, a religious school, that now served as a Taliban base. Informants reported the presence in the camp of a tall, scruffy-bearded commander of obviously high rank. A phone intercept confirmed that it was Hakimullah Mehsud.

Just before dawn, two large explosions leveled the school building and an adjoining house. Among the ten bodies were several Uzbek fighters who were known members of the Taliban leader's personal security team.

Pakistani media rushed to publish the news online: Hakimullah Mehsud, the man who had helped prepare Balawi for his suicide mission, had been inside the compound when the missiles struck and was believed to be buried in the rubble. One English-language news site posted a large headline on its main Web page. "Hakimullah feared dead," the headline read.

Panetta remained tethered for days to his secure phone, giving orders and receiving reports from the Predator teams. But publicly his role was to lead the agency through a long period of grieving. He and his deputy, Steve Kappes, together attended more than twenty funerals and memorial services, beginning with the gathering at Dover and ending many weeks later with the final burials at Arlington National Cemetery. He traveled to Jordan to reassure top officials of the Mukhabarat, and he met with Darren LaBonte's coworkers in the agency's Amman station, pledging that he would personally see to it that his widow and child were cared for.

It was at Dover that the human dimensions of the disaster became fully clear. Panetta had flown to the Delaware base with General James E. "Hoss" Cartwright, the Marine Corps general and Joint Chiefs of Staff vice chairman, to receive the bodies, and he expected to speak with family members of the dead in private bereavement rooms. But the sheer number of parents, children, and spouses forced the group to move into a large multipurpose room in the base chapel. When Panetta arrived, the room was crowded with mourners. Adults stood in clusters along the walls, while children played or sat in their parents' laps.

"It was shocking to see so many people," one of Panetta's aides said afterward.

Panetta made his way through the crowd, shaking hands and giving hugs. Then he spoke briefly to the group.

"You should know two things," he said. "We will honor your loved ones in an appropriate, dignified way, starting here at Dover. And we will keep up the fight, because that is what they would have wanted us to do."

In Jordan, meanwhile, other CIA and State Department dignitaries gathered in Amman for a royal funeral for Ali bin Zeid, a ceremony that began with the red-carpeted arrival of the Mukhabarat captain's body accompanied by an honor guard of twenty-four elite soldiers in traditional red and white kaffiyeh head scarves. A bagpipe corps led an official funeral procession that included bin Zeid's cousin King Abdullah II, along with Queen Rania and their oldest son, Crown Prince Hussein.

American families gathered to mourn in a series of private services that stretched from coastal Oregon, to Rockford, Illinois, to suburban Boston. Fellow SEALs gathered in a navy chapel in Virginia Beach, Virginia, to salute their fallen comrade, Jeremy Wise; while Harold Brown Jr.'s two oldest children, Paul, twelve, and Magdalena, eleven, played a duet on saxophone and clarinet to honor their father in services in a Catholic church in his boyhood home of Bolton, Massachusetts. Narcotics detectives and motorcycle cops wept over Scott Roberson's coffin in Akron, Ohio, while in an Annapolis, Maryland, cathedral, one of Darren LaBonte's CIA comrades recalled the bravery of the former Army Ranger known as Spartan. The officer compared his former comrade with Leonidas, the ancient warrior-king of Sparta, who, when ordered to surrender his weapons by a vastly superior Persian force, replied, *"Molon labe"*— "Come and get them!" Jennifer Matthews's life was celebrated in separate services at the family's church in Fredericksburg, Virginia, and in the small brick congregation near Harrisburg, Pennsylvania, where she had attended Sunday school as a girl. A hush fell over the packed church at Fredericksburg as Matthews's oldest child, a twelve-year-old girl, stood up to sing, in a fine soprano, lyrics from *Les Misérables*, her mom's favorite musical. *Some will fall and some will live*, she sang. *Will you stand up and take your chance?*

Mindy Lou Paresi, honoring her husband's wishes, made arrangements for Dane Paresi's burial in the same Willamette veterans' cemetery in Portland where he had played army as a boy. The body, dressed in the Green Beret uniform and paratrooper's boots Mindy Lou had carried with her to Dover Air Force Base, made its final cross-country trip in a metal casket. A closed-coffin reception was planned for a close circle of friends and family members, but before it started, Dane Paresi's widow asked to spend some time alone with his body. She prayed quietly for a few minutes, then walked to the coffin and carefully opened the lid. Dane's face was wrapped in gauze, and there were white gloves on his hands.

Mindy Lou needed to fully understand what her husband had endured, so she willed herself to touch his broken body. She caressed his swollen, shrouded face. She felt the empty parts of the glove where fingers were missing. She let her hands pass along the length of his uniform, feeling the broken bones through the fabric.

She kissed her husband one last time and then closed the coffin.

On February 5 the families of the dead officers and hundreds of their CIA colleagues gathered at Langley for a last tribute. A massive winter storm was bearing down on the capital as the motorcades arrived carrying the elites of Washington's national security community, from the Pentagon to Congress to the White House. In the CIA's marbled foyer, a large group of parents, spouses, and young children sat in folding chairs in front of a dais as a string ensemble played an adagio. Facing them from the platform was President Barack Obama, flanked by Panetta and Kappes.

The president spoke first, at one point addressing the children in the front rows.

"I know that this must be so hard and confusing, but please always remember this: It wasn't always easy for your mom or dad to leave home," Obama said. "But they went to another country to defend our country. And they gave their lives to protect yours.

"They served in secrecy, but today every American can see their legacy," he continued. "For the record of their service is written all around us. It's written in the extremists who no longer threaten our country—because they eliminated them. It's written in the attacks that never occurred—because they thwarted them."

Panetta's words were largely aimed at the slain officers' CIA family.

"We are on the front lines," he began. "We will carry this fight to the enemy."

The agency's secret cables had brought initial reports of successes in northern Pakistan, but in recent days the storm clouds had again gathered, with warnings of new threats from al-Qaeda cells from East Africa to the Arabian Peninsula and signs of renewed resilience by al-Qaeda's leaders. The agency confirmed that Hakimullah Mehsud had narrowly escaped the attempt on his life and was again furiously threatening to find ways to kill Americans. Osama bin Laden had just resurfaced with a new audiotape praising the attempted bombing of the Detroit-bound passenger jet on Christmas Day and promising that Americans would "never dream of peace." Sheikh Saeed al-Masri, minus one of his bodyguards, was living somewhere in the Pakistani hills, listening for the buzzing of Predators and plotting his next move. The war was far from over.

"Our resolve is unbroken," Panetta continued, "our energy undiminished."

After the speeches a CIA officer sang a mournful ballad, and the crowd slowly filed out of the headquarters building. It was now dusk, and the first clots of thick snowflakes started to fall.

18

MEMORIAL DAY

Arlington, Virginia—May 21, 2010

Nearly five months passed without a proper burial for Elizabeth Hanson, but at last it was happening. There had been hurdles to overcome, including initial Pentagon resistance to burying non-veteran CIA officers in the nation's most prestigious military cemetery. Leon Panetta, who was accustomed to plowing through bureaucracies when he needed to, called on his old friend Robert Gates, a former CIA director and now the Obama administration's defense secretary. Soon it was settled: Though a civilian, Hanson would receive the Arlington burial her family wanted. The date for this, the last of the Khost interments, was set for May 21, and Panetta, as always, would be there.

But the date arrived to find the agency's senior leadership unusually distracted. That same morning the CIA director returned home from two days of urgent meetings in Islamabad with Pakistani government officials. Panetta and National Security Adviser James L. Jones made the trip together to share information about a young Pakistani-American charged with trying to blow up New York's Times Square with a car bomb on May 1. The suspect, an out-of-work financial analyst named Faisal Shahzad, had told police he had received training for the bombing attempt during a 2009 trip to Pakistan's border region. Eventually a video turned up of the

Bridgeport, Connecticut, suspect embracing his Pakistani sponsor, Hakimullah Mehsud.

The car bomb, fortunately, had been a flop, but U.S. intelligence officials were stunned to discover Mehsud's fingerprints all over the plot. A year earlier, Hakimullah Mehsud had been an obscure aide to a semiliterate tribal gangster living in the remote mountains of northwestern Pakistan. Now, catapulted into Taliban leadership by the death of his cousin Baitullah in a CIA missile strike, Hakimullah Mehsud had managed to threaten American lives in the heart of its greatest city. Was this what Mehsud meant when he warned that his fighters had "penetrated the terrorist America"? How many other bombers were on their way or perhaps already here?

But Panetta had even bigger things on his mind as he climbed into his limousine for Hanson's graveside service. All morning his aides had been calling about a possibly momentous discovery, something unexpected that had emerged from the day's trolling for terrorist suspects. The picture from the Pakistani tribal belt was still coming into focus, but the agency's targeters believed they had located an al-Qaeda operative they had been seeking for a long time.

It was Sheikh Saeed al-Masri, the No. 3 terrorist commander and the man who had presided over Humam al-Balawi's suicide attack at Khost.

Panetta, still exhausted from his overnight flight, snapped to attention. He flung questions at the counterterrorism chief. *What do we know? How did we find him? How certain are you?*

The reply from Langley: *Not certain enough. Not yet.*

From his car, Panetta thought through the possible implications. Sheikh Saeed al-Masri—if that was who it was—would be one of the important terrorist figures ever to fall into the CIA's sights. At the moment he was the most prominent al-Qaeda operative after Osama bin Laden and Ayman al-Zawahiri. As a practical matter, he was more influential than either one of them.

As the big black car rolled into Arlington National Cemetery for Hanson's burial, the CIA's robot planes were prowling the sky over a house outside Miranshah, waiting. What an amazing ending to a truly awful chapter in the agency's history, Panetta thought.

But was it really the sheikh?

Panetta phoned the White House to relay the latest information to Rahm Emanuel, the president's chief of staff.

"It's not a 'go' mission yet," he said.

The questioning started before the dust had even settled at Khost. How could it have happened?

Surviving officers in Khost relayed the known facts within hours of the explosion, and the base's Special Forces team prepared its own separate report summing up what was immediately obvious. A CIA double agent—in fact a triple agent—had managed to gain access to the agency's secure base with an extraordinarily powerful bomb strapped to his body. He was able to come within a few dozen feet of a group of sixteen intelligence operatives before blowing himself up. Immediate intervention by experienced battlefield medics and surgeons had saved lives, but ten people had been killed, including the bomber and the CIA-trained Afghan driver.

The hard questions would take longer to sort out. Panetta's senior staff focused on the key decisions and began tracing the steps backward, from Khost to Kabul and Amman and, inevitably, Langley. Panetta shared what he knew with White House advisers, including White House Chief of Staff Rahm Emanuel and National Security Adviser James L. Jones. Both he and Steve Kappes recounted the details in closed-door sessions with the Senate and House intelligence committees. Lawmakers had been sympathetic but also distracted by the near disaster that had occurred in the skies over Detroit on Christmas Day. Thus there would be no formal congressional inquiry into the events.

Panetta, with the White House's blessing, decided to launch two investigations of his own. One was a task force of veteran CIA officers experienced in counterterrorism and counterintelligence. A second, independent review was led by a pair of longtime Washington hands known and respected within the intelligence community, former United Nations ambassador Thomas Pickering and Charles E. Allen, a former CIA manager who had served as intelligence chief for the Department of Homeland Security during the second Bush administration. The two teams would examine thousands of secret cables, memos, and e-mails, and interview surviving CIA officers as well as their coworkers and superiors, from Khost to Kabul, Islamabad, Amman, and Langley.

Nearly a year passed before the teams' reports were completed. In the intervening months scores of former intelligence operatives and terrorism experts offered their own judgments, drawing from the scant details available. In op-ed pieces, news articles, and blogs, commentators focused on two perceived failures, missteps that were said to have contributed to the disaster at Khost while pointing to deeper flaws in the country's premier intelligence agency. Several of the agency's retired executives pinned the blame on Khost base chief Jennifer Matthews and, more broadly, the CIA managers in Langley who had approved her promotion to a frontline post despite her lack of experience in a war zone. Other observers argued that the fatal errors in judgment at Khost stemmed from the agency's growing aversion to risk. Even in Iraq and Afghanistan, these critics noted, many CIA officers lived in secure compounds where no one ever got hurt, while relying on technology and foreign allies to do the dirty work of finding and destroying terrorist threats. Somewhere along the way, basic rules of spycraft, including time-honored procedures for assessing and running informants and double agents, had been all but forgotten.

The criticisms hit at legitimate problems within the CIA. But they did not fully capture what had gone wrong at Khost in the hours before New Year's Eve.

The agency's Khost review did confirm numerous missteps. It concluded that Jennifer Matthews and her Khost team—with the support of more senior officials at Kabul and Langley—failed to follow standard safety procedures in their meeting with Balawi, apparently out of an eagerness to secure the informant's coopera-

tion. Warnings that might have alerted the CIA to Balawi's deception were never passed along, in part because the messages weren't
entirely trusted, investigators concluded. Critical insights were not
shared with decision makers because they were expressed in private
e-mails and text messages that never became part of the agency's
reservoir of knowledge about Humam al-Balawi. At the same time,
expectations were raised in high-level meetings in Washington
before key facts were known.

As a result, both Matthews and senior managers at Langley
believed that Balawi was a trusted Jordanian agent, investigators
found, and the cautions raised by those who knew him best—Ali
bin Zeid and Darren LaBonte—were trumped by the "evidence"
the officers could see with their own eyes: the words and images
Balawi e-mailed from inside al-Qaeda's tent.

"All they had seen and read, plus the urgency of getting to the
top leadership of al-Qaeda, led to a situation in which the major
preoccupation was the good health and safety of the man who was
intent on becoming a suicide bomber," said Ambassador Thomas
Pickering, coleader of the independent review.

The agency's investigators recommended significant reforms, several of which were quickly implemented by Panetta and his team.
The agency raised its standards for training and experience for overseas managers, even though the investigators concluded that inexpe-
rience was not a decisive factor at Khost. CIA officials also tightened
security procedures for their overseas bases and established a system
of "red teams" to probe the agency's defenses as an enemy would do,
as well as internal reviews to guard against double agents and spies.

No single person or failure caused the disaster at Khost, the
investigators found. Yet just as had happened before the September 11 terrorist attacks, managers at every level were blinded to
warnings and problems that would seem screamingly obvious in
hindsight.

After September 11 a bipartisan commission sought to distill in
a single report why so many government departments had failed to
prevent al-Qaeda's plot to turn commercial jets into missiles against
the Pentagon and the World Trade Center. The 9/11 Commission

identified scores of tactical mistakes by the CIA, the FBI, and others, but it said the larger lapse was the agencies' inability to conceive of the inconceivable.

"The most important failure was one of imagination," the panel said in its 2004 report.

The suicide attack on Khost, while hardly comparable in scale, shared in at least this one root cause. Before December 30, 2009, no one at the CIA had dreamed that an informant would set up a meeting with his handlers just so he could kill them along with himself. Over the course of the CIA's first sixty-two years, a multitude of double agents, informants, and spies had lied, defrauded, betrayed, stolen money, or skipped town. Not one had ever blown himself up.

Balawi, through the power of his manufactured evidence, put himself on a path that would inevitably end with a confrontation. Foresight might have limited the number of deaths, yet even the most powerful and prescient observer could not have constrained the two singular forces that collided in Khost in the fading light of December 30, 2009.

One was the mind of Humam al-Balawi, a man who scudded and wove between towering waves, unsure of his destination and never exactly what he seemed.

The other was the eagerness of war-weary spies who saw a mirage and desperately wanted it to be real.

Arlington's marble headstones had lain beneath a thick blanket of snow when Leon Panetta visited in January to preside over the burials of Jennifer Matthews and Darren LaBonte. Now the cemetery was ablaze with color, from crimson tulips and pink dogwood blossoms to the emerald green of new grass, all bathed in brilliant sunshine. More than three hundred people, including a large contingent of Elizabeth Hanson's CIA friends, trooped quietly through the rows of headstones to stand with her parents and brother at her graveside. Two of them walked with crutches because of leg wounds suffered in the bombing at Khost.

The crowd gathered beneath a giant oak tree that shaded the spot where Hanson's ashes, in a mahogany box bearing the CIA seal, was to be buried. An honor guard folded an American flag, which was presented to Hanson's mother. "She guarded the flag, and now the flag guards her forever," the military chaplain said.

As the eulogies were spoken, Panetta's chief of staff, Jeremy Bash, stood near the back of the crowd with an eye on his muted cell phone. The wait was nearly over. It was time for a decision, and this one would be harder than most.

Near the Pakistani town of Miranshah, two of the agency's drones had been monitoring the same mud-brick building for hours, watching for any sign of movement. The man inside was believed to be Sheikh Saeed al-Masri, but the truth was, the agency was less than sure. Earlier in the spring the CIA's targeters had come close, but the sheikh slipped away before the Predators were in place. This time a tip led the agency to a cluster of buildings a few miles northwest of Miranshah. The structures were watched for days as counterterrorism officers narrowed down where precisely al-Masri was staying and who else shared the space with him.

The CIA did know that there were noncombatants in the compound, because at least two women and several children had been seen entering. The risks were grave this time, but the potential prize was huge: al-Qaeda's No. 3 commander, on this day of all days.

If it was really him.

The service ended with no further word from Pakistan. Panetta paid his respects to Hanson's family, and the CIA director's black car pulled out of the cemetery and headed north, away from Washington and toward Baltimore. Panetta had an appointment at the National Security Agency, the government's electronic eavesdropping service, and the hunt for al-Masri would follow him there.

Panetta had scarcely arrived at the NSA building when he was summoned to one of the agency's secure phones. The CIA's counterterrorism chief had fresh news, not all of it good.

"We think we've got this guy, but there may be some collateral damage," the chief was saying, referring to the women and children believed to be in the building the agency's drones were watching.

Panetta's heart sank. Nothing was coming easy with this one. He called Emanuel's office again. The White House was nervous too.

"It's your decision," Panetta was told.

The CIA director sat quietly for a moment, the day's events replaying in his brain. He picked up the phone again and called his counterterrorism director.

"Look, I need to know how certain you feel about the target," he began. "This is really important."

"Eighty percent," the counterterrorism chief was saying. "Maybe ninety percent, in terms of knowing we have the right target."

The numbers weren't the ones Panetta was hoping for. But this might well be the best chance the agency would ever get.

"I don't see how I can't do it," he finally said. "Go ahead."

Panetta hung up the phone and tried to focus on his meeting. Later in the afternoon he received reports about the missiles' deadly flight and the utter destruction of the targeted building. He learned of the recovery of bodies, and he was given the news—painful to contemplate for him—that two women and a child were among the dead. As for the fate of al-Masri himself, there was only silence out of Pakistan. Nothing more was learned during the rest of the day, or the following morning, or the day after that.

Then, on Memorial Day, the agency's surveillance network picked up the first snippet of conversation hinting of a momentous change in al-Qaeda's highest ranks. The terrorist group had lost one of its leaders, and the formal announcement would be posted soon on one of the usual jihadist Web sites. Al-Masri, the operational commander, had been targeted by a CIA missile at a safe house near Miranshah on May 21 and was now dead.

Panetta immediately picked up the phone and called his friend Emanuel at the White House.

"Rahm," he said, "we just took out Number Three."

The whereabouts of No. 1, bin Laden, and No. 2, Zawahiri, remained unknown.

EPILOGUE

On May 1, 2011, the same fierce desire to avenge September 11 that led to a terrible miscalculation at Khost produced a long-sought victory. Less than one year after al-Masri was confirmed dead, the hunt for bin Laden also ended.

Bin Laden, the CIA discovered, had been hiding not in the dusty borderlands between Afghanistan and Pakistan, but in a green valley town in Pakistan called Abbottabad, noted for its pleasant weather, shopping malls, and top-rated golf course. There, a half day's drive from the Afghan border, his followers had constructed a palatial compound for the al-Qaeda chief, far from the buzzing CIA drones and shielded from neighbors by twelve-foot walls topped with razor wire.

Bin Laden set up housekeeping within the compound in 2005, joined by three of his five wives and at least two of his eighteen children. The house had no telephone or Internet, but it had a shaded garden for morning strolls and a balcony with its own seven-foot-tall privacy barrier so the terrorist mastermind could sun himself in seclusion. His third-floor bedroom window afforded a view of cabbage fields, grazing cattle, and craggy hills, while the satellite TV served up a daily diet of Arab-language soap operas and news shows. In March 2011, in his sixth year inside the compound, he quietly marked his fifty-fourth birthday, a middle-aged man with graying locks and a thickening waist, his once-towering global ambitions now confined to a space smaller than a soccer field.

Unknown to him, even this small sanctuary was soon to disappear.

Thousands of miles away in another green suburb, tiny scraps of data, collected and studied by scores of different people over nearly a decade, had been assembled like a giant puzzle to reveal a possible answer to one of the most vexing mysteries of the age. For the first time since the attacks of September 11, 2001, the CIA believed it knew where to find bin Laden.

The trail of evidence stretched across three continents. It started in Pakistan, where security forces captured a pair of midlevel al-Qaeda operatives with knowledge of the terrorist group's inner workings. It wound through a secret CIA prison in Eastern Europe, where the interrogation of one of the men yielded a partial name. It picked up intensity in Langley, Virginia, where Jennifer Matthews and her colleagues in the CIA's bin Laden unit poured over the new data searching for patterns and connections. In 2007, it reached the office of then-CIA director Michael V. Hayden, who was briefed by his senior counterterrorism advisers one morning about a potentially momentous discovery: They had learned the name of the trusted al-Qaeda courier who served as bin Laden's personal connection to the outside world. All that remained was to find the man who would lead them to bin Laden's door.

"We think we've found a path forward," one of Hayden's briefers said.

The task of locating bin Laden's courier could take months or even years, Hayden knew, but he considered the discovery important enough to warrant a full airing during one of his regular meetings with President George W. Bush and his national security advisers. True, there had been other promising leads—some of them more akin to Elvis Presley sightings than intelligence tips, Hayden thought. This one seemed more promising than most, but it was not, he cautioned, a breakthrough.

"There is rarely a 'eureka' moment," Hayden has said. "It's one grain of sand at a time."

Indeed, the progress in finding the courier remained agonizingly slow. The man had first come to the CIA's attention soon after the September 11 attacks, when investigators learned of bin Laden's preference for using personal couriers to send messages, rather than relying on e-mail or phone calls that could be electronically tracked. Captured Afghan fighters spoke of a particularly favored courier, a young Pashtun businessman who was known within al-Qaeda circles by his jihadist name, Abu Ahmed al-Kuwaiti. But it took the CIA several years and a series of lucky breaks—including the arrests of the two al-Qaeda operatives in Pakistan in 2004 and 2005—before the agency discovered his real name: Sheikh Abu Ahmed. Still, CIA officials had no idea where to find him.

In 2007, with Hayden at the helm, the CIA embarked on a massive search for the mysterious courier. The National Security Agency, with its computer networks and global eavesdropping capabilities, swept phone and Internet lines for the name. At the CIA's Counterterrorism Center, Elizabeth Hanson's team of targeters assembled a profile of the man and scrubbed interrogation transcripts for clues that might lead to a family member, business connection, or hometown. The search was still active in the closing weeks of 2009 when Matthews and Hanson, by then at Khost, turned their attention to another possible path to bin Laden's inner circle, the Jordanian agent Humam al-Balawi.

A few weeks after Elizabeth Hanson was laid to rest, the CIA finally hit pay dirt. In early summer 2010, the NSA was conducting routine phone surveillance of a suspected Pakistani terrorist when a man named Sheikh Abu Ahmed came on the line. Within days, the CIA had tracked Abu Ahmed to the Pakistani city of Peshawar and identified his car and license plate. Then, in August, agency operatives followed the man to his principal residence, a suspiciously large, highly secure compound in Abbottabad with high walls capped with razor wire. Many of the dwelling's features stood out as strange, including its lack of a phone or Internet connection, and the owner's penchant for burning his trash rather than hauling it to the street. The three-story main building appeared to be shared by at least three families, including a tall, bearded man who, intriguingly, had never been seen outside the walls.

Beginning that month, the CIA turned its full attention to discerning the bearded man's identity.

Through the fall and winter, in a process closely tracked by CIA director Leon Panetta and his top aides, the agency studied the dwelling, using satellites, sophisticated listening gear, and spies on the ground. More than once, agency cameras captured the image of the mystery man pacing inside the compound's walls. Everything about him fit bin Laden's description, but his face could not be clearly seen.

Around the time of bin Laden's birthday in March 2011, Panetta gave the first of several presentations to the White House's national security team. There was no hard proof, he acknowledged, that the occupant of the Abbottabad compound was the terrorist leader. Panetta himself judged the probability to be no better than 60 to 80 percent.

But that, he argued, was close enough.

"When you put it all together," Panetta recalled telling White House officials, "we have the best evidence since Tora Bora. And that makes it clear that we have an obligation to act."

He continued: "We're probably at a point where we've got the best intelligence we can get."

Just after midnight Afghanistan time on May 2, a warm, humid night with the barest sliver of a moon, a pair of specially modified U.S. MH-60 helicopters slipped across the border on their way to Abbottabad. The choppers sprinted across 120 miles of Pakistan, skimming treetops and hugging mountain ridges to avoid detection by Pakistani radar. Only a few dozen Americans knew about the flight, and many of them were seated at that hour around a conference table in the White House's Situation Room, watching anxiously as the mission unfolded on large TV monitors. Appearing on a separate screen was Panetta, who was tasked with narrating the events from his command center across the Potomac River in Langley.

President Barack Obama, wearing an open-collar dress shirt and casual jacket, leaned forward in his seat, his elbows resting on his knees. He frowned at the screen and said little as Panetta reviewed again the likely contours of the mission, as well as the formidable risks. Obama understood these well; three days earlier, in the same room, the president's national security team had given him a long list of possible outcomes, many of them frightful. If there was to be any U.S. strike on the compound, a missile lobbed from a Predator or stealth bomber would be safer for Americans, Obama was told. And yet, a bomb would almost certainly kill women and children, inflame Pakistanis, and leave Americans in doubt about whether they had succeeded in hitting their intended target. On the other hand, sending American soldiers into the compound could be even more perilous. U.S. soldiers could be captured or killed by al-Qaeda, drawn into gun fights with local civilians, or blasted from the sky by Pakistani military jets whose pilots would know nothing of the secret U.S. mission. Alternatively, the Americans might successfully fight their way into the Abbottabad compound only to find they had nabbed a different tall, middle-aged man, one with a passing resemblance to bin Laden.

Obama weighed the risks overnight in his private quarters before deciding to roll the dice. He would send in the Navy SEALs, highly trained commandos who hailed from the Virginia Beach base that Blackwater guard Jeremy Wise had once called home.

Now a nervous hush fell over the Situation Room as the president and his advisers followed the movement of the two Black Hawks on the TV monitors. The choppers, carrying about two dozen commandos and crew members, thundered into Abbottabad on schedule just after 1:00 A.M. but immediately ran into trouble. One helicopter was to hover over the main house while the commandos rappelled from ropes onto the roof. Instead, the chopper malfunctioned and landed hard in an outer courtyard, its tail rotor hopelessly damaged after striking a wall during the descent.

The commandos from both birds then clambered over the walls

into the main courtyard, only to come under automatic rifle fire. One of bin Laden's protectors who lived in the compound had been roused from his bed by the commotion and began spraying bullets in the direction of the black-clad figures pouring over the walls in the dark.

The Americans with their night-vision equipment quickly overwhelmed the defender, killing the shooter and a woman who was caught in the crossfire. Two other men were killed as the commandos stormed the main building, including one later described by U.S. officials as an adult son of bin Laden.

The minutes ticked by, and still the SEALs had seen nothing of the man they were seeking. The commandos scoured the compound in two teams, one of which began methodically clearing the rooms on each floor of the main house. From that moment and continuing for what seemed like hours, the TV monitors in the Situation Room essentially went dark.

"Once those teams went into the compound, I can tell you that there was a time period of almost twenty or twenty-five minutes where we really didn't know just exactly what was going on," Panetta recalled afterward. "There were some very tense moments."

It would be days before the full details were known about the bloody struggle that ensued on the compound's third floor. Working slowly to avoid booby traps, one of the SEAL teams picked its way through a maze of barriers on the staircase until they found themselves outside the entrance to the last of three separate living quarters. After breaking the door, the two lead commandos burst into the room in time to see a dark-robed figure charging toward them. One of the men squeezed off a round, and the figure, a woman, dropped to the floor, wounded in the leg. Behind her in the dim light the Americans could perceive a tall man with a long, gray-flecked beard, wearing loose-fitting Pakistani-style pajama pants and kameez tunic. The man was neither cowering nor armed but standing defiantly. SEAL training demanded a split-second judgment. There was no hint of surrender. Was the man wearing a bomb?

The first shot caught the bearded man squarely in the chest. The next one pierced the side of his forehead near the eyebrows, blowing out the front of his skull.

For the listeners at the White House and in Langley, the muted sounds of struggle were impossible to interpret. More minutes passed without a further sign, and then, finally, a male voice came through the speaker.

"Visual on Geronimo," the voice said, using a prearranged code. Bin Laden's identity had been confirmed.

Within minutes, the SEALs were safely in their choppers—a third one had been dispatched to replace the broken bird—carrying with them a large cache of computer equipment taken from the compound, as well as bin Laden's bloodied corpse.

The entire operation had lasted forty minutes. Moments later, when the helicopters crossed into Afghan air space and out of range of Pakistani interceptors, the group in the Situation Room burst into spontaneous applause.

"We got him," Obama finally said.

The following morning, as millions of Americans awoke to the news of bin Laden's death, Panetta paused in his Langley office to compose a brief message that would be distributed that day to CIA employees around the world. It was in large part a congratulatory note, commending the agency's men and women for achieving a goal that had eluded them for nearly a decade.

"Today, we have rid the world of the most infamous terrorist of our time," Panetta began.

Then, in a somber turn, Panetta paid special tribute to CIA officers who had not lived to see their work bear fruit. "Our heroes at Khost," he wrote, "are with us, in memory and spirit, at this joyful moment."

The fight was not yet over, Panetta knew. There would be a new No. 1 at al-Qaeda. Almost certainly, there would be retaliatory attacks, perhaps major ones. But not on this day.

It was a balmy May morning with brilliant streaks of sun, just like the one a year earlier in Arlington, and Panetta allowed himself a moment to bask in the achievement. The world had been made to feel a bit safer, at least for a time, and the quiet pledges made at eight American and Jordanian gravesides had been fulfilled.

"A promise," Panetta wrote, "has been kept."

AFTERWORD

Beginning on May 2, 2011, and continuing for months afterward, CIA analysts swarmed over Osama bin Laden's computer files and papers for a chance to peer directly into the al-Qaeda leader's brain. They studied his handwritten journal in which he scribbled lists of future targets and calculated how many people would die. They examined the wooden box where he stashed his pornographic videos. They scoured computer disks and thumb drives where he stored tens of thousands of electronic records, a nearly complete archive of the communiqués, field reports, and private conversations between the terrorist commander and his deputies scattered throughout South Asia, North Africa, and the Middle East.

One name stood out among the others. *Atiyah.*

The al-Qaeda religious scholar and adviser known as Atiyah abd al-Rahman was everywhere in the document cache. Indeed, he appeared to be bin Laden's main link to the outside world in his final years. He was known simply as Atiyah—Arabic for "gift"—among both his comrades and CIA operatives, and his main job was to keep the old general informed about the group's sinking fortunes, from constant money shortages to the relentless toll of CIA drone strikes. Between such gloomy recitals, Atiyah fantasized with his boss about a future grand strike against the

United States, the long-awaited follow-up to September 11 that would reverse al-Qaeda's decline and rally its scattered armies. Again and again, Atiyah would suggest a name, a new recruit who might be ready to begin organizing such a feat. Not yet, bin Laden would reply.

The Atiyah who emerged from the documents was startling, and not just because of his unexpected climb to a top perch next to bin Laden's ear. The CIA had a history with Atiyah, and a special reason for regarding the man with particular loathing. Two years earlier, it had been Atiyah's unlined face and youthful beard that appeared next to Humam al-Balawi's in the first phony video the Jordanian spy had sent his handlers from Pakistan. Atiyah had played a star-ring role in luring the seven American operatives to their deaths at Khost.

Now, amid the tumult that followed bin Laden's death, Atiyah had surfaced again, in an entirely new light. It was clear that Atiyah was not merely the bait for Balawi's suicide plot. He was a co-author. And his involvement in the Balawi affair, analysts now understood, stretched back to the very beginning—long before Balawi's first tentative steps on Pakistani soil.

Any lingering doubt about Balawi's identity and intentions was sloughed away in the face of the new revelations. Balawi was, and had always been, a triple agent. And Atiyah was the missing piece of the puzzle.

Exactly when and how Atiyah and Balawi first connected is unclear, but U.S. and Jordanian officials believe it happened in 2008, when Balawi was rising to prominence as the Internet essayist Abu Dujana Khorasani. Atiyah, a Libyan who had joined the jihadi movement in hopes of overthrowing his country's dictator, Colonel Moammar Ghadafi, had gained renown by then as one of al-Qaeda's rising stars, an original thinker who, like Balawi, was in his thirties and spoke the language of the Internet generation. At some point Balawi decided to try to contact Atiyah through intermediaries he had met online. And Atiyah, against all reasonable expectation, chose to write back.

The two men struck up a secret correspondence that continued over several weeks. But it did not remain secret for long. American eavesdroppers picked up the exchange and, suddenly, in late 2008, the search for the Islamist writer known as Abu Dujana took on new urgency. In an element of the Balawi case that would remain closely held for years, U.S. and Jordanian intelligence officials became increasingly alarmed about the blogger's contact with a known al-Qaeda figure, and poured new energy into the effort to find him. Abu Dujana, the writer, was already regarded as a dangerous subversive; now, because of his acquaintance with Atiyah, he also was viewed as potentially valuable.

The connection would grow in significance in the weeks to come. Hours after his arrest in January 2009, Balawi was confronted about his relationship with Atiyah in the interrogation room of the Mukhabarat's Knights of Truth. Balawi had no choice but to confess to having had contact; the Jordanian spy agency had copies of his e-mails. But what else could the doctor provide, his questioners wanted to know. Would Balawi consent to contact Atiyah again, as the Mukhabarat watched?

Yes, Balawi finally said, as he collapsed emotionally on the third day of his interrogation. *I will.*

The particulars of how he would assist his new Jordanian minders were still unclear when Balawi was sent back home to brood over his options. Much later, in retelling the story in Pakistan, Balawi said he felt his destiny was being guided by a divine hand: In one of their last exchanges before his arrest, Balawi said, he had confided to Atiyah about wanting to travel to Pakistan to fight alongside al-Qaeda. And Atiyah had agreed that he should.

If you decide to come, I will help you, Atiyah wrote back, according to an account written two years later by Abu al-Hassan al-Wa'ili, one of the Libyan's deputies.

Balawi did he as promised, sending messages to Atiyah from

Amman during the icy weeks of late winter 2009 while under the Mukhabarat's microscope. Then, after agreeing to travel to Pakistan as a spy for the Jordanians, Balawi wrote again to say he was on his way to the land of jihad and would seek to join Atiyah there.

Thus, when Balawi landed in Pakistan in March, one specific mission outranked all others: finding Atiyah. Balawi had been promised a hefty cash reward even if he could achieve only this feat. And while the odds for success were still judged to be long, they were not remote. There was at least a plausible path to al-Qaeda for Balawi if he could survive the journey.

Nearly five months would pass before Atiyah's protectors would allow such a meeting. After landing in the Pakistani frontier city of Peshawar, Balawi threw away the stethoscope the Jordanians had given him, fearing that it contained a tracking device. Then he began the slow, perilous climb through the tiers of lower-ranking Taliban emissaries who could grant access to Taliban leader Baitullah Mehsud and, with luck, to al-Qaeda itself.

The death of Mehsud finally presented the chance he had been waiting before. On August 8, 2009, he scribbled a note to be passed to Atiyah, making arrangements for the encounter. (A scanned copy of the note was posted on a Web site nearly three years later by al-Wa'ili).

"By Allah, I have yearned to meet you, Sheikh," Balawi wrote. He ventured a modest pun: "I spent two months conspiring with the enemies of Allah to kill you. So, when I meet you I will squeeze you to my chest."

Within weeks, working with Atiyah and under the supervision of Sheikh Saeed al-Masri, the outlines of what became the Khost plot began to form. Atiyah posed with Balawi for the fake video that was e-mailed to the CIA late that same month. Then the two worked together on revising their plan when it became clear that bin Zeid would not be lured into Pakistan for a meeting. Al-Wa'ili's account described Atiyah as "the most important pillar" in the suicide plot after Balawi himself and a "second hero of the operation."

The account acknowledges that many in al-Qaeda's camp continued to doubt Balawi, despite Atiyah's obvious enthusiasm, until the very end. One night shortly before Balawi departed for his mission, one of the jihadists who shared the same house became suspicious after seeing Balawi slip out of his bedclothes in the middle of the night to go outdoors.

"He searched the bag of Abu Dujana and openly confronted him," al-Wa'ili wrote in his account. Bawali replied that he had gone outside to pray.

Yet, al-Qaeda kept a wary eye on Balawi and sent spies to follow him on the first leg of his journey. On December 30, operatives secretly videotaped Balawi as he met the CIA's Afghan driver at the Pakistan border crossing at Ghulam Khan, Wa'ili wrote. They continued to watch until the two men crossed into Afghanistan and disappeared over the mountains, headed for Khost.

The CIA's interest in Atiyah soared in the wake of Balawi's suicide attack, and soon the U.S. government was offering $1 million for his capture. But there were other important targets as well, and the agency's leaders were interested above all in the name at the top of the list: Osama bin Laden.

The Langley team that led the hunt was identical—almost to a person—to the one that had overseen the disaster at Khost. News accounts would describe the operation's final phase as remarkably harmonious, as querulous agencies put aside rivalries to plan the risky, ultra-secret assault on bin Laden's hideout. In fact, some on the CIA side chafed at the exclusion of intelligence officers from the Navy SEAL team that carried out the raid. The CIA's paramilitary officers—many of them highly trained special-forces officers, hardened from years of experience in Afghanistan—burned for a chance to avenge their comrades lost at Khost.

"There were guys who just wanted to be part of it," said one officer who knew several of the dead at Khost.

However, there was little doubt about the spy agency's ownership of the bin Laden mission, from the discovery of the hideout to the exploitation of more than a million electronic and paper pages seized from the compound.

The records revealed no imminent plans to attack the West, nor did they provide the agency with specific coordinates for Atiyah or any of the handful of other al-Qaeda commanders believed to be still hiding in Pakistan. But they offered instead a far deeper look into al-Qaeda's plans and thinking than had been possible before, as well as a rare yardstick for measuring the successes and failures of the agency's ten-year-old war against the terrorist group.

The insights hidden within bin Laden's long missives were both reassuring and troubling. The documents showed how fearful al-Qaeda had become of the pilotless drones that were now the backbone of the CIA's counterterrorism effort. But they also showed, yet again, the limits of waging war by remote control.

"It was clear that drones had imposed a high price on al-Qaeda," said Bruce Riedel, a thirty-year veteran of the CIA who served as an adviser on terrorism to President Obama. "It's premature to count them out, because al-Qaeda still has powerful allies and a base of support that allows them to be more resourceful than they otherwise would be. This is one of the lessons Khost."

Thus, he said, the fight continues, sometimes with success but always with the risk of miscalculation or overconfidence.

"Drones," he said, "are a brilliant weapon. But they are not a strategy."

A final bit of unfinished business awaited the CIA early on August 22, 2011, a brutally hot, muggy morning when yellow dust from newly harvested wheat fields clung to the valleys like a large suffocating cloud. A few miles east of the Pakistani town of Mir Ali, a small car bearing foreign visitors pulled into a village called Norak and into the mud-brick compound of a tribal elder. Several men gathered in a courtyard to talk, oblivious to the presence of a Predator drone circling high overhead. Two missiles pierced the humid air and slammed into the courtyard with an explosion that demolished the car and crumbled one of the buildings.

Among the four bodies recovered was that of a slim, young-looking man with a mustache and wispy beard, and a boy believed to be the man's son. The death of Atiyah abd al-Rahman was officially confirmed weeks later by bin Laden's successor, Ayman al-Zawahiri, the last survivor among the original planners of the Khost operation.

Zawahiri, his gray beard now nearly white, had turned sixty in a year that witnessed not only the death of bin Laden but also a string of uprisings throughout the Middle East. In Zawahiri's native Egypt, boisterous but mostly peaceful crowds had overthrown the country's secularist dictator, something al-Qaeda had dreamed of doing by force. Once Zawahiri's name had evoked fear around the world, and the mere chance of capturing him had led the CIA into its worst stumble in a quarter century. Now he was in hiding, enfeebled and nearly alone. Every few months he would dutifully appear again, a shrinking figure on a small screen, to deliver his tirades against the West. But his words were all but ignored by the youths who surged into the central squares of Cairo, Tunis, and Benghazi. History itself had passed him by.

The old physician looked tired as he stood before a video camera to read a long tribute to Atiyah. He praised his disciple as a "fighter for Islam," and he said that Atiyah had spent his last evening watching in fascination as rebels in his native Libya encircled Tripoli. Atiyah had even recorded a message of encouragement addressed to "my brothers" in Libya, saying he longed to join them but could not, because of the "jihad I am in, against our enemies, your enemies, Islam's enemies: the Americans and the Christian NATO alliance."

Atiyah was killed before the message could be transmitted. Two days later, under assault by a rebel force backed by NATO airpower and protected by American drones, Tripoli fell.

ACKNOWLEDGMENTS

A project of this size is always a collaboration, but in this case there are numerous individuals without whom this book quite literally could not have been written. Some of them are generous colleagues who assisted me in Afghanistan, Pakistan, and the Middle East, sometimes exposing themselves to risk. Others are current and former government officials who shared my belief in the importance of this story. Still others are relatives and spouses of slain officers who gave me their trust and shared precious and often painful memories. Several sources in the latter two groups were extraordinarily generous with their time and insights, meeting with me a dozen times or more. Yet, some of them can never be acknowledged by name because they are restricted from speaking publicly by secrecy rules or confidentiality agreements. To each of them I owe an enormous debt of gratitude.

I have been privileged over the past fourteen years to work for a world-class news organization that nurtures journalists and supports their professional growth. I am grateful to the *Washington Post* and its editors for granting me a leave of absence to work on this book, and for offering encouragement and support in countless other ways. Special thanks go to Washington Post Company board chairman Donald E. Graham and publisher Katharine Weymouth, who offered personal encouragement along the way, as well as executive editor Marcus Brauchli, managing editor Liz Spayd, and national editor Kevin Merida. I am especially indebted to my immediate supervisors, national security editor Cameron Barr and deputy editor Jason Ukman, for their kindness, patience, and advice. A great many current and former *Post* colleagues assisted me in this journey, but I am particularly grateful to David Hoffman, Peter Finn, R. Jeffrey Smith, Ellen Nakashima, David Ignatius, Greg Miller, Karen DeYoung, Steve Coll, Bob Woodward, Jeff Stein, Walter Pincus, Robert Miller, Michel du Cille, Rajiv Chandrasekaran, Karin Brulliard, Josh Partlow, Dana Priest, Glenn Kessler, Mary Beth Sheridan, John Pomfret, and David Finkel. Several colleagues and friends read some or all of the manuscript and offered helpful suggestions and feedback, including Cameron Barr, David Rowell, Jeff Leen, and a friend from the clandestine world whose expert advice, unflagging enthusiasm, and extraordinary kindness sustained me through many a rough patch. Many others provided critical technical assistance and insight, including Rita Katz of SITE Intelligence Group, Ben Venzke of IntelCenter, Jarret Brachman, and numerous current and former members of the intelligence and defense agencies of the United States, Jordan, and Pakistan. Suzanne Kelly, a talented author and CNN producer who shared my fascination for this story, is owed special thanks for her ideas, inspiration, and selfless generosity.

I was fortunate to have the help of several extraordinarily talented, hardworking assistants and collaborators both in Washington and abroad. I was ably assisted in Jordan by the ever-resourceful journalist, translator, "fixer," and occasional hotelier, Ranya Kadri; in Turkey by Mahmut Kaya; in Afghanistan by Hazrat Bahar; and in Pakistan by the indefatigable Haq Nawaz Khan and another Pakistani journalist whose name cannot be revealed for security reasons. I benefited immeasurably from the friendship and assistance of one of print journalism's great news researchers, the incomparable Julie Tate. My wonderful agent, Gail Ross, together with her partner, Howard Yoon, saw the potential in my ill-formed proposal and guided me through an anxious first foray into the publishing world with grace and good humor.

Doubleday and its staff embraced my project with energy and enthusiasm, and worked tirelessly over many months to bring it to fruition. I am enormously grateful to editor in chief William J. Thomas, assistant editor Stephanie Bowen, and the many others who provided critical help with photos and illustrations, editing, legal counsel, and marketing. Throughout this journey I was blessed with one of the best gifts any writer can have: a truly great editor. Doubleday's Kris Puopolo brought extraordinary talents to this endeavor and was a true partner and collaborator at every stage of the process. Her vision and passion made the book immeasurably better, and her patience and wit kept me sane through long weeks of reporting and writing.

I am eternally indebted to my family and friends, whose faith and support sustained me. Among my friends, Paul Scicchitano is owed special thanks for his encouragement and his insights into the publishing world. My parents, Eugene and Barbara Warrick, sister Gena Fisher, and mother-in-law Theresa Jordan were tireless boosters who helped my family during my trips abroad. My wife, Maryanne, cheerfully bore many additional burdens during my yearlong project and was an invaluable partner, offering inspiration and advice at the earliest stages as the idea took shape, as well as research and logistical help, and numerous incisive suggestions on structural changes to the manuscript. My children, Victoria and Andrew, tolerated my absences, virtual absences, abbreviated vacations, missed recitals and ball games, and general distractedness with understanding and grace. We have a lot of catching up to do.

A NOTE ON SOURCES

This book is the result of a year's worth of conversations with men and women who, by necessity, live and work in the shadows. A great many of the primary sources were either active members of intelligence agencies—chiefly the Central Intelligence Agency and Jordan's General Intelligence Department, but also others—or members of the military Special Forces units. Some were trusted sources developed over years of reporting on intelligence matters for the *Washington Post*. Others were current or former senior officials in intelligence agencies who agreed to discuss the Khost tragedy and the larger war on terrorism on the condition that they not be quoted or identified directly as sources. The insistence on anonymity, while unfortunate, could be broadly justified by the classified nature of the events and programs at the center of the story. The Khost base, its primary mission, and even the identities of many of its operatives are protected under U.S. government secrecy provisions. Moreover, America's use of unmanned aircraft to strike terrorist targets in Pakistan, though a well-known fact in both countries, is officially a classified program that cannot be publicly acknowledged by CIA or White House officials. Finally, in addition to government sources, several relatives of slain officers asked not to be associated by name with specific anecdotes and facts. These requests were driven by con-

cern that the speaker might unwittingly divulge sensitive information or complicate ongoing interactions with intelligence agencies.

Because so many sources are anonymous, I have gone to great
lengths to separately corroborate each of the essential facts in this narrative, conducting more than two hundred interviews in the places
where the events occurred—Afghanistan, Jordan, Turkey—and in
various locations in the United States. Memories and documents,
including private e-mails and texts, were shared by intelligence officials and operatives from three countries. Other recollections and
important contextual details were provided by current and former
members of the George W. Bush and Barack Obama administra-
tions, as well as diplomatic officials and U.S. military personnel who
either served at the Khost base or were colleagues or friends of the
fallen officers. Relatives and friends of each of the individuals killed
in the Khost attack provided critical, and often enthusiastic, support. In attempting to understand the thoughts and motivations of
Humam al-Balawi, I relied on interviews with family members and
former colleagues of his at the Marka clinic or elsewhere, as well as
a large body of interviews, essays, and video statements by Balawi
himself. I also spoke directly, or through my assistants in Pakistan
and Afghanistan, with members of the Taliban and other jihadist
groups who either met with Balawi or were personally informed
about his activities during his ten months in the Pakistani tribal
region.

Despite the diversity of viewpoints, the sources agreed in most
cases on the essential details. On the rare occasions when differ-
ing accounts could not be reconciled, I made judgments based on
which source appeared to have a clearer view of the facts in question.
Where sources could not be named in the text or footnotes, I sought
to explain the source's relationship to the characters and events as
clearly as possible while honoring promises not to reveal identifying
details.

NOTES

Chapter 1: Obsession

9 The man was called Osama al-Kini: The details of the CIA's operation against al-Kini were provided in author interviews with two current and two former agency officials with direct knowledge of the events.

12 "This is now a bona fide threat to the homeland": Author interview with former U.S. government official present at the White House meeting.

13 "If you had to ask for permission": Ibid.

13 "simultaneous notification": The basis of the new U.S. policy was described to the author in interviews with two former senior intelligence officials involved in the policy discussions, and confirmed separately by a congressional official briefed on the policy change at the time.

15 a massive truck bombing: For details on the Marriott Hotel attack, see Bill Roggio, "Bombing at Islamabad Marriott Latest in String of Complex Terror Attacks," *Long War Journal*, Sept. 21, 2008, http://www .longwarjournal.org/archives/2008/09/bombing_at_islamabad.php.

15 a commander named Sheikh Saeed al-Masri: Details of al-Masri's expanded role within al-Qaeda beginning in 2007, as well the competition among rival commanders, were supplied to the author in interviews with one former and two current CIA officers involved in counterterrorism operations during the period.

17 Hayden's initial meeting with his successor: Events described to author in interviews with two intelligence officers who witnessed the exchange.

Chapter 2: Haunted

20 chief liaison on counterterrorism to Britain: Details of Matthews's experiences in London and her previous work at CIA headquarters and Thailand were recounted in author interviews with eight former agency colleagues as well as two relatives who were in frequent communication with her during the relevant periods.

20 sophisticated double suicide bombing: Separate accounts of the attack were obtained from International Security Assistance Force incident logs for Afghanistan's eastern district on Jan. 19, 2009, and an interview with a Khost regional police commander who investigated the incident. The ISAF records were first posted by the anti-secrecy Web site WikiLeaks in July 2010.

22 Inspector General, had launched a wide-ranging investigation: For details of the redacted report, see CIA Office of Inspector General, "Report on CIA Accountability with Respect to the 9/11 Attacks," June 2005, http://www.foia.cia.gov/docs/DOC_0001499482/DOC _0001499482.pdf.

23 list of names remain classified: For a fuller description of the CIA's deliberations over the release of names, see "CIA OIG [Office of Inspector General] Timeline" at HistoryCommons.com, http://www.historycommons.org/timeline.jsp?investigations:_a_detailed_look=complete_911 _timeline_cia_oig_9_11_report&timeline=complete_911_timeline, accessed on Sept. 30, 2010.

27 attempted to distill his advice: Author interview with former senior CIA official.

Chapter 3: The Doctor

28 The raiding party gathered: Details of Humam al-Balawi's arrest, detention, and interrogation were provided in author interviews with two family members present during the relevant events; three current Jordanian intelligence officers and one former intelligence officer who were present during the events or were given detailed briefings; and a senior CIA officer who was similarly briefed. Additional details were drawn from Balawi's videotaped statements about his arrests, as provided to the author by SITE Intelligence Group, a private group that monitors Web sites associated with extremist groups and provides

analysis to government agencies, news organizations, and other customers on a restricted-access basis.

32 *"Your handcuffs will be as silver bracelets"*: English excerpts from Balawi's Internet blogs as Abu Dujana al-Khorasani were provided, along with analysis, by Jarret Brachman, a terrorism expert, author, and government consultant.

32 He was also an instant hit: For analysis of Balawi's impact as jihadist blogger, see Brachman's monograph "Abu Dujana al-Khorasani," in publication.

33 Defne, began to worry: Insight into Balawi family dynamics is provided in press interviews by Defne Bayrak, including her February 5, 2010, interview with al-Jazeera Television's *Today's Interview* program. English translation courtesy of SITE Intelligence Group. Additional corroboration provided in author interviews with two of Defne Bayrak's journalist colleagues in Istanbul, Turkey.

33 Abu Dujana was a seventh-century Arab warrior: For more on Balawi's namesake, see "Abu Dujana, Stories of the Sahaba," as reprinted in http://www.articlesbase.com/spirituality-articles/abu-dujana-stories -of-the-sahaba-1532056.html.

35 Code-named Turbulence, it is a five-hundred-million-dollar-a-year network: For an authoritative account of the NSA's secret data-collection network, see James Bamford, *The Shadow Factory* (New York: Anchor Books, 2008).

35 he was known among his peers as Sharif Ali: Biographical details about Ali bin Zeid and his interaction with the Balawi case were shared with the author in interviews with three bin Zeid family members and two of his Mukhabarat colleagues.

37 "He wasn't flirty like some of the others": Author interview with former patient of Balawi's, Marka refugee camp, Amman, Jordan.

38 so closely reflected Zawahiri's own views: Author interview with Jarret Brachman.

38 coordinated attacks on hotels in Amman: For details on the Amman hotel bombings, see Hassan Fattah and Michael Slackman, "Hotels Bombed in Jordan; at Least 57 Die," *New York Times*, Nov. 10, 2005.

39 Zarqawi, who had spent five years as the Mukhabarat's prisoner: For more on Zarqawi's radicalization and later exploits, see Lee Hudson Teslik, "Profile: Abu Musab al-Zarqawi," Council on Foreign Relations

backgrounder, "Profile: Abu Musab al-Zarqawi," CFR online, June 8, 2006.

Chapter 4: Humiliation

41 He was in a small cell: In addition to the primary sources on Balawi's interrogation as described in Chapter 2 notes, further insights into the Mukhabarat's detention facility and procedures were provided in author interviews with two former Mukhabarat officers and an Amman jihadist who related his personal experiences in repeated incarcerations and interrogations.

44 Balawi remembered his dream: Balawi describes his dream while in Mukhabarat custody in a Dec. 26, 2009, videotaped interview obtained by SITE Intelligence Group. English translation courtesy of SITE.

46 On the third day of Humam al-Balawi's incarceration: Circumstances of Balawi's release described in author interviews with two Balawi family members in Amman, Jordan.

Chapter 5: The Informant

50 The report bore an Arabic caption: Report described to the author in interviews with a Jordanian and a U.S. intelligence officer who reviewed its contents.

51–52 with a known terrorist organization in Turkey: The Balawis' interaction with the IBAD-C was described to the author by two of Defne Bayrak's colleagues, who were aware of the couple's contacts with the organization at the time. For more on the group, see http://www.globalsecurity.org/military/world/para/eastern-raiders.htm.

52 "I liked his personality": Defne Bayrak interview with al-Jazeera, Feb. 5, 2010, op. cit.

52 peculiar to privileged young adults: For more on this phenomenon, see Delia Lloyd, "Smart Bombers: Do Universities Breed Terrorists?" *Politics Daily*, Jan. 2010, http://www.politicsdaily.com/2010/01/19/smart-bombers-do-universities-breed-terrorists/.

53 The couple named their older girl: Author interview with a Balawi family friend, Istanbul, Turkey.

56 a promise to redraw the country's counterterrorism priorities: For

an insider's view of the administration's early priorities, see speech by White House counterterrorism adviser John Brennan, "A New Approach to Safeguarding Americans," Aug. 6, 2009, before the Center for Strategic and International Studies, as published on the White House's Web site, WhiteHouse.gov., http://www.whitehouse.gov/the _press_office/Remarks-by-John-Brennan-at-the-Center-for-Strategic -and-International-Studies.

58 Balawi was gradually checking out of his old life: Details about Balawi's activities in his final weeks in Amman were described in author interviews with two family members and a colleague at the Marka clinic.

59 bin Zeid tucked a case of dog food under his arm: Balawi describes his meetings and discussions with bin Zeid in his Dec. 26, 2009, interview, SITE, op. cit.

61 *I think we should talk to our father about this*: Airport departure described in author interviews with two Balawi family members.

Chapter 6: Targets

62 *Nuclear devices*: This unreported event was described in author interviews with two senior intelligence officials and a separate interview with one Obama administration official, all of whom were actively involved in the response to the threat.

65 "Are you sure this was the right choice?": Author interview with a U.S. official present during the White House exchange about Panetta's candidacy.

65 Panetta's stance on the so-called torture memos: Peter Finn and Joby Warrick, "Under Panetta, a More Aggressive CIA," *Washington Post*, March 21, 2010.

66 change a missile's trajectory in midflight: Capabilities of advanced munitions used by Predators described in author interviews with two current and one former senior intelligence official.

66 inadvertently killed nine people: Ibid. For alternative views on civilian casualties, see Peter Bergen and Katherine Tiedemann, "Revenge of the Drone," New America Foundation, Oct. 19, 2009, http://www .newamerica.net/files/appendix1.pdf.

66 "I don't take it lightly": Account of Panetta's personal views and experiences described in interviews with three senior intelligence officials

and an Obama administration official who participated in conversations in which the matters were discussed.

67 that group included Hanson: Hanson's work duties, personality, and character described in multiple author interviews with five former agency colleagues and two family members.

70 the top items on the agenda were Mehsud: New details about National Security Adviser James L. Jones's trip to Pakistan described in author interviews with two senior intelligence officials involved in preparatory meetings for the visit.

71 The Taliban leader was officially blamed: Although Mehsud denied involvement in the Benazir Bhutto assassination, communications intercepts pointed to his foreknowledge of the attempt on her life. See Joby Warrick, "CIA Places Blame for Bhutto Assassination," *Washington Post*, Jan. 17, 2008, http://www.washingtonpost.com/wp-dyn/content/article/2008/01/17/AR2008011703252.html.

72 Before sunrise on June 23: Details of the June 23, 2009, operations described in author interviews with two intelligence officers briefed on the events. For more on the attacks, see Bill Roggio, "Scores of Taliban Killed in Second US Strike in South Waziristan," *Long War Journal*, June 23, 2009, http://www.longwarjournal.org/archives/2009/06/seventeen_taliban_ki.php.

74 "It created a havoc": Unsigned report by *Dawn* news staff, "Missile Attacks Kill 50 in South Waziristan," *Dawn*, June 24, 2009, http://news.dawn.com/wps/wcm/connect/dawn-content-library/dawn/news/pakistan/04-suspected-us-drone-strikes-swaziristan-qs-03.

Chapter 7: The Jihadist

75 Humam al-Balawi arrived alone: Accounts of Balawi's early weeks in Pakistan were provided in author interviews with three U.S. and two Jordanian intelligence officials briefed on the events.

76 "You have made us proud": bin Zeid's words, as recalled by Balawi in Dec. 26, 2009, video interview, op. cit.

76 *I want to study medicine*: Defne Bayrak's account of her husband's explanation for his travels to Pakistan, as told to al-Jazeera in Feb. 5, 2010, interview, op. cit.

78 from his Taliban interviewer: Interview excerpts, as published in "An Interview with the Shaheed," posted by al-Sahab Web site on Feb. 28, 2010; English translation courtesy of SITE Intelligence Group.

79 The two had a mutual acquaintance: Descriptions of Balawi's relations
    with Mehsud and his early interactions with the Pakistan Taliban pro-
    vided interviews with a Tehrik-i-Taliban member and two Pakistani
    intelligence officers who later investigated the Balawi affair after the
    Khost bombing. Additional insights are drawn from Balawi's accounts
    of his meetings with the Taliban chief.

79 Qari had beheaded a kidnapped Polish geologist: For a descrip-
    tion of the incident, see Bill Roggio, "Taliban Feud over Murder
    of Polish Hostage," *Long War Journal*, Feb. 11, 2009, http://www
    .longwarjournal.org/archives/2009/02/taliban_feud_over_mu.php.

80 *I could go to FATA*: Description of Balawi's offer of his spying services
    in Pakistan provided in author interviews with two Jordanian and four
    U.S. intelligence officials. A detailed account of Balawi's meetings and
    conversations with bin Zeid about the assignment is related in Balawi's
    Dec. 26, 2009, videotaped interview, op. cit.

81 the "father of smoke": For more on the terrorist Imad Mughniyeh and
    the circumstances of his death, see Matthew Levitt and David Schen-
    ker, "Who Was Imad Mughniyeh?" Washington Institute for Near
    East Policy online, Feb. 14, 2008, http://www.washingtoninstitute.org
    /templateC05.php?CID=2716.

81 who had killed Abdullah Azzam: For more on the influential cleric
    and the circumstances of his death, see Aryn Baker, "Who Killed
    Abdullah Azzam?" *Time* (June 18, 2009), http://www.time.com/time/
    specials/packages/article/0,28804,1902809_1902810_1905173,00
    .html.

83 the logistics of Balawi's journey came together: Details about the
    arrangements for Balawi's insertion into Pakistan were described by
    two Jordanian and three U.S. intelligence officials personally knowl-
    edgeable or privy to classified briefings on the events.

84 he could make out a familiar form: Balawi describes his encounter
    with the guard Ahmad, a disabled Taliban fighter, while sleeping out-
    doors in a videotape essay titled, "O Hesitant One: It Is an Obligation!"
    posted by al-Qaeda's media arm, as-Sahab, April 30, 2010; English
    translation courtesy of SITE Intelligence Group.

85 "We pray to God": For a fuller description of the interview with Bai-
    tullah Mehsud, see Nick Schifrin, "More Dangerous than Osama: Mil-
    itant Leader Claims He Is Fighting a 'Defensive' Jihad to Destroy the
    White House," Brian Ross Reports, Jan. 28, 2008, ABC News online,
    http://abcnews.go.com/Blotter/story?id=4199754&page=1.

85 capturing an entire garrison: For a discussion of Baitullah Mehsud's
    defiance of Pakistan's government, see "Baitullah Mehsud," a Times
    People Topic, *New York Times*, Aug. 25, 2009, http://topics.nytimes
    .com/top/reference/timestopics/people/m/baitullah_mehsud/index
    .html.

85–86 the real target would be a decoy: This controversial story was described
    in detail by an official of the Pakistan Tehrik-i-Taliban Pakistan (TTP),
    the main Pakistani Taliban alliance, and related separately by two
    other Taliban associates, suggesting that it is a widely shared story
    that was used to establish Balawi's credibility. There is no independent
    corroboration of the event by the CIA or other U.S. sources.

86 "Every drone strike": Quote related in interview with Taliban official
    close to Mehsud.

86 his every move was being recorded: Detailed description of the attack
    on Baitullah Mehsud provided in author interviews with three U.S.
    intelligence officials involved in the planning or oversight of the opera-
    tion.

Chapter 8: Pressure

89 Taliban leader was "alive, safe and sound": "Taliban Ask Gov't
    to Prove Mehsud Death Rumors," AFP/Reuters, in *Nation* online,
    Aug. 11, 2009, http://www.nation.com.pk/pakistan-news-newspaper-
    daily-english-online/Politics/11-Aug-2009/Taliban-ask-govt-to-prove-
    Mehsud-death.

89 his staff was caught up in the drafting of a proposal: Details of the
    CIA's proposal for strengthening its campaign against al-Qaeda, and
    of the White House's reaction to the plan, were provided in author
    interviews with two senior intelligence officials and one administra-
    tion official involved either in the planning meetings or in the pre-
    sentation.

90 helicopter gunships swept the Taliban's valley: For a discussion of
    the Pakistani offensive in South Waziristan from its faltering start in
    June 2009 to its final phase in October, see Bill Roggio, "What Lies
    Ahead in Waziristan," *Long War Journal*, Oct. 17, 2009, http://www
    .longwarjournal.org/archives/2009/10/analysis_what_lies_a.php.

90 touched off several bloody rounds of: *Wall Street Journal* online, Aug.
    10, 2009, http://online.wsj.com/article/SB124976257139816985.html.

90 Shadow Army, a paramilitary force: Bill Roggio, "Al Qaeda's Paramilitary 'Shadow Army,'" *Long War Journal*, Feb. 9, 2009, http://www.longwarjournal.org/archives/2009/02/al_qaedas_paramilita.php.

92 technology had helped turn the tide against Iraq's insurgents: Bob Woodward, "Why Did Violence Plummet? It Wasn't Just the Surge," *Washington Post*, Sept. 8, 2008, http://www.washingtonpost.com/wp-dyn/content/article/2008/09/07/AR2008090701847.html.

93 "We don't know for a fact where Osama bin Laden is": Defense Secretary Robert Gates interview with George Stephanopoulos on ABC News' *This Week*, Dec. 5, 2009, http://blogs.abcnews.com/george/2009/12/where-is-bin-laden-secretary-gates-says-no-intel-in-years.html.

93 One of the most promising involved: Details of CIA discussions and activities during the six-year search for bin Laden's courier were described in interviews with two current and two former intelligence officials with direct knowledge of the events.

93 The Taliban's defeat had been engineered by a small group of CIA officers: For perhaps the most authoritative description of the CIA-led offensive, see Gary Berntsen, *Jawbreaker: The Attack on bin Laden and al-Qaeda* (New York: Crown Publishers, 2005).

94 "will have flies walking across their eyeballs": Jane Mayer, *The Dark Side: The Inside Story of How the War on Terror Turned into a War* (New York: Anchor Books, 2009).

94 shut down for good: Mark Mazzetti, "C.I.A. Closes Unit Focused on Capture of bin Laden," *New York Times*, July 4, 2006, http://www.nytimes.com/2006/07/04/washington/04intel.html?_r=1.

95 She arrived in Kabul in August: Details of Hanson's time in Afghanistan provided in author interviews with two agency colleagues and two family members.

Chapter 9: Chief

99 attempted to bury an IED: An account of the premature mine explosion is contained in International Security Assistance Force incident logs for Afghanistan's eastern district for Sept. 19, 2009, and released publicly by the anti-secrecy Web site WikiLeaks in July 2010.

99 She would be safe at Khost: A detailed description of Matthews's experiences and conversations during her early weeks at Khost was provided in author interviews with eight former agency colleagues as well

as two relatives who were in frequent communication with her during the relevant periods.

102 "the only women in a sea of men": A narrative of Matthews's early years in the CIA was drawn from accounts provided in interviews with six agency colleagues who knew her professionally and socially during that period, with additional insights provided in interviews with family members.

105 The officers . . . drew up contingency plans for killing bin Laden: For an authoritative account of pre–September 11 failures in the pursuit of al-Qaeda, see the final report of the so-called 9/11 Commission, *The National Commission on Terrorist Attacks upon the United States*, http:// govinfo.library.unt.edu/911/report/index.htm. Report released in July 2004.

105 "We're at war now, a different kind of war": Former CIA counterterrorism director Cofer Black's words as remembered by a former CIA officer, in John Kiriakou and Michael Ruby, *The Reluctant Spy* (New York: Random House, 2010).

107 the case became the center of a roiling controversy: See Mayer, *The Dark Side: The Inside Story of How the War on Terror Turned into a War*, loc. cit.

107 Zubaida was never truly an al-Qaeda leader: For an assessment of Zubaida's role in al-Qaeda, see Peter Finn and Joby Warrick, "Detainee's Harsh Treatment Foiled No Plots; Waterboarding, Rough Interrogation of Abu Zubaida Produced False Leads, Officials Say," *Washington Post*, March 29, 2009.

108 Teams of SAD officers and Special Forces commandos spearheaded the assault: See Berntsen, *Jawbreaker: The Attack on bin Laden and al-Qaeda*, loc. cit.

109 They arrived in Khost at 2:00 A.M.: An account of the CIA's first days at Khost was provided in author interviews with one current and one former agency officers who were present at Khost during the events.

110 Green Beret sergeant named Nathan Chapman: For more on Chapman, see the Special Forces tribute site to him: http://www.quietpros .com/Afgan/chapman_nathan_ross_5sfg.htm.

110 Haqqani had spent years on the CIA's payroll: For a comprehensive history of the network and its founder, see Jeffrey Dressler, "The Haqqani Network," Afghan Report No. 6, Institute for the Study of War, October 2010, http://www.understandingwar.org/report/haqqani-network.

113 "It's just rudimentary, baseline, box-checking training": Author interview with retired CIA instructor who led training courses and exercises for CIA officers at Camp Peary, near Williamsburg, Virginia.

113 There were three thousand of these soldiers in the eastern half of Afghanistan: For an account of the CIA-trained Counterterrorism Pursuit Teams, see Bob Woodward, *Obama's Wars* (New York: Simon & Schuster, 2010).

Chapter 10: The Double Agent

115 first big score as a spy: Details of Balawi's video attachment and the reaction within the CIA were described in interviews with three current intelligence officials who participated in meetings to discuss the finding, and one former U.S. intelligence official who reviewed internal memos and notes about the events.

116 a top aide to bin Laden: For more on Atiyah Abd al-Rahman, see Craig Whitlock and Munir Ladaa, "Al-Qaeda's New Leadership," *Washington Post* online special, accessed Jan. 7, 2010, http://www.washingtonpost.com/wp-srv/world/specials/terror/rahman.html.

117 "You have lifted our heads": bin Zeid's reaction to Balawi's apparent success as a spy, as described in Balawi's Dec. 26, 2009, videotaped interview, op. cit.

118 serve up graphically detailed descriptions of the damage: Descriptions of Balawi's assistance to CIA targeters in the fall of 2009 were provided in author interviews with three U.S. and two Jordanian intelligence officials.

119 code-named Agent Hero: For an official account of the double agent Colonel Penkovsky's espionage achievements during the Cold War and his eventual execution in Russia at the hands of the KGB, see his official CIA profile at https://www.cia.gov/news-information/featured-story-archive/2010-featured-story-archive/colonel-penkovsky.html.

119 Indonesian terrorist ring known as Jemaah Islamiyah: For a detailed description of the terrorist group, see the profile "Jemaah Islamiyah" at HistoryCommons.com, at http://www.historycommons.org/entity.jsp?entity=jemmah_islamiyah.

119 "I have to be there for Ali": Darren LaBonte's comments, biographical information, and friendship with bin Zeid described in author inter-

views with two CIA colleagues as well as with members of the bin Zeid and LaBonte families.

Chapter 11: Dangle

126 The Jordanian had made direct contact with the deputy commander of al-Qaeda: Details of Balawi's e-mails about his reported interaction with Zawahiri, as well as the internal reaction to his messages, were described in author interviews with U.S. intelligence officials who participated in meetings convened to discuss the e-mails, and one former U.S. intelligence official who reviewed internal memos and notes about the events.

127 "we have a chance to go after Zawahiri": CIA director Leon Panetta's words, as recalled in author interviews with two intelligence officials and one administration official who attended the meeting.

128 the al-Qaeda version of a mad scientist: See Lawrence Wright, *The Looming Tower: Al-Qaeda and the Road to 9/11* (New York: Alfred A. Knopf, 2006).

128 "To kill Americans and their allies": Ibid.

130–31 an alleged 2003 plot to attack New York City's subway system: See Ron Suskind, *The One Percent Doctrine: Deep Inside America's Pursuit of Its Enemies Since 9/11* (New York: Simon & Schuster, 2006).

131 Zawahiri was known to have visited the same province: For a description of the failed assassination attempt on Zawahiri, see analysis by Bill Roggio, "Zawahiri, and al-Qaeda's Future Plans," *Long War Journal*, Jan. 15, 2006, as posted by http://threatswatch.org/analysis/2006/01/zawahiri-and-alqaedas-future-p/.

131 "Bush, do you know where I am?": Andrew Buncombe, "Zawahiri Taunts Bush in New Videotape," *Independent*, Jan. 31, 2006.

132 a series of options for a meeting with Balawi were weighed: The CIA's internal debate over the meeting with Balawi was described in author interviews with three CIA officers who participated.

133 "government was crying out for information": Interview with the author.

133 Balawi became increasingly insistent: Negotiations with Balawi over the details of his meeting with the CIA and bin Zeid recounted in author interviews with two Jordanian and three U.S. intelligence officials.

134 "We need to go slow on this case": LaBonte's words and his bosses' response, as described in interviews with two CIA officials briefed on the exchange.

135 "But it's my case": The Jordanian intelligence agency's effort to replace bin Zeid as the case officer for Balawi was confirmed by CIA director Leon Panetta in a press briefing on Oct. 19, 2010. Additional details about the internal discussions and events preceding bin Zeid's departure for Afghanistan were described in author interviews with two Jordanian and two U.S. intelligence officials, as well as with bin Zeid's and LaBonte's families.

Chapter 12: Rehearsal

139 She would join them via Skype: Details of Matthews's experiences during Christmas week were provided in author interviews with two CIA colleagues and two family members.

141 the most important ops plan of her life: Matthews's plan and the various reactions to it were described in author interviews with two senior U.S. intelligence officials, three CIA colleagues, and two former Special Forces officers with personal knowledge of the events.

144 no formal counterintelligence review for Balawi: The CIA's internal review, as described by Panetta on Oct. 19, 2010, confirmed deficiencies in the agency's counterintelligence review of the case. Additional insights provided in author interviews with two senior intelligence officials.

144 they had found Balawi's behavior suspicious: Author interview with Pickering, op. cit. at Langley, Virginia.

144 everything seemed wrong: LaBonte's and bin Zeid's concerns about the Balawi case were described in author interviews with two CIA colleagues and family members with whom they discussed their feelings in the final days of December.

146 "Sometimes it's your job to say something": Dec. 21, 2009, e-mail from Jeremy Wise to former navy colleague, provided to author.

147 *Stay far away from this*: Roberson's words, as recalled by Khost colleague and recounted in author interview with the Khost colleague.

149 "Pray for me": Hanson's words as recalled in author interview with family member.

Chapter 13: The Triple Agent

150 very different from the vests he usually made: For the initial account of the making of Balawi's suicide vest, see Sami Yousafzai and Ron Moreau, "Inside Al Qaeda: Nine Years After 9/11, Osama bin Laden's Network Remains a Shadowy, Little-Understood Enemy," *Newsweek*, Sept. 13, 2010. Additional details provided in interview with Pakistani Taliban official.

151 police discovered that they could often distinguish the dead bomber: For a fuller understanding of the forensics of suicide bombing investigations, see Almogy et al., "Suicide Bombing Attacks: Update and Modifications to the Protocol," *Annals of Surgery*, vol. 239, no. 3 (March 2004).

152 outlandish theories about how the CIA's missiles found their targets: Specifics provided in interviews with two Taliban associates and a Pakistani law enforcement official.

153 Balawi's days started at 5:30 A.M.: Details about Balawi's training camp experiences, including his leg injury, as well as al-Qaeda's internal debate over his trustworthiness, were provided in interviews with two Pakistani Taliban officials.

155 If you do not march forth, Allah will punish you with a painful torment: For an example of al-Masri's rhetoric, see his "Message to the People of Pakistan," on March 26, 2009. English translation provided by www.nefafoundation.org.

155 Some in the group had been interrogated in U.S. detention camps: Conclusion reached by CIA investigators of the Khost attack, as described in author interviews with two participants in the review.

157 "All praise is due to God, the bait fell in the right spot": Balawi's words in his Dec. 26, 2009, videotaped interview. English translation provided by SITE Intelligence Group.

159 Among the dead was Abdullah Said al-Libi: For more on this attack, see Bill Roggio, "Al Qaeda Shadow Army Commander Thought Killed in Dec. 17 Strike," *Long War Journal*, Jan. 8, 2010, http://www.longwarjournal.org/archives/2010/01/al_qaeda_shadow_army_2.php#ixzz1AMkm70vc.

159 "what is going on in the head of a martyr": Balawi's words in essay titled "The Last Writing of Abu Dujana al-Khorasani," released Feb. 26, 2010, by al-Qaeda's online magazine *Vanguards of Khorasan*. English translation courtesy of SITE Intelligence Group.

161 "We will get you, CIA team": Balawi's words in English in a video-

taped suicide message posted on Feb. 28, 2010, by al-Qaeda media arm, as-Sahab. Video provided courtesy of Ben Venzke and IntelCenter, http://www.intelcenter.com/.

Chapter 14: No God but God

162 There was a weightier matter: Dane Paresi's views about the Balawi case and life at Khost were described in author interviews with two of his Khost colleagues, a family member, and a third person, a former military comrade with whom he spoke in December 2009.

166 he finally arrived at Ghulam Khan: Details of Balawi's transit through Pakistan to Khost were provided in interviews with three current and one former U.S. intelligence official.

169 "wants to go on a martyrdom-seeking mission": Hakimullah Mehsud's and Balawi's statements in a joint video appearance first broadcast on Jan. 9, 2010, on al-Jazeera television. English transcript provided courtesy of SITE Intelligence Group.

169 "These are the hired dogs": Balawi's words in his Dec. 26, 2009, video, op. cit.

171 "Are you going to perform jihad and get yourself killed": Balawi offers insight into his anxieties over his mission in his essay "The Last Writing of Abu Dujana al-Khorasani," op. cit.

Chapter 15: The Martyr

174 witnesses to the explosion: The immediate aftermath of the explosion and the initial efforts to save the wounded were described in author interviews with three U.S. intelligence officials privy to after-action reports.

175 Alley was nearing the end of his shift: Author interview with Dr. Josh Alley. For more on Alley's recollections of the day, see his blog at http://www.joshalley.com/node/158.

Chapter 16: Fallen

178 Hayden happened to be in Langley: Accounts of the reaction to the Khost bombing at Langley were described in author interviews with three +intelligence officials and one administration official present at the time.

181 grim task of locating wives and parents: The circumstances surrounding notification of the CIA and Jordanian families were described in
author interviews with family members.

Chapter 17: Resolve

186 "A successful epic": Al-Masri's reaction to the bombing in a statement
posted on jihadist Web sites on Jan. 6, 2010; English translation courtesy of SITE Intelligence Group.

187 "We claim the responsibility for the attack": Tom Cohen, "Taliban
Factions Compete for Credit in CIA Bombing Deaths," CNN online,
Jan. 3, 2010.

187 "Our fidaeen have penetrated the terrorist America": Hakimullah
Mehsud's words in a videotaped statement recorded April 4, 2010;
English translation courtesy of *Long War Journal*, http://www
.longwarjournal.org/threat-matrix/archives/2010/05/full_text_of
_hakeemullah_video.php.

187 CIA's senior managers gathered in the director's office: Account of CIA
meeting related in author interviews with two agency officials present
at the meeting.

189 CIA Predator carried out the first retaliatory strike: Details of the
missile strikes in late December and January were provided in author
interviews with two senior agency officials who participated in meetings in which the strikes were discussed.

190 "Hakimullah feared dead": "Hakimullah Feared Dead in SWA Drone
Attack," *OnePakistan* online, Jan. 15, 2010, http://www.onepakistan
.com/news/top-stories/29848-hakimullah-feared-dead-in-swa-drone
-attack.html.

191 the human dimensions of the disaster became fully clear: The events at
Dover were described in author interviews with two CIA officials and
four family members present at the time.

192 a series of private services: Private memorials described in author interviews with family members who participated.

193 "they went to another country to defend our country": Remarks by
President Obama and Leon Panetta at Feb. 5, 2010, memorial service,
as recorded by CIA and posted on the agency's Web site at https://www
.cia.gov/news-information/press-releases-statements/press-release-2010/
president-and-cia-director-speak-at-memorial-service.html.

Chapter 18: Memorial Day

195 proper burial for Elizabeth Hanson: Details of the service provided in author interviews with two CIA officials and a family member present for the burial on May 21, 2010.

196 they had located an al-Qaeda operative: CIA effort to target al-Masri described in author interviews with two senior agency officials privy to the details.

198 pair of longtime Washington hands: Author interviews with Thomas Pickering and Charles E. Allen.

199 the major preoccupation was the good health and safety of the man: Author interview with Thomas Pickering.

200 "The most important failure was one of imagination": 9/11 Commission report, op. cit.

Epilogue

203 Bin Laden set up housekeeping: Details of Osama bin Laden's hiding place, as well as the May 1, 2011, Navy SEAL raid that led to his death, were compiled from official White House and Defense Department statements and from interviews with two Obama administration officials briefed on the events.

204 "We think we've found a path forward": Details of CIA discussions and activities during the six-year search for bin Laden's courier were described in interviews with two current and two former intelligence officials with direct knowledge of the events.

206 "When you put it all together": Leon Panetta interview with Jim Lehrer on PBS *NewsHour*, broadcast May 3, 2011.

208 "Once those teams went into the compound": Author interview with Panetta, May 3, 2011, and ibid.

209 "we have rid the world of the most infamous terrorist of our time": May 2, 2011, e-mail from Leon Panetta to CIA staff, provided to author.

Afterword

211 Atiyah abd al-Rahman was everywhere: Atiyah's role within al-Qaeada and other details gleaned from the bin Laden data were confirmed in author interviews with two intelligence officials with access to the materials.

213 The connection would grow in significance: The deeper links between Balawi and Atiyah were first described in "Abu Dujana al-Khorasani, The Full Story of the Khost Operation," an essay written by self-proclaimed al-Qaeda operative Abu al-Hassan al-Wa'ili and posted online by al-Fajr Media Center on December 30, 2011. The original text as well as an English translation was provided by SITE Intelligence Group. Further details about the links between the two men were described in author interviews with one Jordanian intelligence officer and two former U.S. intelligence officers.

213 one of the Libyan's deputies: Al-Wa'ili essay, op. cit.

214 "I have yearned to meet you, Sheikh": Al-Wa'ili essay, op. cit.

215 "He searched the bag of Abu Dujana": Al-Wa'ili essay, op. cit.

215 "There were guys who just wanted to be part of it": Confidential interview with U.S. intelligence official.

216 "drones had imposed a high price on al-Qaeda": Author interview with Bruce Riedel.

216 A final bit of unfinished business: Details of Atiyah's death provided in author interviews with two U.S. intelligence officials.

217 He praised his disciple: See Ayman al-Zawahiri's recorded message posted on December 1, 2011; downloaded from Jihadology.net, at http://azelin.files.wordpress.com/2011/12/ayman-al-e1ba93awc481hirc4ab-e2809ceighth-installment-of-a-message-of-hope-and-glad-tidings-to-our-people-in-egypte2809d-en1.pdf.

217 "jihad I am in": Atiyah's posthumously released message, "Tidings of Victory in the Month of Patience," posted August 30, 2011, by al-Fajr Media Center. English translation provided by SITE Inelligence Group.

INDEX